W9-CCV-526

WRITING WITH COMPUTERS
in the Early Grades

WRITING WITH COMPUTERS
in the Early Grades

Edited by
JAMES L. HOOT
STEVEN B. SILVERN

Teachers College, Columbia University
New York and London

Published by Teachers College Press, 1234 Amsterdam Avenue,
New York, NY 10027

Library of Congress Cataloging-in-Publication Data

Writing with computers in the early grades.

   Bibliography: p.
   Includes index.
   1. English language—Composition and exercises—
Study and teaching—Data processing. 2. Word processing
in education. I. Hoot, James L., 1949-   .
II. Silvern, Steven B.
LB1576.7.W75   1988   372.6   88-18477
ISBN 0-8077-2920-5
ISBN 0-8077-2919-1 (pbk.)

Manufactured in the United States of America

93 92 91 90 89 88   1 2 3 4 5 6

This volume is dedicated to teachers of children in the early grades who persevere in making school a more developmentally appropriate and humane environment in which to learn.

Contents

Preface   ix

Acknowledgments   xi

PART I   Word Processing for Young Writers

1   Word Processing as a Tool for Developing
Young Writers: An Overview   3
James L. Hoot and Steven B. Silvern

2   The Early Development of Writing Abilities:
Two Theoretical Perspectives   10
Colette Daiute

3   Word Processing in the Writing Process   23
Steven B. Silvern

PART II   Getting Started in the Classroom

4   When Word Processors Come into the Classroom   43
*Marilyn Cochran-Smith, Jessica Kahn,
and Cynthia L. Paris*

5   Preparing the Classroom and the Children
to Use Computers   75
Ruth J. Kurth

6   Language Experience as an Introduction
to Word Processing   90
Terry S. Salinger

PART III   Word Processing with Special Needs Children

7 Word Processing in the English
   as a Second Language Classroom   107
   Mary A. Johnson

8 Word Processing with Learning Disabled Children   122
   Catherine Cobb Morocco and *Susan B. Neuman*

PART IV   Support Programs and Developing Issues

9 Talking Word Processors for the Early Grades   143
   Teresa J. Rosegrant

10 Computer-Based Feedback for Editing
    in the Early Grades   160
    Ernest Balajthy

11 Keyboarding in the Writing Process:
    Concerns and Issues   181
    James L. Hoot

12 Computer Writing Programs:
    Linking Research with Practice   196
    Carolyn L. Piazza

About the Editors and the Contributors   219

Index   223

Preface

During the past decade, overzealous educators enamored with the power of microcomputers suggested that these technological devices would quickly transform the educational system at all levels. While such ambitious claims have in most cases fallen short of the rhetoric, some areas of promise are beginning to emerge from developing research. Perhaps one of the most promising uses of computers with younger children involves word processing.

The purpose of this volume is to explore the potential use of the microcomputer, programmed as a word processor, for improving writing in the early grades. While word processors have been around for quite some time, those designed specifically for the younger writer are just beginning to emerge. While most of the information in this volume can be directly applied to children of all ages, our primary focus is word processing in the early grades. We consider the early grades to be those in which children are just breaking into print, that is, Grades K-4.

The volume is divided into four major sections. Part I provides an introduction to word processing as a writing tool for younger children. Part II suggests specific directions for maximizing word processing in the classroom. Part III explores word processing with very young special needs students. The volume concludes with Part IV, which describes support programs for teachers to use in conjunction with word processing, as well as discussing developing word processing issues.

Acknowledgments

We would first like to thank the contributors who so willingly shared their expertise in this volume. Thanks also to Nancy Myers, Pat Glinski, Chris Bogan, Carlene Hoot, and Rosemary Sansone, who helped in various stages of manuscript preparation. We would like to express our appreciation to Sue Liddicoat and Nina George at Teachers College Press, for their superb editorial assistance, and to Myra Cleary for her excellent copyediting. In addition, a special debt of thanks is due to Carole Saltz and Sarah Biondello of Teachers College Press, for including this book in their collection of quality volumes for teachers of children in the early childhood and elementary grades. Most importantly, thanks to Kathy and Linda for their continual inspiration.

J. L. Hoot
S. B. Silvern

Part I
WORD PROCESSING FOR YOUNG WRITERS

1 Word Processing as a Tool for Developing Young Writers: An Overview

JAMES L. HOOT
State University of New York at Buffalo
STEVEN B. SILVERN
Auburn University

Through the early 1980s, the primary technological concern of most teachers appeared to be simply how to obtain a computer for their classrooms; only 1 child per 100 had access to a computer (Becker, 1984). As we approach the 1990s, more technologically sophisticated and serious professionals are shifting their attention toward how they can use computers to develop literate minds rather than simply occupy minds with questionable, untested software, which has thus far predominated in the early education marketplace. Bork (1987) expressed this developing interest, noting that the real value of the computer "lies not in its decreasing price and increasing capabilities, . . . but rather in its effectiveness as a learning device" (p. 6).

While research to date exploring the "effectiveness" of the computer as an educational tool for younger children is far from definitive, word processing is beginning to show a great deal of promise. Along with the support of an informed teacher, it appears to be a powerful tool for beginning writers.

THE NEED FOR BETTER WRITERS

From the beginning of education in our country, writing has been one of the major skills taught in the early grades. Despite this history, recent long-term assessment of writing abilities "gives clear cause for concern about the writing proficiency of the nation's students" (Applebee, Langer, & Mullis, 1986, p. 7). Administrators and teachers throughout the country are currently receiving increased pressure to rectify this situation at all levels.

Numerous reasons can be postulated for students' inability to convey meaning through writing. One possibility suggested in a national report is that students do not write (Education Commission of the States, 1982). At the secondary level, for example, it has been found that students spend the majority of time in classes designated for "writing" on non-communicative tasks such as filling in blanks and responding with short answers (NAEP, 1982). In the earlier grades, writing periods are generally consumed by extensive practice in reproducing letters.

Throughout our educational system, writing programs have been devoted to the *form* of writing—handwriting, copying sentences and words, and recopying messy text—rather than the *function* of writing—expressing important ideas and messages through print. Without serious attention to changing this pattern, the likelihood of creating more literate children is slim at best. Before exploring how word processors can be used to improve children's writing ability, we will focus on recent developments in our knowledge about the writing process.

WHAT WE KNOW ABOUT GOOD WRITERS

Recent interest in writing instruction has resulted in a great deal of research into activities that encourage children to become good writers. Vukelich (1981), Graves (1981), Daiute (1982), and others have explored the development of writing and suggested that good writers are proficient in three major processes: (a) prewriting (thinking through the tasks at hand), (b) composition (actual writing as well as making decisions about what goes where, stopping and starting, and re-reading), and (c) rewriting (editing and massaging ideas into final form).

The nourishment of the above processes clearly requires a major shift in the manner in which writing is often taught. Emphasis must move away from instruction focusing on the mechanical elements, or form, of writing; rather, the primary emphasis must be on expression of thought. To focus on thought, both teachers and children must emphasize how words convey meaning, not simply how words are formed. Teachers will try to have children focus on the clarity and interest value of what has been written.

This may be done by stating what the writing appears to be about, commenting on its good qualities, and asking questions about how a child may improve the clarity or interest of the writing (see Morocco & Neuman, Chapter 8, this volume). Additionally, because teachers want children to focus on meaning, writing assignments must be meaningful; they must have a purpose beyond fulfilling a requirement. Children must see that what they say is important, and that the clarity and interest value of their writing determine the number of readers who will be interested in it. Further, children must view their writing as work in progress until it reaches a level of refinement that makes it readable.

Successful writing, viewed in the above manner, requires multiple revisions of text. Certainly, multiple revisions may be made on paper, but text revision on paper becomes an immense effort for writers who have difficulty with manipulation of letters and words. Thus, a tool designed to minimize the mechanical features of writing and revision appears likely to support changes in writing instruction. The word processor is such a tool.

USING THE WORD PROCESSOR WITH YOUNGER WRITERS

While still in its infancy and fraught with numerous methodological problems, research in word processing with upper-elementary grade children is beginning to show some interesting results. Specifically, children who write with computers write more, take greater pride in their writing, are less concerned about making mistakes, are more attentive to finding errors, and revise more (Daiute, 1982, 1985; Lehrer, Levin, DeHart, & Comeau, 1985; Rosegrant, 1986; Watt, 1982 and others). Clearly, such outcomes are consistent with process-writing goals.

Until very recently, little research had been done on the use of word processing with children in the early grades (Dickinson, 1985) because developmentally appropriate word processing software programs were unavailable for that age group. Now that such programs designed to minimize the mechanical features of writing for the very young are readily available, a growing cadre of researchers and practitioners are exploring the potential of this tool for assisting children with constructing meaning for print.

Early research (see Cochran-Smith, Kahn, & Paris, Chapter 4, this volume) indicated two features of the microcomputer that make its use suitable for process writing. First, the use of word processors can emphasize that text is temporary in form. What is seen one moment will vanish from the screen the next. Yet with disk storage nothing is lost. Therefore, it is possible to make temporary changes in text to see how it will sound, without losing the form or structure of the original. Text may be copied to different locations on the screen, and each version changed to test the effects of the revisions. Some or all of the text may be erased or removed at will. Salinger (Chapter 6, this volume) and Johnson (Chapter 7, this volume) both suggest that children may have lists of words available on the screen to help them with spelling and organization. When the child is finished, the list is easily removed.

Second, through the word processor, text is easily manipulable. Letters, words, sentences, paragraphs, and chapters may be added, deleted, and moved from one location to another. As children identify needed revisions, they can make them without disturbing the rest of the text (Silvern, Chapter 3, this volume).

THE SCOPE OF THIS BOOK

It is our view that, in the hands of a competent teacher, word processors can be highly effective learning tools. In addition to a basic understanding of relatively recent research on the nature of the writing process for beginning writers, the teacher also needs a basic understanding of the promises, limitations, and support programs for word processors and how these devices can be used in early grade classrooms in a manner that supports developmentally appropriate principles.

This book is organized to provide teachers with information that will help them make appropriate decisions for using word processors with young children. Colette Daiute (Chapter 2) reviews developmental theories that both support process writing and provide reasons for the use of word processors in a developmentally appropriate writing program. Steven Silvern (Chapter 3) discusses the features of process writing and identifies how word processors support each of those features. Marilyn Cochran-Smith, Jessica Kahn, and Cynthia Paris (Chapter 4) report on research that describes how teachers use word processing for instruction and how children word process. This chapter also describes the behaviors children display in using the word processor in the various phases of writing.

After discussing the why and what of word processing, Ruth Kurth (Chapter 5) provides suggestions for setting up the classroom. Advice regarding where computers should be located, when they might be used, and how to facilitate computer use is offered in a practical setting. Terry Salinger (Chapter 6) follows Kurth's management advice with suggestions about how a very familiar language/reading technique—language experience approach (LEA) —can be applied to the word processing environment.

Professionals who work with special needs populations have long recognized the contribution of the computer to individualizing instructional programs and to providing individualized practice. Mary Johnson (Chapter 7) and Catherine Morocco and Susan Neuman (Chapter 8) provide information and advice for using word processing with language variant children and children with learning disabilities, respectively. It is clear from these chapters that the word processor is a valuable tool for the observant, informed teacher because it makes the writing/language development process observable. In effect, the computer externalizes an essentially internal process.

While word processing is not new—reporters have been using computers for years—word processing is new to the early grades. Several improvements to word processing programs have made word processing particularly appropriate in early childhood education. Teresa Rosegrant (Chapter 9) and Ernest Balajthy (Chapter 10) discuss two support elements for early word processing. The "talking" word processor (described by Rosegrant) uses a voice synthesizer, which enables the computer to echo letters, words, sentences, and pages of text (it doesn't talk in the strict sense of the word). This device provides children with immediate hypothesis testing for the spellings that they construct and is a highly appropriate support for children just learning the conventional system of letters. Of course, the talking word processor is a useful proofing device for older children also. Another useful support system is text analysis. Balajthy discusses programs that provide children with information about their text. Essentially, text analyzers are useful for the editing phase of writing because they require children to pause and make decisions regarding the surface features of their text.

The advent of word processing is not without some problems. Most visible of these is the entering of text into the computer using a keyboard. James Hoot (Chapter 11) discusses the issue of keyboarding and provides some guidelines regarding children's learning of the keyboard. Those teachers who wish to address the issue of keyboarding by providing alternative means of entering text (for example, alphabetic keypad or joystick) may wish to read Hoot's chapter to become familiar with the arguments surrounding keyboarding.

Two word processing packages—Quill and Writing to Read—have captured more attention than any other software available. Carolyn Piazza (Chapter 12) analyzes each package in light of what we know about how children learn to write. This chapter provides excellent guidance on what to look for in word processing software and also summarizes the major points of this book regarding the writing process in the early grades and word processing.

SUMMARY

Extravagant (and largely unsubstantiated) claims of zealots favoring early educational technology are beginning to diminish. Informed teachers are now looking toward existing and developing research to guide them in use of classroom computers. As our honeymoon with computers comes to a close, many educators see more clearly than ever that computers by themselves do not ensure learning. As in the case of computer use with pre-kindergarten, kindergarten, and elementary school children, for example, it is even quite possible that classroom time spent in computer activities actually prevents pupils from engaging in activities known to be related to academic success (for instance, educational play activities). In any case, at this time, educators are exploring promising educational uses of computers with children, including the word processor as a tool for supporting writing processes.

How this technological innovation can help promote educationally justifiable practice is just beginning to be studied. This volume will approach the issue of writing with computers in the early grades by exploring research and specific direction for practice.

REFERENCES

Applebee, A. N.; Langer, J. A.; & Mullis, I. V. S. (1986). *Writing: Trends across the decade, 1974-1984, NAEP.* Princeton, NJ: Educational Testing Service.

Becker, H. J. (1984, April). *The social context of microcomputers: It's not just a matter of good software.* Paper presented at the meeting of the American Educational Research Association, New Orleans.

Bork, A. (1987). *Learning with personal computers.* New York: Harper & Row.

Daiute, C. (1982, March/April). Word processing. Can it make good writers better? *Electronic Learning,* 29-31.

Daiute, C. (1985). *Writing and computers.* Menlo Park, CA: Addison-Wesley.

Dickinson, D. K. (1985). *Young children's collaborative writing at the computer.* Paper presented at the meeting of the American Educational Research Association, Chicago, IL.

Education Commission of the States (1982). *Reading, thinking, and writing: Results from 1979-80 national assessment of reading and literature.* Denver, CO: Education Commission of the States.

Graves, R. L. (1981). Renaissance and reform in the composition curriculum. *Phi Delta Kappan, 62,* 417-420.

Lehrer, R.; Levin, B.; De Hart, P.; & Comeau, M. (1985). *Voice feedback as a scaffold for writing: A comparative study.* Paper presented at the meeting of the American Educational Research Association, Chicago, IL.

Rosegrant, T. (1986). Using the microcomputer as a scaffold for assisting beginning readers and writers. In J. L. Hoot (Ed.), *Computers in early childhood education: Issues and practices* (pp. 128-143). Englewood Cliffs, NJ: Prentice-Hall.

Vukelich, C. (1981). The development of writing in young children: Review of the literature. *Childhood Education, 21,* 167-170.

Watt, D. (1982, June). Word processors and writing. *Popular Computing, PS,* 124-126.

2 The Early Development of Writing Abilities: Two Theoretical Perspectives

COLETTE DAIUTE
Harvard University

Six-year-old Amanda sat in a low chair in front of the computer word processor. She searched for the letters of her name one by one on the keyboard, pressed carefully after finding each letter, and chuckled as it appeared on the screen. After pausing thoughtfully for a while, she said, "Now, I want to go here," pointing to a place under the "A" in "Amanda." She then carefully wrote "Amandas buthday parte," hugging herself when she finished.

Seven-year-old Jeff sat in a chair, very close to his teacher, and said, "Let me read you this story." Jeff gestured as he read and held his paper to his chest looking at his teacher's face for a reaction. His teacher smiled and said, "Oh, it sounds like you love your dog. I really like the ending; it's exciting. Can you make the opener a little more interesting?" Jeff energetically put the story into his writing folder, got another piece of paper from the shelf and began writing.

These anecdotes illustrate important developmental facts about young writers. Children can be absorbed in the content of their writing, other people's perceptions of their writing, and the forms that their ideas take on the page or the computer screen. Like Amanda, children feel a sense of excitement and accomplishment through the act of representing objects and sounds with letters. Like Jeff, children can engage in some of the activities of mature authors, but they may also persist in a childlike allegiance to a first draft.

Both these vignettes illustrate that children can tell stories and write them in their own notation, even before they have mastered the alphabet and can print it legibly. Yet the understanding and behavior of young writers are so complex that no one theory of cognitive development has explained them adequately. This chapter reviews two theories of cognitive development that have inspired recent theory and practice in writing. It then explains implications of these theories for designing writing curricula with computers for young children.

PIAGETIAN VIEWS OF THE FOUR- TO EIGHT-YEAR-OLD MIND

Interactions with the Environment

Piaget (1951, 1967) views the child as a little scientist who learns about the world by manipulating objects and, eventually, ideas. Because cognitive ability determines how children understand and interact with the environment, the four-year-old's play with a set of blocks differs from the seven-year-old's. According to Piaget, children construct the world based on the structures of their minds at each stage in their development. For example, a five-year-old child sees a water mill as a wheel with water pouring off it, because the child at this age is capable of focusing on one highly visible variable or step in a process—in this case water coming off a wheel. An eight-year-old child, on the other hand, is more likely to coordinate multiple variables, and thus might perceive the water mill as a set of interlocking gears and wheels propelled by the current in the stream.

Children's minds develop as they construct theories about the world, which change as new stimuli and events become salient. The imposition of stimuli and events on the child is called "accommodation," and the child's construction of interrelationships among beings and objects in the world is called "assimilation." The child accommodates to the various levels of complexity in the water mill differently at different ages, and likewise forms a different description of the water mill at each age, depending on the features that are salient at a particular time in development.

Similarly, young children gradually accommodate to the conventions of written language, but at each stage of accommodation impose their view of writing onto the task. For example, Amanda has learned that letters represent sounds, but she still thinks there is a one-to-one correspondence. In writing "buthday," Amanda has accommodated to the semiphonetic spelling of "day" probably because it is a common word that children learn as a whole, but she has assimilated "buth-" to her rule that words are spelled as they sound.

Decentering

According to Piaget, children are able to interact with other people as an outgrowth of their ability to categorize objects. Sorting a set of multi-colored and multi-shaped picture cards by color and shape involves being able to consider the objects from two points of view and to realize that objects can be defined in terms of several features. As children are able to hold multiple aspects of objects in mind, they develop the ability to differentiate themselves from others in the world. They realize that all objects are not personal extensions and that other people may see objects and events differently. This ability to distinguish oneself from others enables a child to socialize, which requires taking another person's point of view into consideration and eventually coordinating opposing points of view.

Being able to decenter is important to writers. Writers have to evaluate the clarity of what they have written, which is difficult because writers generally know what they have said. Thus, they have to imagine other points of view and to assume these when evaluating a piece. This is difficult for young writers.

Cognitive Structures

The development of the child's mind in Piagetian terms is like a kaleidoscope changing from a simple pattern to a more complex one. Just as a single-colored star pattern in a kaleidoscope evolves into a multi-colored crystal pattern, the child develops from perceiving and acting on one aspect of a task to manipulating several variables and functions (for example, sorting puzzle pieces by color, by shape, and by size). After first viewing objects as static, the child becomes able to understand and to predict transformations as well as multiple categorizations of objects. The basic transformations Piaget has described are addition, subtraction, and reversibility, which underlie mathematics and human relations as well as categorization. The ability to coordinate differing points of view reflects cognitive structure; it involves recognizing that there is more than one way to think about a book, a friend, or even oneself. Comparing and contrasting two opinions about a friend involve the logical operations of addition and subtraction—noting similarities involves summing common features; noting differences involves subtracting the common features. The ability to reverse logical operations is important because it reflects complex transformations and the recognition that changing form does not necessarily imply changing substance.

The logical operations of addition, subtraction, and reversibility in the cognitive structure of the mind apply to writing in several ways. Researchers and teachers have often noted that young writers do little revision of their writing (Bereiter & Scardamalia, 1987; Daiute, 1985; Freedman, 1984). Once the text is written, it becomes a fixed object in the child's mind. When children are asked to revise, they are more likely to add to the end of a text rather than expand it internally, erase repetitions, or reorganize its structure. Revising a text involves not only simple additions and subtractions but also complex transformations, such as moving sentences around for different effects and realizing that such changes can be reversed if they do not improve the flow of the text. Logical operations also determine the young writer's ability to view a text in varied ways, which is eventually necessary in writing. For example, in evaluating one's own writing, it is sometimes helpful to review just the ideas at first. Then on a later pass, it is helpful to try to ignore meaning and to focus on mechanics, such as spelling. Such focusing on different aspects of a text for different purposes requires mentally subtracting out certain aspects of the text and then transforming the text in one's mind back to its multidimensional form.

Although the general progression of abilities that Piaget described has been supported, some researchers have found that Piaget's theory may be too rigid in associating stages of cognitive development with specific ages and in claiming that development occurs at the same time across all intellectual domains. Piaget's theory has also been criticized for its focus on logical operations rather than intuitive or culturally influenced ways of interpreting the world (Donaldson, 1978; Gelman & Baillargeon, 1983). A related problem is Piaget's limited account of the role of social interaction on cognitive development. The developmental theory of the Soviet psychologist, Lev Vygotsky (1978), can be contrasted to Piagetian theory in its emphasis on the role of social interaction in cognitive development.

VYGOTSKIAN VIEW OF THE FOUR- TO EIGHT-YEAR-OLD MIND

While Piaget argued that children develop the ability for true social interactions during the seventh year, when they have become sufficiently decentered to take other people's points of view into account, Vygotsky argued that all development occurs first in social interaction and then in individual cognition. In Vygotsky's view, social interactions around literacy during preschool years are essential for the development of writing skills.

Interactions in Society

Vygotsky was interested in explaining the development of higher psychological processes of human thought. Thus, he focused on unique human activities such as intentional action and speech, which involve an individual as a member of a sociocultural group. The individual's intentions are determined in large part by the exigencies of the cultural setting, and speech is in large part a social activity. According to Vygotsky, voluntary attention, logical memory, and concept formation all begin in social interaction. Children observe the activities and relationships in their communities, interact in increasingly complex ways, request feedback from adults, and finally act as they presume an adult would. Similarly, the social speech that goes on between children and adults as they solve problems while playing games, reading stories, or deciding what to do for an afternoon becomes internal speech, regulated alone by the child after a period of egocentric speech or audible problem solving.

In the second anecdote at the beginning of this chapter, Jeff consults with his teacher by reading her a piece of writing and then responds to her comments. Because of repeated interactions like the one between Jeff and his teacher, the students in his class learn to make comments to one another, offering reactions, emphasizing positive points, and sometimes noting points that could be improved in a piece of writing. The children internalize a "script" for making comments by modeling their speech on the teacher's as they create their own authorship community.

Action, Tool, and Sign

Vygotsky emphasizes the importance of the child's active manipulation of tools, including words as well as objects. Toys, games, puzzles, and stories serve as reference points for social interaction. Such tools for thought are the subject of social speech between children and adults, but they also serve as media for the transition of speech into mental signs that represent concepts and thus as the bases for the child's original language and thought. The sign or symbolic representation of ideas is the core of the child's generalized knowledge. Jeff's teacher's comment, "Can you make the opener a little more exciting," if repeated in several forms about other texts, could lead to Jeff's generalized understanding that a written text should begin with a statement that grabs the reader's attention. Such mental signs occur, according to Vygotsky, only through working and playing with objects, including language, in social settings.

WRITING INSTRUCTION AND
COGNITIVE DEVELOPMENTAL THEORIES

Recent theories on the development of written language abilities have been grounded in Piaget and Vygotsky. Seldom does an educator find these theorists to contribute complementary insights about early writing. But these theorists' views serve to explain different aspects of writing, and one similar theme can be cited to highlight a way of describing the young writer's task that has not been discussed in recent years.

Theory and practice in writing have been based on several of Piaget's ideas, most notably his characterization of the child as a little scientist who constructs meaning out of a complex environment. Piaget has been credited with showing adults how to comprehend children's unique understanding of the world, rather than simply assuming that they view it less accurately than adults do.

Writing as Process

The recent focus on teaching writing as a process of discovery has been associated with Piaget's theory (Calkins, 1986). The process approach advocates that young children should be encouraged to

discover their own writing topics (Graves, 1982), which is Piagetian in its emphasis on invention. But the emphasis on personal
experience as the basis of all writing development ignores the
Piagetian focus on the manipulation of intellectual material.
Piaget has shown that children make increasingly complex observations about the world around them; thus, they should be able to
write about a variety of topics external to their own experience.
Of course, they do this based on certain limits in the number of
aspects of a topic that they can address at one time. In the Piagetian spirit, the process approach theorists have also said that
teachers should not assign topics. While this tenet is generally
consistent with the view of children as little scientists who will
assimilate aspects of the world to their own point of view, Piagetian research has shown that children can be stimulated to think
logically when given certain analytic tasks. Later research has
even shown that children's thinking advances when they are engaged in challenging tasks involving categorizations and cognitive transformations of objects.

Writing theorists have shown that very young children
can write stories or descriptions if they are not held back by
having to master all the conventions of spelling, style, or punctuation before they are encouraged to write (Bissex, 1980; Graves,
1982).

It also follows from Piaget's theory, however, that children
can begin basic analysis at ages 7 and 8. Thus, with the proper
instruction, chidren can write about themselves analytically
rather than just narratively and can write about topics outside of
themselves. Allowing children to write with pictures (Dyson,
1982) or invented phonetic spellings is also consistent with
Piaget's insight that children perceive the world and express
themselves in unique ways.

In addition, the process approach to writing involves apprenticing children as authors, thereby showing them the strategies
that experienced authors use for planning and revising their texts
rather than asking them to write based on analyzing examples of
good texts. Realizing that composing strategies can be taught
explicitly has been an important advance in writing theory and
instruction, but one limit of the process approach is that teachers
typically rely on general response for writing improvement rather
than text analysis (see Chapter 10), which can be helpful to many
children (Daiute, 1985).

Writing as Communication

Some researchers and curriculum developers think the major problem with writing instruction in the past was that teachers presented writing as an intellectual activity or an act of self-expression. Some theorists believe that introducing writing as an act of
communication, including writing all pieces for specific peer audiences as well as building a peer response phase into the production of each piece, will make writing more accessible to more children (Reil, 1985). The craft that was once characterized by the
image of a person working alone in a candlelit garrett is now often
replaced by an image like the one of Jeff in the anecdote at the
beginning of this chapter. The process approach involves a phase of
feedback from a person who listens to the author reading a piece.

Recent incarnations of the writing as communication approach
have developed with the use of the computer. As described in
Writing and Computers (Daiute, 1985), the class or school newspaper is a popular activity. Children design the goals, storylist, and
format of the newspaper. They also serve as authors and editors
who control the content and form of the pieces. Those who advocate
such a public form of writing say that it increases children's understanding of the purposes of literacy, their motivation to write, and
their mastery of spelling. Similar claims are made by those who
advocate the related but more individual and expressive writing
process approach. Unfortunately, there is no research to confirm
either set of claims or to contrast results of the methods.

Awareness of Language as an Object

Since recent theory has focused on writing as a process of discovering and communicating meanings, the field has overlooked one
important task for young writers. To build a strong foundation as
a writer, one has to develop an awareness of language as an
object. In the Vygotskian sense, this means that children increase
their awareness of language as a sign relating the real-world
object with a cognitive symbol. In the Piagetian sense, this means
distinguishing words from the underlying meanings, feelings,
events, and observations that the words represent. The visual and
verbal manipulation of letters and words on the children's television program *Sesame Street* (Lesser, 1974) heightens children's
awareness of language as an object—an object of thought and

expression. Viewing a text as an object is one step toward being able to make it and rework it creatively.

Sound-letter correspondences, word-meaning correspondences, and the structures of discourse genres have recently been described as low-level concerns that are secondary to meaning and communication. One reason for the lack of focus on language form is the fact that language had once been presented entirely as an object rather than as an extension of one's daily life. In addition, common belief was that children had to master basic building blocks of written language, such as sound-letter correspondences and story form, before they could write. It has recently been shown that children can make stories before they can spell correctly and that subsequent spelling skills do not necessarily suffer because children have been allowed to write whatever symbol they wish to represent their early stories. But, the value of focusing on the forms as well as the meanings of language has not been discussed in recent years. Complementary focus on form *and* content helps children develop written language skills.

Many of children's verbal play as they collaborate on writing tasks centers around testing hypotheses about the nature of written language, from rhyming patterns to discourse genres (Daiute & Dalton, in press). For example, when deciding on characters' names, children played with sound contrasts, such as "Crissy crocodile," "cramped crocodile," "Lile crocodile," "Christopher crocodile," and meaning contrasts, such as "Mr. Dumb" and "Mr. Smart," which reflected the progression of a story in which an unsuspecting owl was hit on the head by some crows, which he later outsmarted. Such verbal explorations help children make discoveries about the structures and meanings in written language. Such language play does not serve an entirely social function. Rather, it focuses on language as an object and on children's need to explore it as such when writing. In different ways, Piaget's and Vygotsky's theories make note of the need to manipulate intellectual objects; especially for Vygotsky, language is an intellectual tool.

THE COMPUTER MEETS THE CHILD'S MIND

Although there are important differences between Piaget's and Vygotsky's theories, both theorists emphasize the importance of rich environments in which children can observe, explore, and manipulate objects and ideas. It follows from both theories as well that writing assignments should be given in a way that highlights the nature of the activity as a discovery process. The computer can be used to enhance writing as a discovery process, as social interaction, and as an aid in the development of logical thought as discussed by Vygotsky and Piaget.

The Computer as a Tool for Discovery Writing

The computer word processor is a tool that can simplify the writing process and thus help children explore more ideas and phrasings than they might with other tools (Daiute, 1985). Since the word processor offers options for making all types of changes without requiring recopying, it would have been the perfect tool for Jeff to use after hearing his teacher's comments.

The Computer and the Social Context of Writing

Many computer applications have been based on Vygotsky's theory that writing builds directly on social interactions about topics relevant to young writers. Educators who use computers generally value them as communication tools (Daiute, 1985). Collaborative writing and peer conferencing, described elsewhere in this volume, can be more easily done on the computer than with pencils or typewriters. Thus, many teachers use the computer to emphasize the social nature of writing.

I recently explored the Vygotskian idea that speech that goes on as one writes with a partner would later be internalized into an elaborated internal dialogue. Such dialogue is so necessary in writing, especially in planning and revising, which involve critiquing one's own ideas or text drafts. Fourth graders who used the word processor to write stories with partners improved their narrative writing, especially their fluency (Daiute & Dalton, in press). Although I did not do as comprehensive an experiment with second graders, I found that they too can collaborate effectively on the computer and that collaboration is much easier with the word processor than it is with paper and pencil.

As discussed in *Writing and Computers* (Daiute, 1985), one of the most popular uses of the computer is to develop and produce a class or school newspaper. The collaborative processes of soliciting articles on different topics (typically modeled on those in adult newspaper sections), and of composing and editing them, are easier on the computer than with the tools traditionally used for such a project. Also, formatting programs like Newsroom and the easy editing features of word processors make it possible for children to produce their newspapers independently of the teacher. Traditionally, teachers had to type all the stories onto a ditto master; in that typing process, the teacher served as the newspaper editor (Daiute, 1985).

In the spirit of Vygotsky, researchers and teachers have also collaborated on electronic mail networks so that children can see the relevance of writing to long-distance communication (Reil, 1985). One networking project involves children in Puerto Rico writing to peers in Hartford, Connecticut, and San Diego, California. Another project involves networking between Cambridge, Massachusetts, and the Soviet Union. The research from such projects is only beginning, but the value of such networking for very young writers will probably be that writing begins in real communication contexts, rather than in exercises such as copying sentences from the blackboard.

There has been little formal research done to test whether children under the age of eight benefit from collaborative writing more or less than older children, so teachers have to follow their own sense of appropriateness of such activities. In spite of the lack of conclusive research, young children enjoy such activities, and enjoyment may be the best predictor of later success with literacy.

The Computer as Transitional Object

The computer can also be used as a context in which to help children view their texts from several perspectives. Prompting programs can help them concentrate on developing goals and contents for their writing. Spelling checkers and word analysis programs can help children shift their focus to form, temporarily.

The first anecdote in this chapter shows Amanda discovering some of the formal conventions of written language and enjoying this discovery so that it could be called "play." As children begin to explore the relationships between sounds, meanings, and written forms, experience with several media can serve them well. Adding a computer to other production tools, such as pencils and crayons, enables children to make a variety of connections between sounds, mental signs, and written forms. They can represent a sound by drawing it with a pencil, by pressing a key on the computer keyboard showing the graphic form of the letter, by checking the computer screen to make sure the letter that appears there is the letter that was pressed, and by hearing the letter sounded out by a speech synthesizer (see Chapter 9).

Once children learn the placement of letters on the keyboard, they can begin to write quickly—at first more quickly than they can handwrite—and thus can accelerate the translation and synthesis of ideas. As the child's production rate increases, it also becomes necessary to slow down to read over and evaluate what has been written (Daiute, 1986). Often, the public appearance of a text on the computer screen provides an impetus for reading and reworking texts. Children spontaneously read and comment on one another's texts on the screen and even decide to make a story together.

SUMMARY

Piaget and Vygotsky have offered concepts for thinking about and observing children's cognitive development. Several concepts reveal some of the complexity of learning to write. Just as no theory has yet explained this process completely, no one composing tool can serve all of the young writer's needs. The computer, however, can be used for a range of writing activities, from communicating to playing with words.

REFERENCES

Bissex, G. (1980). *GNYS AT WRK: A child learns to write and read.* Cambridge, MA: Harvard University Press.

Bereiter, C., & Scardamalia, M. (1987). *The psychology of written composition.* Hillsdale, NJ: Erlbaum.

Calkins, L. (1986). *The art of teaching writing.* Portsmouth, NH: Heinemann.

Daiute, C. (1985). *Writing and computers.* Menlo Park, CA: Addison-Wesley.

Daiute, C. (1986). Physical and cognitive aspects of revising: Insight from studies with computers. *Research in the Teaching of English, 20,* 141-159.

Daiute, C., & Dalton, B. (in press). 'Let's brighten it up a bit': Collaboration and cognition in writing. In B. Rafoth & D. Rubin (Eds.), *The social foundations of writing.* Norwood, NJ: Ablex.

Donaldson, M. (1978). *Children's minds*. New York: W. W. Norton.

Dyson, A. (1982). The emergence of visible language: Interrelationships between drawing and early writing. *Visible Language, 16*, 360-381.

Farr, M. (1985). *Children's early writing development*. Norwood, NJ: Ablex.

Freedman, S. (1984). *The acquisition of written language: Revision and response*. Norwood, NJ: Ablex.

Gelman, R., & Baillargeon, R. (1983). A review of some Piagetian concepts. In P. Mussen (Ed.), *Handbook of child psychology*, Vol. III. New York: John Wiley.

Graves, D. (1983). *Writing: Teachers and children at work*. Exeter, NH: Heinemann.

Lesser, G. (1974). *Children and television: Lessons from Sesame Street*. New York: Random House.

Piaget, J. (1951). *The psychology of intelligence*. London: Routledge & Kegan Paul, Ltd.

Piaget, J. (1967). *Six psychological studies*. [New York: Random House.

Reil, M. (1985). The computer chronicles revisited: A functional learning environment for acquiring literacy skills. *Quarterly Newsletter*, Laboratory of Comparative Human Cognition, University of California-San Diego, 1(3), 317-335.

Vygotsky, L. (1978). *Mind in society*. Cambridge, MA: Harvard University Press.

3 Word Processing in the Writing Process

STEVEN B. SILVERN
Auburn University

Several years ago I read a popular article extolling the features of a word processor. This processor, wrote the author, was extremely powerful. It could record volumes of data and print using any font the writer desired, including foreign and mathematical characters. It was easy too, requiring no training and incorporating no additional keystrokes. It could correct errors with a simple mechanical flip. It seldom broke down, and when it did it was easily repaired. Further, this word processor was so inexpensive, users would not think twice about replacing it should it simply wear out. Finally, the processor weighed less than a gram and could easily fit into a pocket or behind one's ear. The word processor, of course, was a pencil.

This article raised the question, what is a word processor? Of course, a pencil is no more a word processor than a meat cleaver is a food processor. While a pencil may be used to do all the things a word processor can do, the word processor can execute the task faster, more easily, and more neatly than may be accomplished using a pencil (with a few noteworthy exceptions). For example, one may insert text by cutting and pasting, or one may correct errors by erasing and rewriting. But a word processor does not require the mechanical manipulation necessary for cutting and pasting, or erasing and rewriting. Rather, it can create and print "new" text much more easily than can be accomplished with a pencil.

Others may argue that "special" features offered by word processors may be accomplished just as easily, or more easily, with a pencil. For example, I organized this manuscript using a planning program that is offered as part of a word processing package. Obviously, an outline written by hand may work just as well. Other processors offer graphics to go along with the text.

But a child may produce a drawing of a human figure much more easily by hand than through a processing graphics program. These examples, however, do not obviate the fact that text may be manipulated more easily through electronic means than through mechanical means.

Well, what about a typewriter? I've used a typewriter in my classroom for years. Children can take their finished manuscripts to the typewriter and create nice clean copy. No, typewriters are not word processors either. Word processing is not simply entering text onto a computer screen, although that's the way it may appear when one observes computer-assisted typing in an office. Word processing provides two features not easily available through other means—editing features and motivational features.

EDITING FEATURES

The editing features of word processors are not important in and of themselves. As mentioned earlier, one may easily edit manuscripts using a pencil. As a matter of fact, in my role as editor and author I have no problem taking a pencil to a manuscript, deleting and inserting at will. It's actually much easier than doing the same work using a word processor. However, that is not necessarily true for a beginning or novice writer.

There are some differences between experienced writers and beginning or novice writers. Experienced writers have learned the value of critical reading and rewriting. Changing sentences and word order to clarify meaning and tone, while still difficult for experienced writers, is no longer a matter of trial and error. Beginner and novice writers, on the other hand, must experience the process of changing text. They must be able to see and hear the effects of rearranging words and sentences. They must be able to react to their peers' questions and ask their peers about what was meant, what was said, how it was written, and what might be changed.

The difference between experienced and beginning writers broadens even further when one looks at what the finished product will be. Again, using myself as an example, I know that the end result of this manuscript will be a crisp, clean chapter in a book that was typeset by a printer. Furthermore, the printer will do all the tricks necessary to make this manuscript presentable, something I may be proud of. I also know that at least one other person will read this manuscript. I would hate for anyone (other than the secretary who will type this) to see the original form of this manuscript, which is written in a combination of cursive and manuscript letters, including scratch outs, insertions in the margins which run perpendicular to the text, and arrows which lead to other places in the text. In sum, it is a veritable mess which a primary school teacher would find unacceptable (forgive me, Miss Greenhoffer) and which a primary school child would find unreadable. In fact, I do not seriously reread my manuscripts until they have been typed.

This situation is quite different for young children. Lacking a secretary and a printer to turn their rough drafts into a finished product, young children must rely on their handwriting to produce a readable manuscript. Any changes in that manuscript require the entire manuscript to be rewritten. The sheer tediousness of producing a finished product requires focusing on the mechanical aspects of writing—spelling and form. A finished copy is complete; it cannot be changed. And, certainly, it cannot be reproduced for wider distribution. It is no wonder, then, that children tend not to focus on the compositional aspects of writing. I know that I would not write if I were responsible for a finished handwritten manuscript, which I had to recopy by hand for everyone who wanted a reprint.

The word processor, however, changes the writing focus to composition rather than mechanics. Because the text may be easily changed, manuscripts may be viewed as successive approximations. That is, the first draft is simply putting together words that represent the author's beginning ideas. There may be misspellings, and the format will probably be more of a stringing together of sentences/ideas. Run-on sentences containing the ubiquitous "and then" of young children's narrative will be quite common. But the foundation of a manuscript will have been created. This provides material for the author/editor, other author/editors, and the teacher/editor to use in making changes that will result in successively better, more complete approximations of a "final" manuscript. Using the word processor means that children can view writing as having a starting point and an ending point that are distinctively different.

When writing by hand, any changes in the manuscript mean changes in the whole manuscript. Because the entire manuscript has to be altered, all changes should be noted before rewriting. This view requires the young child to think about a manuscript (even if it is only two sentences) in its totality—something that is extremely difficult. It is much easier for the young child to focus attention on individual pieces. In some cases, the smaller the piece the better (almost reminiscent of mind-sized bites; cf. Papert, 1980). Using the word processor, the child may focus on a small portion of a manuscript and make changes affecting only that portion. The child may examine particular word usage by inserting alternative word choices. Again, it must be emphasized that, because only one word in text is being changed, the task of editing is not overwhelming. Confining editing to small portions of text produces two impressions important to children's editing. First, it makes editing appear to be a manageable task. Second, it encourages writing as a steplike process that begins as a generation of ideas and is finalized only after a series of steps in which the first manuscript is progressively refined. The refinement, however, is a gentle process of "what would happen if I changed this word, or rearranged this phrase?"

One of the functions—find and replace—available in most word processors may also be used for analyzing small portions of text that frequently recur in children's writing. For example, the conjunction "and then" or simply "and" is overused in children's writing. The find function, without replacement, may be used to demonstrate how frequently a word is used in a particular piece. Find and replace may then be used to determine if the particular wording of each occurrence may be changed. In this process children learn that they have greater control over their manuscripts. An example of this process is provided by six-year-old Elaine.

> *First Draft*
> One day I went to the zoo. And I saw a monkey. And he was jumping. And then I saw a snake. And it hissed at me. I fun there.
> *Second Draft*
> One day I went to the zoo and I saw a monkey. (remainder unchanged)
> *Final Draft (after several editorial passes)*
> One day I went to the zoo and I saw a monkey. He was jumping. Then I saw a snake, and it hissed at me. I had fun there.

By using find and replace, Elaine was able to reduce her initial reliance on the conjunctive "and." She was also able to reconstruct her simple sentences into more complex sentences. All of these changes occurred as a result of several passes through the manuscript.

Another feature of word processors is that a story may be stored in separate files. This allows children to create different versions of the same story (Rosegrant, 1986). The children may then read their stories critically to determine which version of the story sounds best. (This is also known as backing-up work—if the version you are working on gets lost or accidentally mangled in some fashion, at least you have the most recent version stored separately through which you can recreate your editing. This will be discussed later in the chapter.) Using dated drafts stored in separate files allows the child to compare and contrast stylistic changes. It also permits children to see the cumulative effects of editing. In addition, the drafts provide teachers and parents with objective data on the child's writing progress.

To this point I have been discussing editing features that allow children to focus on composition. However, the "public" access of writing on the word processor provides for additional focus on composition (Bruce, Michaels, & Watson-Gegeo, no date). There are several forms of public access. The most obvious form is the public nature of the video screen. Children may easily look over the shoulder of the author to read what is being written. Public viewing of work-in-progress potentially affects both the current work and the work to be done by the authors viewing the screen. The manuscript in view may be changed because of comments made by onlookers. Children may question a word, phrase, or even the visual structure of the text, and these comments may lead the author to make changes. Onlookers may change their ideas or initial purpose for a manuscript, based on what they read or the comments of others gathered around the screen. This public access, then, permits and may even encourage "professional" talk among classroom authors.

A second form of public access is that afforded through the storage of text on a "public" disk. Some word processors contain a library for stories/articles and a bulletin board for messages (Rubin & Bruce, 1983). These are accessible by subject and by author. Before children write a story on a particular subject they can access the library to see what has already been written. The computer will display keywords, which the children may use to see library holdings. For example, Rebecca might want to write a story about her dog. Among the keywords displayed might be PETS and ANIMALS. Looking under ANIMALS produces stories about snakes, horses, and sharks. She decides to check the keyword PETS. Here Rebecca sees that Tommy and Ellen have written stories about their dogs, Jack has written about his cat, and Amanda has written about her fish. Rebecca decides to read all of these stories to get some ideas about what she wants to write, which will be similar to the stories about pets, and also to consider how she might make her story different from the others. In this way, some children may use the work of other authors as building blocks for their own work. Rebecca's story will then be saved in the library to help inform and influence other authors. Similarly, children may want to read the work of their friends. That is, they may choose to get ideas based on other authors' works rather than based on a topic.

Yet another aspect of public access is the potential for producing multiple copies. Because children do not normally have access to copying machines, any copies of their manuscripts, prior to word processing, must be produced using the same process as fifteenth-century monks used—copying by hand. Using word processors, however, children may produce several copies of the same text and thus may share their work simultaneously with several people. This kind of sharing may lead to copy editing meetings where groups of children work together to edit text. Using copy editing meetings children may learn to be better editors through working with their peers. An interesting application of the copy editing meeting using a word processor would come when two children have differing suggestions regarding the same portion of text. In this instance, multiple copies of both versions of edited text could be produced easily. The editors could then read and compare both versions as part of their editorial meeting.

A final aspect of public access is the opportunity, afforded by some word processing programs, for children to read works-in-progress and leave comments for the author (Rosegrant, 1986). Using this feature, the teacher and children may read each other's unfinished manuscripts on the computer. When they have suggestions for revision or questions about the text, a comment block may be used to save the comments. The author will see them the next time the text is edited and will, of course, have the option of using the comments or ignoring them.

The focus of writing may be simple text editing, or it may be communication. When children have only the option of producing clear, readable text by hand, the focus must be text editing. This is because errors mean recopying the text. In this case, the communicative purpose of writing is overshadowed by the technical purpose of writing. However, when children have the option of word processing, text editing becomes a secondary concern. Mechanical errors are easily corrected, and clean copies of text may be produced without tedious recopying by hand. Word processing, then, allows children to focus on the communicative purpose of writing. In addition, the public access of word processing may be used in a variety of ways to help children focus on the communicative purpose of writing. Another way to focus on the communicative purpose is by using the word processor in a way that is "motivational."

MOTIVATIONAL FEATURES

There is nothing about word processors that is inherently motivational. Some say simply being a "new" piece of equipment might make it motivational. Newness, however, is not a function of the word processor. Other researchers note that, for children who already feel comfortable writing with a pencil, the word processor may actually interfere with the composing process (Daiute, 1983). That is, these children tend to focus on learning to use the word processor and lose sight of their writing. Ultimately, the motivation for writing is not within the word processor, but rather in what the word processor can help young authors accomplish. Children write more effectively when they are writing for a purpose, when they know that someone (besides the teacher) will be reading what they write (Graves, 1983). The word processor is a tool that helps create text in a form that many people may read. It allows children to format text for several different purposes. It is because it is a tool for purposive writing that the word processor is valuable.

The purposive writing that children engage in may vary widely. For example, children may write stories to be filed in the library, articles to be published in the school newspaper, items to be published in the class newsletter, notes to be posted on the computer's bulletin board, signs and banners for use in the classroom and throughout the school, and greeting cards and invitations. Again, this kind of purposive writing can be and has been accomplished without the use of the computer. However, the specialized software available, which allows children to experiment easily, focuses attention on what is being communicated rather than on the technical aspects of getting something on paper. Reports from research on word processing (Borgh & Dickson, 1986; Dickinson, 1985; Neuwirth, 1984; Rosegrant, 1986; Rubin & Bruce, 1983, 1984; Russ-Eft, 1984) support the idea that word processing facilitates purposive writing.

In addition to motivating children to write, purposive writing may direct children's attention to the role of voice in writing. Essentially, children may become aware that they can make the same manuscript sound/read differently by changing the style of the manuscript. They may also become aware that different kinds of writing require different voices. And, finally, they may become aware that knowledge of the audience reading the manuscript may change the voice used.

A library in which different stories on the same topic are filed allows children to see how similar things may be said differently. For example, two children wrote reviews of a recent episode of *Fraggle Rock*. One child chose to focus on the message, which was that everyone can do something well. The second child focused on the believability of the story. A third child, reading both stories, observed that the second child's review, "sounded more like real talking." Similarly, the same kind of writing about two different events may take on different voices. In this case two children wrote reviews of television programs—*Fraggle Rock* and the *Go-Bots*. The *Fraggle Rock* review contained long leisurely sentences, while the *Go-Bots* review contained short, choppy sentences conveying intensity. By having easy access to similar types of stories on the same or similar topics, children can see how different writing styles create different effects. Further, some children may consciously choose a different voice from that of a previous author, in order to emphasize the distinction of their text from another author's text. For example, two children wrote "commercials" for a certain brand of soap. The first child focused on the attributes of the soap (that is, it smelled nice and didn't sting your eyes). After reading that "commercial" a second student chose to use a personal recommendation format (that is, Bob and Susie used the soap and said, "Everyone should try it!"). In changing styles of presentation, the child also changed the voice to reflect a less formal, more familiar presentation.

In regard to voice, children may also become aware of the need to change voice based on the audience they are writing for. In one class, children created the text for their project books on a word processor. Some children created two versions of this text;

one version was for other children in the class who were familiar with the terminology of the project, and the second version was for people who were not involved in the project. The second version contained more definitions of terms so that the reader would be able to easily understand the project. To create the second version, the children simply made a copy of the first, and inserted definitional phrases where appropriate.

For example, Jennifer wrote:

I made a checker pattern by using white loops for the warp and red loops for the weft.

Her second version read:

I made a checker pattern by using white loops for the warp, the strings that run the long way, and red loops for the weft, the strings that cross the warp.

It also may become apparent to children that the writing voice changes based on the format of what is written. That is, how information is stated depends on the amount of space available. A letter may be longer than a notice, and a notice may be longer than an invitation. For example, Katie posted the following message on the word processor bulletin board:

Attention! Attention! Attention!
Everyone is invited to my birthday party. It will be on Friday, May 2, 1986, at two o'clock. My Mom is bringing cupcakes to school for everybody in the class. We will make frosting and you can choose your own color. Mrs. Adams says we can play games and win prizes. Mom is bringing prizes, too.

Contrast the above message with the sign Katie made using a popular graphics and text software package:

Katie's Birthday
May 2, 1986   2:00
Cupcakes and Prizes

It is clear that Katie had to change the chatty nature of her bulletin board message to meet the terse requirements of constructing a sign. Both formats provide an opportunity for children to engage in purposive writing, and both formats allow children to use and construct different writing voices.

Closely related to the format/voice motivation of word processing is the ability of the child to control the format of the text. Using a dot matrix printer, children may be able to control the printing style, visual layout, and inclusion of graphics in the text.

As children become more sophisticated in using word processors, they may learn that different print fonts are available for printing their text (depending on the hardware and software configuration, changing fonts may be a matter of adjusting the printer or changing a software code). In addition, children may add emphasis to certain words by using underlining, italics, or boldface. The size of the print font may be changed so that the title may be larger than the rest of the text and printed in boldface. Such control, and the ease of such control, is highly dependent on the hardware and software configuration. For example, some configurations may be manipulated very easily by pointing to a menu item and touching a button. The effects of the menu choice are immediately visible on the screen. Other configurations require learning a series of keystrokes, codes, and hardware switches. Obviously, the former setup is more conducive than the latter for young children to change print style.

Children may also change the visual layout of their text. Straight text, of course, would rely on a simple paragraph setup. But in creating books or newsletters, children may want their text to look more formal. They may accomplish this by using a justified layout, where both right and left margins are aligned. Also, for a more formal look children may choose to have their text in a two-column format. Once again, depending on the setup, this may be easily accomplished or may be fairly complex. In terms of classroom management, the formatting just described may be handled in various ways, depending on the difficulty level. For configurations that are driven by pointing at a menu, young children can manipulate this very successfully. For more difficult procedures, the teacher can create the proper manipulations to achieve the desired results. For example, Friday may be designated as newspaper/book day. On that day, the teacher will set up the computer so that all text will be formatted to be justified and in two columns. Alternatively, every classroom has its own "computer expert," that is, the one child who has a particular affinity for working with the machine. The expert has incorporated the notion that operating a computer is simply executing a series of commands in a precise order. The "expert" may be taught the appropriate series of commands to accomplish the various printing tasks, and, when necessary, the other children will call on the expert for assistance. A classroom may have several experts, such as an italics expert, a font type expert, and a font size expert. Some skeptics may doubt that very young children can carry out this function, but in my work teaching four- and five-year-olds Logo, I have witnessed several children in each class voluntarily taking on the expert role. We had shape experts, that is, individuals who could help others make a particular shape; naming experts, who helped name and recall procedures; and saving experts, who helped save work to a disk.

Visual layout may also be formatted in other ways, such as centering a text. Children's poetry using Cinquain is particularly appropriate for a centered layout, as demonstrated by the following example (Petty, Petty, & Becking, 1976):

Sam
Warm, friendly
Licks my face
To show his love.
Puppy

By using the tab key, children may arrange words on the screen to make a design. Other programs permit children to format how the text will look. These programs are generally available for creating greeting cards and signs.

Still other programs provide motivation by allowing children to illustrate their text using graphics. The motivation lies particularly in creating or borrowing pictures and designs that are not plausible for children to create on their own. Again, the greeting card/sign programs have libraries of pictures that children may borrow, or they may use a graphics editor that gives them great control over what is drawn. There are also programs that give complete flexibility over creation and placement of text and drawing. Children may use a screen turtle to illustrate their text, or they may enter a controlled graphics editor to create a picture (although the size of the picture here is limited).

There is one other formatting/motivational feature not yet discussed—screen editing. Screen editing is like magic: A child can make a word or sentence disappear and then reappear in a different place. Words or sentences may be repeated over and over again, without typing them each time. If children do not like a pattern, they can shift it, move it, or wipe some or all of it out. All of this can be done without creating an incorrectable mess. Different versions of text may be tried using different layouts. Best of all, the appearance of magic gives the child the motivational feeling of being in control.

Word processors, then, provide children with a tool that allows them to focus on the content of a composition rather than the mechanics. Furthermore, these devices are highly motivational because they encourage purposive writing and allow control over how the writing is produced. These are the good aspects of word processing. Are there any problems?

PROBLEMS WITH WORD PROCESSING

As with anything, problems are a matter of perception. Something is only a problem if you perceive it as a problem. Obviously, for me, there are no problems associated with children's word processing. Sure, there are little annoyances, but nothing that can't be handled—no roadblocks. I realize, however, that that is not everyone's perception. In considering what people might perceive as problems, I identified three possible problem areas: learning to use the tool, illicit writing and "cheating."

Learning to Use the Tool

Learning to use the tool consists of learning to physically operate the computer and learning to operate the word processing software. I have observed children as young as two years old in a day care context physically operate a computer correctly. These computing tots learned to locate the appropriate floppy disk, remove the disk from its protective sleeve, and gently insert the disk correctly into the disk drive. (If you think about it, the procedure for handling disks is virtually the same as that for handling cassette tapes. And both procedures are orders of magnitude easier than handling LP records.) The tots were then able to turn on the monitor and the central processing unit of the computer. In fact, my 17-month-old learned the sequence by observing—there was no effort to teach her to use the computer. In my experience with toddlers, preschoolers, school-aged children, and adults, I have found the children to be infinitely more cautious and attentive to detail than the adults. As a matter of fact, after working with over a thousand children, I have never known one to destroy or lose a disk. I wish I could say the same for adults.

The next aspect of physically operating a computer involves using the keyboard. Hoot (1986, Chapter 11 this volume) notes that there is little available research regarding the desirability of young children learning a "touch" system of keyboarding. People responsible for teaching touch typing/keyboarding are loathe to have children interact with a keyboard until they can learn the touch system. It is feared that keyboarding strategies, other than correct touch strategies, will form "bad habits" which will interfere with teaching and learning the touch system. There is, however, a long tradition of research that indicates that children and adults discard inefficient actions and thoughts in favor of more efficient ones. Using this research as a base, it is probably safe to assume that inefficient keyboarding strategies will be discarded when there is a need and/or realization that keyboarding may be accomplished more effectively. Of course, some people never adopt a touch system, but continue to keyboard using some system that they developed themselves. It is important to note that people who continue to use an efficient system have no "need" for a more efficient one. My point is that it is probably not necessary for children to learn to type prior to using a word processor. In the process of using a word processor, children will develop more and more efficient (though not perfect) keyboarding strategies. From my own experience, children between the ages of 4 and 12 years all become more and more fluent with the keyboard as they use it. Granted, it is painful for a skilled keyboarder to watch the tedious hunting and pecking of the novice, but after a few short weeks the novice is capable of accomplishing much. The actions are still not pretty, but they are effective for what the child is attempting to do.

The alternative question is: Is it any harder for a child just learning to form letters to hunt and peck than it is to produce the letter using a pen or pencil? It may be observed that pressing a key seems to be far less tedious than attempting to form a letter.

Another issue related to using the computer as a tool is maintaining the text created on disks. The possibility of losing text is very real. There are numerous reasons why text may be lost: The disk to which the text was saved was full; there is a bad sector on the disk; an incorrect command was given; a file was deleted by mistake; the electricity was cut off (power failure or plug pulled); or the author simply forgot to save the text. Naturally, any text lost is a tragedy, but the loss may be eased if an earlier version of the text has been saved. Children may be taught to save their work periodically (make "back-ups") so that if the latest version gets lost, there is still something to work from. Experience, as usual, is the best teacher. Lose your work once, and you become fanatical about making back-ups. Of course, losing one's work is not confined to using the computer; paper may be lost also. It is easier to back up work on the computer than it is to back up handwritten work.

Another category of problems relates to learning to use word processing software. Essentially, these problems relate directly to the difficulty associated with the word processing software itself. There are, however, programs designed for use by very young children, which are not at all difficult to learn (see Chapter 2).

Another problem relates to the incompatibility of different programs. Many children have learned word processing programs at home. In these cases, it is natural for the children to expect the word processor in school to operate like the one at home. Experienced teachers know that this is not an insurmountable problem. There are always discontinuities between home and school which need to be resolved; a different word processing system is just another discontinuity.

Illicit Writing

Some teachers fear that the word processor will be used for purposes of illicit writing—writing that is not sanctioned by classroom teachers. Illicit writing may take the form of writing notes, jokes, or funny pictures. It is also possible to perceive this same writing as an attempt to communicate—as another form of purposive writing. If writing is not perceived as illicit by the teacher, then all forms of writing may be perceived as "serious" by the students.

Related to the concern over illicit writing is a fear that the children will use the word processor to avoid assignments. Essentially, this fear is based on the idea that children will sit at the word processor in order to look busy. The problem here is easily avoided, particularly if, as in most classrooms, there is only one computer available. This makes computer time extremely valuable. Children who finally get to the computer could hardly use it to waste time. Further, other children waiting to get to use the computer will brook no "messing around." There is strong personal and peer pressure to accomplish what you need the computer for and then get off. This is particularly true if children expect the same courtesy in return. In our program with four- to seven-year-olds, one child started monopolizing the computer by typing in the text of a storybook. The other children objected strongly. As a group, the children decided that once the screen was full (24 lines of characters) the writer had to save the work and let someone else use the machine. The children themselves enforced this rule, and the teacher was never required to remind them of it.

Because computer time is valuable, many children work in pairs to collaborate on a story. In paired work, whether at the computer or elsewhere, there is a greater potential for off task behavior. Once again, the children jealously guard computer time—so off task behavior is easily handled through peer pressure. I have heard children say, "If you don't know what you want to write, think about it at the writing desk; we're ready to write our story!"

"Cheating"

With the ready availability of other people's work, teachers have a very real fear that children will cheat on an assignment by copying another child's file. Actually, dealing with this problem provides an opportunity to have children express pride and value in their own creativity and originality. Teachers can support this feeling by expressing pleasure in each child's work. Stress may be placed on accomplishing a task as opposed to accomplishing a task at a specific time. In this way, children may submit work-in-progress and avoid the stressful situation of not having their assignments complete. Further, ready access provides a direct lesson in eschewing plagiarism. How does it feel to have someone else take your work? How would you feel if you claimed something that you hadn't really created?

There is also a fear that by collaborating, children are cheating—that the product of two is not a representation of either child's work. This is a fear that is born out of ignorance regarding cooperative work. It has been demonstrated time and again that children in a cooperative learning setting learn more than children in competitive or isolated settings. Further, researchers from a constructivist position have shown that one of the crucial factors in learning is social interaction with one's peers. Essentially, through social interaction children see that there are possibilities for more than one point of view. In addition, during social interaction children tend to accept more mature arguments and move (cognitively) in the direction of the child with the more mature argument. Collaborative work at the computer, then, rather than presenting a problem, presents an opportunity for fruitful learning.

SUMMARY

Word processing may be seen as a tool that allows children to experiment more easily with the process of writing. As such it allows children to focus on the content and the purpose of writing rather than the mechanics. It provides an environment where editing is valued rather than avoided. It creates an opportunity to share writing with parents and peers, not just teachers. And it provides motivation because it gives meaning to one's work by allowing the text to take various forms both in voice and layout.

As in any classroom situation, there are also problems that may be associated with word processing. These problems, however, are not insurmountable.

REFERENCES

Borgh, K., & Dickson, N. P. (1986, April). *The effects of computer-generated spoken feedback on children's writing with a word processor.* Paper presented at the meeting of the American Educational Research Association, San Francisco.

Bruce, B.; Michaels, S.; & Watson-Gegeo, K. (no date). *Reviewing the black history show: How computers can change the writing process.* Cambridge, MA: Bolt, Beranek & Newman.

Daiute, C. (1983). Writing, creativity, and change. *Childhood Education, 59,* 227–231.

Dickinson, D. K. (1985, March). *Young children's collaborative writing at the computer.* Paper presented at the meeting of the American Educational Research Association, Chicago.

Graves, D. (1983). *Writing: Teachers and children at work.* Portsmouth, NH: Heinemann.

Hoot, J. L. (1986). Keyboarding instruction in the early grades: Must or mistake? *Childhood Education, 63,* 95–101.

Neuwirth, C. M. (1984). Toward the design of a flexible, computer-based, writing environment. In W. Wresch (Ed.), *A writer's tool: The computer in composition instruction.* Urbana, IL: National Council of Teachers of English.

Papert, S. (1980). *Mindstorms: Children, computers, and powerful ideas.* New York: Basic Books.

Petty, W. T.; Petty, D. C.; & Becking, M. F. (1976). *Experiences in language: Tools and techniques for language art methods* (2nd ed.). Boston: Allyn & Bacon.

Rosegrant, T. J. (1986, April). *It doesn't sound right.* Paper presented at the meeting of the American Educational Research Association, San Francisco.

Rubin, A., & Bruce, B. (1983). *Quill: Reading and writing with a microcomputer.* (BBN Report No. 5410). Cambridge, MA: Bolt, Beranek & Newman.

Rubin, A., & Bruce, B. (1984). Learning with Quill: Lesson for students, teachers, and software designers. In T. E. Raphael & R. E. Reynolds (Eds.), *Contexts of school based literacy.* New York: Longman.

Russ-Eft, D. F. (1984, April). *Reading and writing: Ideas for courseware development and research.* Paper presented at the meeting of the American Educational Research Association, New Orleans.

Part II
GETTING STARTED IN THE CLASSROOM

4 When Word Processors Come into the Classroom

MARILYN COCHRAN-SMITH
JESSICA KAHN
CYNTHIA L. PARIS
University of Pennsylvania

A growing number of reports have explored the potential benefits of microcomputers in writing programs. Such studies, however, are highly speculative; they suggest promising directions for research but are based on limited empirical evidence. Hence we know very little about the details of what actually happens when word processors come into classrooms.[1] We know little about how children learn to word process and how they use word processing in conjunction with their developing writing strategies. We know little about how these strategies change over relatively long periods of time. We know little about the ways teachers choose to introduce and provide instruction in word processing. And we know little about similarities and differences in children's writing and word processing across grade levels. This chapter addresses these issues from a practical classroom perspective.

The comments that follow are based on an ethnographic study of what happens when word processing is introduced into

---

[1]Most of the software currently available for writing instruction is based on a segmented, skills approach to literacy. Word processing, on the other hand, depends on the active manipulation of the writer as he or she uses language in order to communicate. For this reason word processing offers particular promise for writing instruction in elementary classrooms and is in need of empirical exploration.

The three-year study, "Microcomputers and Writing Development," on which this chapter was based, was funded in part by University of Pennsylvania grants from IBM and UPS to the Literacy Research Center at the Graduate School of Education.

the early elementary grade curricula.[2] Over a two-year period, extensive classroom data were obtained from nine public school classes from kindergarten through fourth-grade levels. Each classroom had at least two IBM Personal Computers. The children used Bank Street Writer, a word processing package especially designed for use by children and one of the most readily available to classroom teachers.

As we began our study, we wanted to know about the potential value and roles of word processing in children's efforts to communicate in writing. The research project was established, therefore, in a school and a school district that had a process approach writing curriculum. Teachers were required to include regular writing times in their reading/language arts programs and to help children carry writing through all of its stages from pre-writing to publishing. Teachers at the school were also informed about recent research in writing and regularly attended inservice programs on writing.

WHEN TEACHERS INTRODUCE WORD PROCESSING

Although all the teachers in our study had received the same training in writing instruction, worked within the same district curriculum policies, and taught children of similar backgrounds and abilities, each teacher created very different conditions within her classroom for children to begin to use word processing in their writing. We found that these differences had less to do with differences in ages of the children or extent of experience of the teachers, than with assumptions the teachers made about children, teaching, and learning.

Teacher's underlying assumptions were revealed in their classroom routines and instructional strategies. Specifically, assumptions were revealed through (a) the ways in which teachers introduced word processing to the children, (b) the ways teachers allocated space and time to word processing and managed indi-

---

[2]Ethnographic research is interpretive; it seeks to uncover the meaning perspectives of the participants in particular situations. Within the ethnographic perspective of this study, it was assumed that the ways children used word processing for writing would be related to, and embedded within, the larger context of the classroom environment, the reading/language arts curriculum, the rules and constraints of the school system, and the teachers' perceptions and assumptions about all of these.

vidual children's access to the word processor, and (c) the kinds of writing instruction and assignments that teachers gave. Teachers' talk about children, writing, and computers, which was sometimes consistent with their behavior and sometimes not, supported, refuted, and/or extended our inferences about their assumptions.

For example, in order to understand the decisions teachers made about the space and time that the word processors would occupy in their classrooms, it was necessary to consider the underlying values and assumptions these arrangements reflected. The placement of the equipment and furniture in some classrooms suggested that teachers believed that writing at the word processor was a solitary and private activity rather than a collaborative one. One chair was placed in front of each computer, and screens were positioned so that children could see each other's work only by getting up from their chairs. Other teachers seemed to believe that writing was a collaborative activity to be shared with a teacher or a peer. In these classrooms seating was available for two at each computer, suggesting to the researchers and to the children that writing could be a shared activity.

The teachers' decisions about scheduling and the beliefs they expressed in discussions were consistent with their physical arrangements. The teachers who assigned one child at a time to each computer also talked of their beliefs that children could not or would not want to share a computer. Those who assigned pairs of children to work together at the computer, or who allowed children to elect to work in pairs, spoke often of the value of peer teaching and helping in both writing and word processing.

As the teachers planned their first uses of the word processor in their classrooms, and as they modified and adapted these initial procedures, we found that their judgments and decisions were influenced by assumptions about: (a) writing, (b) children as learners, (c) effective teaching and teachers. The ways teachers introduced word processing need to be understood as expressions of these assumptions.

Writing theory and research over the last 15 years has prompted a shift in the emphasis of classroom writing instruction from written products to writing processes (see, for example, Graves, 1983; Calkins, 1983, 1986). Many school districts have implemented what is commonly understood to be a "process approach" to writing instruction. With this approach, children develop their writing from prewriting and drafting stages through revising, editing, and publishing stages. By school district mandate, the teachers who participated in our study had been taught a "process approach" to teaching writing. They were required to use methods derived from this approach, to follow the district's curriculum schedule, to use writing topics and activities prescribed for each grade level, and to provide the building administrator with writing samples to document their compliance with these requirements. Despite these constraints and the similarity of their training, there was considerable variation among the teachers' assumptions about the nature of the writing process. These assumptions significantly affected the ways that the teachers introduced word processing and subsequently encouraged children in their classes to use it.

As mentioned above, writing was seen by some teachers as a solitary activity and by others as a collaborative activity. The number of children permitted at the computer, rules for behavior while writing, and the nature of writing assignments reflected the teachers' differing views. Children in one classroom, for example, were sent to the computer in pairs to prepare interviews of each other and to help each other as they did so. In other classes, children always worked alone at the computers on their own individual pieces of writing.

Research in writing processes suggests that writing is a recursive process. Some of the teachers in our study, however, taught writing as a linear process. In their classrooms, one step followed the other in unvarying order—prewriting, drafting, revising, editing, publishing. Every child was expected to follow the same sequence, often within the same time period. Teachers who taught writing as a linear process also taught word processing in a linear fashion. They introduced a limited number of word processing skills at a time within a predetermined sequence. When children asked about a word processing skill before it had been introduced, they were generally told to wait until the whole class received the planned instruction in that skill. In classrooms where writing was viewed as a more recursive process, however, children moved freely in and out of drafting, revising, and editing phases of writing. In these classrooms, the children's writing itself determined the sequence in which skills were taught. Writing skills were taught to individual children as needs arose within individual children's writing; word processing skills were taught in the same manner. The way each teacher taught word processing was consistent with the way she taught writing.

What was and was not considered "real writing" also influenced how teachers selectively rewarded certain uses of the word processor by the children. One teacher of very young children, for example, consistently rewarded children for using invented phonetic spellings or memorized conventional spellings for words in both their paper and pencil writing and their writing at the word processor. This same teacher, however, did not reward "pretend writing" (that is, children's early attempts to imitate conventional writing by using wavy scribbles across a page or series of letter-like forms) or children's attempts to copy words from books or from labels and signs posted around the classroom. She described some of the children's activities at the computer as "writing" and some as "just playing." Printed copies of the "writing" were hung on walls or saved by the teacher; the others were sent home.

For example, a five-year-old boy working at the word processor typed short groups of letters carefully separated by single spaces so that his lines of print resembled the contours of conventional writing (Figure 4.1). As he wrote, he used both hands without looking at the keyboard, in much the same way as a skilled touch-typist would. After a few keystrokes, he pressed the space bar with his thumb. As the cursor reached the end of each line on the screen, he emphatically pressed RETURN as one would the carriage return on a typewriter. As he pretended to write, imitating the look of adult texts, he demonstrated that he knew a great deal about the conventions of print. But because his teacher did not understand the contribution of pretend writing (either with paper and pencil or at the word processor) to later writing development, she did not acknowledge children's use of the word processor to imitate adult writing.

Although all the teachers in our study had been taught that children should take ownership of their writing, and none refuted this position, actual classroom practice suggested that other assumptions were influencing teachers' behaviors. In some classrooms, for example, children used word processors only in response to teachers' assignments. Children were told what to write about, their drafts were edited by the teacher, and then they were sent to correct their errors on final copies. In other classes, by contrast, children were assigned topics and permitted to write anything that fit within the boundaries of the topic. Editing consisted of the teacher evaluating drafts and making suggestions for improvement, which the children then incorporated into their final copies.

Figure 4.1   A Kindergartener's Imitation of Adult Writing

```
kwok    san    kan                        20           gfg
e                    eggs       fhjsscds
tgrtyfft                   12345678919            gdhut
gfgr      gfghg       gr74
29,y6re            frtjifd2hyri       y6rdh
   gt5utytub            vdtgrh54       vcgfh
yrdgfcjghfytjh                jjjjjjjjjjjjjjjjjj
    hghglkuyyghjg       55555555      hg
tryutuigh            bfgfkvbnvffgkbf
 gytiiyr476ihk           hgjhjuy7jghcv.
dfjhj         gdyt32jbn       29         ffghg7
bvnvh         gfhguhui6tgjg        hgjgy
hfytygubcmv            hyebnvbtr877rtr666ry
qycnmb           543ghjfdghjk'hgt/y
frtrt5r7hg          t44ugjghhgkjv.mm.,bfht
    ,.yr759tu,v           geyr85777757h
gtyytukhughn     64n        hgjghkgkgkjjy—n
m        jkgjtyuy54t       gfyfukr4ggj
hngj6dv         yhyfgguijbvhg6570
tryrkfhrotophijghyt          yutiut89
gtr7t43kgkb            t77tyk          ibm
 tytryfgf6ehh8790—bfn          htu2wq
yy656567h5fbymibymiun            sawfth
=yfdhbcz        fuifjghyu57tutj   yyhgy
gftryrrdgcg         gdtrurufgft54gkjnbvc
gjvf       ygu554j,n      nr43ihk
ht76875655hgj       2165jghhgtfyt54hgg
5hfgfgg;          tfyguytgy77yug
fgkhkhhb5v6i,p.6075/ghgry6utgrj
 yu643fbv;k            yrut6r7r
ffgfutighhh64nghggfuyhhghtufut75hjhjh
6b50—8p79uyvi                utu796
hhhhhhhhhhhhhhhhhhhhhhhhhhhhhhhhhhhhh
hhhhhhhhhhhhhhhhhhhhhhhhh    hgut
hut869t8j6868j6          77777777777777777
77777777777777777777777777777         j
```

In yet other classes, writing at the word processor was made available as an option at free choice times when children had opportunities to write for their own purposes. At these times children selected their own topics and genres (for example, jokes, lists, and so on). When writing assignments were given by the teachers in these classes, children were given more freedom in selecting topics and in completing their pieces to their own satisfaction. Children produced their finished pieces with only occasional help offered by, or requested of, a teacher or peer. Help consisted of responses to a child's writing, some coaching in form or content, and assistance with word processing procedures, but the children remained in control of their own writing. One teacher believed that ownership of writing was crucially important for young foreign and language-delayed children in their first experiences with seeing their own words in print. She instructed an aide to "let them hunt and peck for any of the letters they know as you take their dictation. I want them to feel ownership of their writing . . . no matter how long it takes."

Teachers' assumptions about the nature of the writing task defined the range of possible experiences that children might have at the computers. The word processing skills that children were taught and the nature of the writing that they did at the machines varied according to their teachers' assumptions about the writing process.

Children as Learners

The assumptions that teachers held about children, concerning both their writing abilities and their capacities for managing their own behaviors, also influenced the word processing experiences that teachers made available. For example, one teacher believed that young children could not yet revise their writing. Consequently, she did not teach children the revision capabilities of the word processor. She expected children to make editorial changes only.

Other teachers seemed to believe that children could learn even difficult word processing skills when they needed those skills to reach goals that were important to them. These teachers looked to the children's needs at the moment to determine what instruction would be given. For example, when children were drafting letters on the computers and needed to arrange dates and signatures properly, they were taught to indent with the word processor, a skill that the teacher had not intended to teach, but one that the children learned with ease. This on-the-spot instruction supplemented the teacher's planned direct-group instruction. In other classrooms, however, individual, as-needed instruction formed the core of word processing instruction. Teachers who approached word processing in this way assumed that children's interests and needs ought to determine what should be taught, when it should be taught, and how it could be taught. Children were assumed to be initiators of their own learning, rather than only passive receivers of instruction.

Teachers' assumptions about children's abilities to use the word processor and to manage their own behavior influenced the direction and supervision children received while working at the word processors. Several teachers allowed the children to use the machines only when an adult was available to supervise their work. These teachers anticipated that the children would not be successful without close adult supervision. Other teachers sent children to the computer in pairs to assist each other, assuming that children could manage their own behavior and solve their problems independently.

Teachers' assumptions about children's learning styles greatly influenced differing approaches to introducing word processing skills to the children and the kind and extent of direction that accompanied their assignments. One teacher, for example, believed that children learned best when the discrete steps of a task were presented separately, practiced in isolation, and then later applied to actual tasks. This teacher taught both the writing process and word processing in this manner. All the children in her classroom were given direct instruction in prewriting as a discrete step in the writing process, and in PRINT procedures as a discrete skill at the word processor. Children then practiced these skills by brainstorming a list of ideas and printing their lists. Later they were expected to apply these skills by using them in their writing.

Teachers' instructional practices also reflected differences in their assumptions about the extent and nature of individual differences among children's writing and word processing abilities and learning styles. Teachers who taught the same writing and word processing tasks to the full class assumed that all children learned in the same manner. Other teachers based their instruction on the assumption that groups of children would vary in their writing and word processing abilities and learning styles. Consequently groups of children with different reading levels and/or prior computer experiences were given different instruction and assignments writing at the computer. Still other teachers expected each child to differ. These teachers supplemented group instruction with many opportunities for individual coaching at the computer, or with chances for children to use the computer on their own.

Teachers and Their Teaching

The teachers in our study acknowledged and valued the great differences among themselves, as teachers. One teacher described herself as having "always loved to write," while another made it clear that she hated to commit anything to writing—even appointments to a calendar. One teacher claimed that some of her colleagues "loved" computers, but suggested that she and others just "liked" them. There were many differences among the teachers in their attitudes and practices related to their own writing and to

computers. These and other assumptions about themselves—
about their roles within the school and about their status among
their colleagues—also influenced the ways the teachers approached using word processors in their writing program.

For example, one of the teachers had had considerable computer experience prior to the beginning of our project. She had
taken an active role in teaching other teachers in her building and
in her district to use computers. She was acknowledged as both
the computer expert and an instructional leader in her school. She
was proud of this identity and worked hard to share her expertise
with others. Interestingly, this teacher chose not to introduce
word processing to her class until she had mastered all aspects of
the software and had planned carefully sequenced word processing lessons for the children. On one level, her caution seemed at
odds with both her status as expert and her considerable computer expertise. At another level, however, her caution was un-
derstandable: Because of the centrality of her own and others'
perception of her as a computer expert and instructional leader,
she would have risked more by not being immediately successful
at using the word processor in her writing program. A measured
and deliberate approach was used. In contrast, other teachers
with not nearly as much computer expertise or experience took
advantage of their "beginner" status and started to use the word
processor during the first days of the school year. These teachers
freely tried out, assessed, and modified or abandoned procedures
as they moved through the first few months of the year.

For other teachers, who expressed doubts about their abilities to use the word processor in their writing programs, lack of
computer expertise was played out differently. These teachers
began word processing instruction by having student interns and/
or researchers work with children individually, teaching whatever these assistants felt was needed at the time. As the year
progressed, however, these teachers became more confident as
teachers of both writing and word processing, and they became
very responsive to the children's needs and interests. They had
clear ideas about what they wanted the children to accomplish at
the word processors, and began to spend more time at the word
processors instructing the children themselves. As these teachers'
assessments of their own abilities changed, so did the instruction
that they provided for their children.

Through both their actual words and in their classroom
procedures, each teacher expressed her assumptions about effec-

tive teaching. Some believed that effective teaching took place in a relatively quiet classroom so that individual children could concentrate and the teacher's directions could always be heard. Others believed just as strongly that the working noise of busy children was an indicator of good teaching.

Many of the teachers' assumptions about effective teaching were grounded in their beliefs about effective teachers' roles in decision making in the school district and in their own classrooms. Some believed that effective teachers acted on decisions made by others, while others believed that effective teachers shared decision-making power with colleagues and children or retained decision-making power for themselves.

Teachers who assumed that effective teaching was achieved by following the curriculum and methods decided on by the school district expressed concern that the time and effort required to introduce the word processor made it difficult to also complete the required curriculum. Word processing was introduced in these classrooms as an addition to the existing curriculum, in keeping with the teachers' belief that their first responsibility was to meet the school district's curriculum goals. Other teachers believed that effective teaching was possible only when teachers themselves made decisions about curriculum content and method. These teachers distinguished their goals for the children from the school district's goals and introduced word processing in ways that helped them meet their own goals as well as the school district's goals. In these classrooms, word processing was integrated more fully into the teachers' curricula.

Assumptions about how effective teachers distributed decision-making power in their own classrooms also affected the ways that word processing was introduced. Some believed that effective teachers took strong leadership roles in their classrooms. One such teacher believed that to be an effective teacher, she should know what each child was doing, what each child had done, and what each one was capable of doing at all times. Consequently, she controlled what the children were taught to do on the word processors, when they received instruction, and in what sequence skills were introduced. She controlled access to the machines by a system of timed, sequenced turn-taking. She retained much of the decision-making power. On the other hand, another teacher measured her effectiveness by the degree of independence her children demonstrated at the word processors. Her children participated in decision making in the classroom— the children decided when they no longer needed a peer coach while they worked; they could ask for and receive instruction as they needed it or became curious; and they were encouraged to look to each other as well as to the teacher for instruction. She shared leadership and decision-making power with the children.

Summary

In summary, each teacher created unique conditions under which her children learned to use word processing. These conditions can be understood when each teacher's assumptions about writing, about children, about effective teaching, and about themselves as teachers are taken into account. The teacher who was the instructional leader and computer expert planned her initial use of word processing in her writing program in carefully measured steps. She also believed that children learned best when instruction was presented linearly, in discrete steps, and she believed that effective teachers retain control of most instructional decisions. In her classroom, she scheduled children's time at the word processor, determined what word processing skills they would learn, and assigned the writing tasks in which these word processing skills would be applied. Her assumptions about how children learn and about the importance of being successful from the outset as computer expert and instructional leader were both expressed in the carefully planned and controlled classroom that she created for the children.

Another teacher, the newest member of the faculty, taught word processing skills both in planned group lessons and in response to needs at the moment. She continually revised and amended her plans to match the needs she saw in the children. Her status as a new teacher and a word processing novice permitted her to experiment and learn as she did so, and to share the process of learning about word processing with the children without losing status. Her decisions to share responsibility for learning to word process with the children were in keeping with her assumptions that children can and should share responsibility for initiating learning and teaching, and that an effective teacher empowers children to be self-directed.

Given the same word processing materials, the same administration, the same curriculum requirements, and the same colleagues, student population, and community, each teacher created very different conditions for children using word processing in their classrooms. This variation related less to the ages of children they taught, than to who the teacher was and what she believed, valued, and understood about teaching and learning. No two teachers brought the same set of assumptions to the task of introducing word processing into their writing programs.

Our study makes it clear that teachers' assumptions significantly effect the ways teachers implement and create curricula. It also demonstrates that there is great variation among assumptions and practices, even within a small group of teachers. Educational research and policy that proceed without attention to the unique conditions for learning are fundamentally problematic.

WHEN CHILDREN USE WORD PROCESSING

The possibilities and advantages of word processing have to be taught and learned by teachers and children alike. How this instruction takes place and what difficulties are encountered and surmounted are important issues.

Getting Started

When word processors first come into classrooms, there is an initial period during which children learn the rudiments of word processing. Asking teachers or children to learn to word process and to compose a piece of writing at the same time is too difficult and is ineffective. This seems to hold true for both children and adults. During initial training sessions, for example, when teachers were asked to write a poem using the word processor, they found the task to be too difficult. Instead, they devoted their attention to learning the mechanics of word processing and simply ignored the poetry assignment. Later in their training they were asked to write journal entries at the computer. They were able to complete this task, partly because they were more secure about journal writing but also because they were, by then, more adept at word processing.

Children, too, need time to learn word processing skills, without the added burden of a writing task. Having to attend simultaneously to two separate cognitive tasks—learning to word process and composing a piece of writing—makes both tasks more difficult. Second graders in one class generally took an hour to compose their first pieces at the computer, requiring instruction both in writing and word processing. Fourth graders, on the other hand, drafted with paper and pencil and then used word processing time for transcribing. In the first year of our study, one second-grade teacher gave mini-lessons in word processing (for example, typing in "My name is ___") to practice capitalization, spacing, and finding the "period" key. When the children who had had the lessons went to the computer for their own writing, they had fewer struggles. We shared this information with the rest of the teachers at the start of the study's second year. As a result, one of the new teachers planned a series of skills lessons, in which she supplied the text and children practiced skills. She found only two or three lessons were necessary to help children get started.

For every group of adult and child learners involved in this study, there was a period at the onset of word processing instruction during which efforts were directed toward mastery of word processing skills. Third and fourth graders had less difficulty learning to use word processing for writing than second graders, but kindergarteners and first graders needed to learn less about word processing to get started. At first the kindergarten and first-grade children used the computer for typing in streams of letters, not needing to learn the shift key or punctuation keys for this sort of exploration. They learned, as young children do, by playing. The word processing learning period requires that teachers commit time and energy to teaching word processing without apparent results in children's writing. Indeed, expectations and/or requirements that writers extensively use the revising or reorganizing capabilities of word processing during this period are ineffective and counterproductive.

Conceptual "Bugs"

Computer users had individual conceptions of what word processing was and how it worked. These conceptions, frequently inaccurate or incomplete, led to strategies that caused problems during the learning period. Conceptual "bugs" seemed to spring from two sources: equating keyboard-and-screen with pencil-and-paper, and inexperience with keyboards.

New users of word processing brought to the machine their experience of writing on paper with pencil, assigning to the screen all the qualities of a piece of paper. They did not expect the word processing package to allow insertion of words by moving text nor did they expect that the word processing package would close up spaces as they deleted words. Paper cannot do those things. New users thought that the screen was a representation of the printout. They tried to format the screen, with margins and skipped lines, as though it were paper. They did not know that word processors have a wrap feature, and they worried about having room to type at the right-hand edge of the screen. The differences between paper-and-pencil writing and keyboard-and-screen writing needed to be demonstrated and emphasized, more explicitly perhaps for older students who had more experience with paper and pencil.

Inexperience with keyboards brought another set of problems for new computer users. New users did not understand that the RETURN key functioned as a carriage return or that the cursor marked the place where a typed letter would appear. Spaces were also a problem. New users were uncertain about how to put them in and take them out. Capital letters were a real stumbling block for young children. They approached the SHIFT key as though it were a test of reflexes, and tried to hit it at the same moment as the letter to be capitalized.

Composing and Keyboarding

While composing at the computer can be very difficult, this seemed to vary from grade to grade, and even from child to child. Kindergarten children who came to the computer with a message to type took as long to think of the next letter as they did to find it on the keyboard. They composed deliberately, inventing spelling and finding letters on the keyboard at the same pace. Children who composed and wrote slowly were less hampered by unfamiliarity with the keyboard. Some second graders, on the other hand, had great difficulty holding a sentence in their heads while searching the keyboard for the letter they needed. A group of fourth graders beginning to use word processing could compose more quickly than they could type, so lack of keyboarding skills made writing irritatingly slow for them. Pencil and paper were much faster. Writing at the computer seemed to be a matter of making the music of composing fit the dance of keyboarding. The ease with which children began composing with word processing was both a developmental issue and an instructional one. Children who knew the keyboard layout, though not correct fingering, found word processing less frustrating simply because they required less time to find the letters. The third-grade class that spent five minutes a day practicing locating the keys on the keyboard seemed to compose more easily and more quickly than classes that had no keyboard instruction. Familiarity with the keyboard helped these children get both music and dance into synchrony.

Monologues and Dialogues

When they were learning to use word processing, children in every grade talked to themselves. We heard running monologues that supported the learning process. Such social talk is what Vygotsky (1962) describes as an aid to learning. Children verbalized letters and keystrokes, rehearsed spellings as they transcribed from pencil and paper drafts, reminded themselves of letters as they searched for them on the keyboard (for example, running a finger across the keys and mumbling, "R-R-R- where's the R?"), and announced or verified their own actions as they performed them (for example, hitting the DELETE key and saying, "Delete, delete, delete!").

Running monologues served to focus children's attention to word processing activities and also provided valuable spelling practice, particularly when children were transcribing from pencil-and-paper drafts. For example, one beginning reader in second grade transcribed a story about an elephant. By the third time he said the word, he could transfer the spelling "elephant" to the screen without referring to his paper. In third grade, this same child talked less, no longer needing the aid of a monologue to support his word processing and spelling skills. We found this pattern at every grade level, that is, as the children became more familiar with word processing, they talked less. This is consistent with Cioffi's findings (1984) that primary-grade children composing with pencil and paper talked aloud whenever they had difficulty assembling their ideas or spelling words and that less able children talked more. We also found that children worked their way out of difficulties by talking themselves through them.

In addition to talking to themselves as they mastered word processing, children also talked to each other. Conversation among the kindergarten children at the beginning of the school year was primarily social as they gathered around the computer. As the year progressed, their computer dialogues changed; they had debates about the nature of print and language. Older children collaborated, particularly in their first experiences writing with word processing, exchanging information about computers and about language. Two children seated side by side, working on their separate writing projects, stopped to confer; "How do you get a capital?" "Hold down that fat arrow." They compared what they could do. A second grader who figured out that holding down an arrow key would make the cursor move quickly across the screen was eager to show her discovery to the child next to her. Word processing knowledge became a valuable commodity.

The Computer Expert

Computer knowledge entitled some children to new status in the classroom—as computer "expert." In every classroom there was a child who had figured out how to print and save almost as quickly as the teacher. This child was called on to help others. The computer expert gained prestige by demonstrating his or her mastery in this new realm. Sometimes this child was more interested in establishing authority over the system commands of word processing (demonstrating ability to print and save other children's work) than in using it for writing. The computer expert, not necessarily the smartest or the most reliable child in the class, had to know what every key did before starting to type. Other children learned as much of the system as they needed for writing a particular piece, and used those keys and commands consistently. One second grader mastered three keys for making changes: the left and right cursor movement arrows, and the DELETE key. She used them exclusively and effectively.

We wonder whether the computer expert uses one kind of learning style which seems to be especially compatible with computers and word processing. In addition to giving attention to technical detail, the computer expert also seemed to approach the computer more systematically than other users who were more random in their strategies. When something unexpected happened, the computer expert looked for a cause. Some children, on the other hand, come to the computer in much the same way as one second grader we observed, who seemed to have no system whatsoever. This child approached each new day at the keyboard as though he had never been there before. Although he was very bright, he did not seem to realize that what had worked at the computer before might work again. For example, he consistently began typing without checking to see where the cursor was. When words appeared where he did not want them, he began to press letter keys as well as the RETURN, ESCAPE, and DELETE keys, without watching what they did. He acted as if he thought some key would work eventually, if only he could get lucky.

Similarly, another child listened as the researcher explained the DELETE key to the child sitting next to him. The second child then tried this out on his computer. Because the cursor was at the end of his piece, however, the DELETE key did not do what he expected. Rather than search for explanations, he said, "That key doesn't work on this computer."

Some adults are equally unsystematic in their approach to the computer. They complain, "I did the same thing I did yesterday, but today it didn't work." These people assume that the computer is arbitrary and beyond their control. While the computer experts of the second and fourth grades may not truly know how a computer works, they do have respect for its systematicity.

COMPUTERS AND WRITING PROCESSES

Once the rudiments of word processing are mastered, teachers and children must construct ways of integrating word processing into their writing programs. Frequently this is constrained by scheduling requirements and lack of sufficient equipment. Some schools have established writing labs in which classes have access to computers for scheduled time periods, but in most schools, the computers are scattered, in ones and twos, throughout the building. This reality shapes in large measure the role computers can play in the writing process.

Even within the above constraints, however, we found that the computer was used throughout the writing process, with some uses predominating in particular classrooms. Computer use takes its energy and direction from the ways in which teachers fashion their classroom writing practices, but we have also observed ways in which the presence of the computer has subtly reshaped the writing program.

In the process writing programs now in place in many elementary schools, writing is viewed as a recursive activity, entailing a repertoire of strategies: *prewriting* (ideas for writing are gathered), *composing or drafting* (a first product is created), *revising* (the piece is refined and reworked), *editing* (grammar, punctuation, and spelling are corrected), and finally *publishing* (the work is made available to an audience of readers).

Children are urged to conference with their teachers or with each other, in order to assess the clarity and effect of their writing. The notion of a repertoire of strategies leads to a conception of writing that is more fluid and less linear than more traditional approaches to composition. The word processor can do much to facilitate this conception (Green, 1984). In our study, we observed children using word processing to support many writing strategies—prewriting, composing, dictating, transcribing, revising, editing, and publishing.

Prewriting

We observed very little prewriting activity on the computer. One second grader, however, was able to use the computer for both prewriting and composing. He came to the computer, typed in a word list, composed a poem drawing from the word list, and then erased the word list from the screen. He seemed to know when he began that his prompts need never be seen on his printout. No other child in any grade used that strategy spontaneously, although the teacher taught it successfully to another, less skillful second grade writer. Instruction enabled this child to benefit from another child's sense that the screen was erasable and impermanent, and that the computer may be useful for prewriting as well as composing.

Many of the difficulties we have observed in composing with word processing seemed to result from inadequate prewriting activities rather than lack of skill with word processing. Sensing this, one second grade teacher reviewed the steps for making a sweet potato plant with two children before sending them to the computer. Her efforts were rewarded when the children produced a clear, concise description in about 20 minutes.

Because of the limitations of access to the computer, some teachers made a special effort to prepare children to compose before they began their turns at the computer. This preparation made a difference: Third graders who came to the computer with prewriting notes composed more easily. On or off the computer, time spent on prewriting activities seems to aid composing. Working with only one or two computers for the whole class, teachers seemed to relearn this lesson out of necessity.

Composing

As discussed earlier, composing and keyboarding simultaneously are generally difficult for second graders. Many of them prefer to compose on paper. But for kindergarten children, composing can be hampered by the physical process of producing letters. One kindergarten child composed this story on the word processor, with invented spelling:

yns pn on thm dr ys a hs
(Once upon a time there was a house)

At this point in her handwritten journals, the child was not inventing spellings of words or composing meaningful messages. Rather, she was copying words and producing random strings of letters, perhaps too occupied with mastery of letter formation to attend to story writing. It is unlikely that she could have produced this sentence with pencil and paper. On this occasion, word processing seemed to both facilitate the child's composing and add to her teacher's appreciation of invented spelling. When the child produced this story on the computer, her teacher viewed her invented spelling as meaningful and as representing her attempt to make sense of sound–symbol correlations.

Dictating

Dictation by a child to a teacher is a way of separating composing issues from keyboarding issues. If the teacher is a fast typist, dictation can be done more quickly with word processing than with pencil and paper. In addition, a child often can more easily see a screen as the teacher types than he or she can see a piece of paper as the teacher writes. Several second graders who lacked keyboarding skills chose to dictate their stories to an adult typist at the keyboard rather than type their stories themselves. That way they could produce whole thoughts without attending to the mechanics of transposing those thoughts to either paper or to screen. In either case, dictation provides a concrete model of speech-to-writing relationships and acts as a bridge between oral and written language.

One first-grade teacher in our study frequently encouraged the children to dictate their messages orally as she typed them at the computer. These children depended on this assistance from the teacher for a while, but as their keyboarding and language skills developed, they insisted on doing their own typing.

Transcribing

In addition to composing and dictating at the keyboard, the children also transcribed their prewritten pencil-and-paper drafts onto the computer screen. Although teachers would have preferred to have children compose at the keyboard, that was not

possible due to the constraints of limited equipment and scheduled writing workshops. So children drafted on paper as they
waited for their turns at the computer and then transcribed those
drafts.

Teachers found that transcribing did have some value—it
provided an opportunity to practice spelling. Children transferred
words from paper to screen, letter by letter, generally saying the
letters aloud as they typed them. Some children made changes as
they transcribed, perfecting spelling, adding words and phrases,
and correcting mechanics. In this way they were involved in a
combination of revision and editing, partly because of their concern to have it right for the computers. Other second and fourth
graders did all their composing, revising, and editing on paper,
and came to the computer only at the end of the process, to
transcribe their final copies onto the computer screen. In these
cases the computer functioned as the "ultimate typewriter"
valued for its attractive final copy.

Revising

One of the often-cited advantages of word processing is that it
provides for ease of revision by facilitating the alteration of sentence structure and sentence order within or at the end of a piece.
Revision is a skill that children understand differently at different ages (Calkins, 1983; Graves, 1983). The ability to revise develops gradually, as children have more experience in writing and
have opportunities for feedback on their writing from a variety of
readers. Revision can be done easily and cleanly on computers
with word processing.

Some children used the considerable capabilities of word
processing to make major revisions in their writing. Children who
understood how to revise their writing appreciated the capabilities of word processing. For example, a second grader dictated his
story to a researcher and then announced that his sentences were
in the wrong order. Because he expressed the need to rearrange
his thoughts, the researcher felt he could use the MOVE command
and taught it to him.

As a writer, the child was able to think about organizing his
content differently and, with the researcher's help, was able to
use word processing to facilitate that reorganization. Even though
he was moving sentences around on the screen, he always had a

legible piece of writing which he read and reread. This helped him to maintain control of his ideas.

The ease with which revising can be done on the word processor made children less resistant to the whole notion of revision. They were relieved that they did not have to recopy their work. But the fullest possibilities of word processing were not exploited by young children who had no conception of the nature or purpose of revision. This is to be expected from what we know about young children in process writing classrooms (Calkins, 1983). Children have to see the need for revision. Gaining this understanding is partly a developmental process, but the writing program can also nurture this view.

Editing

The teachers and children in our study willingly approached the task of editing on the word processor. With word processing, mechanical perfection is relatively painless, and teachers and children kept returning to the computer to correct mistakes. One child insisted that the researcher correct a spelling mistake in his poem since it was displayed for Back-to-School night. Some children were intrigued by the REPLACE function with which they could locate consistently misspelled words and correct them quickly. Others developed quick, effective strategies for changing lower to upper case or inserting punctuation. All approached the editing job cheerfully.

Publishing

Word processing makes publishing effortless and attractive. Teachers need not do laborious typing in order to publish their children's work, and so they publish more of the children's work. In the classrooms we studied, children asked for copies of their own and others' stories. This was a powerful factor in the classroom, and it demonstrates one way in which computers shape writing and reading programs. Printouts became reading material for the children—more legible, more easily reproducible than handwritten copy—enlarging the audience for children's writing, multiplying opportunities for feedback among children, and creating reading texts. Word processing extended and enriched the writing process on many levels.

ROLES OF THE COMPUTER

Our observations of children from kindergarten to fourth grade in a variety of writing situations point to two important roles for the computer: as facilitator and as equalizer.

Facilitator

Word processing facilitated the production of writing. Kindergarteners wrote faster with word processing than with paper and pencil because it was easier. Instead of taking twenty minutes to produce a handwritten sentence, they could type that sentence in five or ten minutes. After older children developed facility with keyboarding, it was easier for them to type than to write by hand. The result was that they wrote for longer periods of time on the computer, commenting that it was easier to push a button than draw a letter. They were more willing to extend their thoughts, because, as one child said, "My hand doesn't hurt when I type."

Word processing also facilitated peer conferencing, generating fascinating discussions about the content and nature of print. The public screen is apparently irresistible. It has been reported that in some classrooms children informally conferenced as they waited around the computer screen for their turns at the word processor (Bruce, Michaels, & Watson-Gegeo, 1985).

In the classrooms we studied, children paused as they passed the computer to read the work-in-progress. One child pointed out misspelled words. Another commented that certain varieties were missing from one writer's list of fruits and vegetables. A fourth grader recognized herself as a character in another child's story. All of this feedback helped to sharpen and focus the writing in progress.

Making the mechanical tasks of writing easier changes the ways in which writing is practiced. Revision and editing are made less tedious, so teachers and children are willing to rewrite and edit more often. Recopying is no longer necessary, eliminating a task that has little meaning and is frequently counterproductive. Dictation goes more speedily, and therefore teachers use it more extensively with children. Word processing facilitates publishing, and as a result many children can have legible copies of each other's work quickly and easily. When public conferencing takes place around the computer and when children can generate multiple copies of their work, the lines of communication about writing change. Children receive comments from other children as well as from the teacher. Children have increased opportunities to see how other children approach a topic, choose vocabulary, and use punctuation. These opportunities are often limited when children produce only one handwritten copy. In all these ways, computers can facilitate aspects of the writing program. Making desired practices easier makes them more likely to happen.

Equalizer

In addition to being a facilitator, the computer is also an equalizer. It can be used to bypass a child's poor or labored handwriting in the composing process, and it can make each final product look as good as every other one. The computer changes the writing task by taking the focus off the physical process of letter formation and spacing, and freeing children to concern themselves with communicating messages. This shift in emphasis can produce a difference in a child's writing. For example, early in the school year, one second grader wrote beautiful pencil-and-paper drafts. His letters were carefully drawn and very dark. It was clear that he put a great deal of effort into producing his handwriting, perhaps thinking that handwriting and writing were somehow related or even equivalent. This child seemed to think that his writing was good if it looked good. Figure 4.2 provides an example of his early writing.

As the year progressed, the teacher encouraged this child to use the word processor and to concentrate on the content rather than the form of his message. By mid-year, his handwriting was no longer labored and crafted; it was even a little sloppy. But, as Figure 4.3 illustrates, his stories also had more detail and more interesting sentence structures. By spring, the same child was composing stories entirely through word processing. Figure 4.4 is one of these stories. This piece, full of detail, shows real growth. The child took risks with difficult words. We believe that the child put more effort into content partly because he knew the computer would produce neat copy. Indeed, he told the researcher that he liked word processing because he knew it would always look nice and that he could always "fix stuff." The teacher who encouraged this child to use word processing wanted him to understand that writing is about content, not appearance. Having a word processor did not create this understanding in the child, but it did seem to make it easier for him to separate handwriting issues from writing issues.

Figure 4.2   A Second Grader's Beginning-of-Year Writing: "A Rainy Day"

IV-6-85,

A Rainy Day.
The boy is kraye
a uqlppe beatse
It is raing.
The boy is wrheg
a raincolea.
The boy is happy.

Summary

Children have to learn that writing with word processing means manipulating text electronically instead of physically. If they conceptualize screen and keyboard differently from paper and pencil, they can begin to utilize all the advantages of the new tool.

Figure 4.3   A Second Grader's Mid-Year Writing: "Elephants"

```
1-31-86.
Elephants
Baby elephants run fast,
They   go near the
water  wher its hot,
Elephants are tall,
When baby elephantscant
find Their mother other
elephants take the job
```

In addition to using word processing to its fullest, children have
to know something about the writing process. If they understand
writing as a recursive process for the purpose of communication,
they will focus on validating their messages. We have found that
teachers and children exploit the possibilities of word processing
just as far as they need them to implement their notions of how

Figure 4.4   A Second Grader's End-of-Year Writing: "The Firefighters"

```
The Firefighters
        Firefighters  put  out  fires.
Firefighters  clam  latters  to  save
poeple  in  the  house. Firefighters
fight  fires. Firefighters  save
poeple. Sometimes  firefighters  wear
gasmasc  to  pirtact  them  slfe  from
somke. firefighters  yus  a  ax
to  barc  wendos. Firefighters  are
string. Firefighters  are  till. The
firefighters  tols  and  aqtmnt  are
hos  gasmasc  extingwersh  lifenet
pocple
```

writing works. We have also found a reciprocal relationship between learning to word process and learning to write. This relationship both enriches and deepens teachers' and children's understandings of literacy and language. Teaching word processing and process writing together creates a situation in which the nature of writing becomes clearer as the capabilities of word processing are mastered, and the capabilities of word processing have more value as their purposes in the writing process are more fully understood.

IMPLICATIONS FOR RESEARCH

We began our study with the assumption that meaningful inquiry into children's uses of word processing for writing would require careful and systematic observation over relatively long periods of time within actual classroom settings. The findings of our study confirm this assumption and especially emphasize the necessity of long-term classroom computer research. Over the course of two years, we found that the ways that children used word processing for writing and the ways that teachers instructed children to use word processing changed dramatically.

During the first year of the study, for example, both re-searchers and teachers were initially disappointed by the appar-ent inability of children to use many of the capabilities of word processing. We had expected upper-grade children to begin to appreciate and utilize the capabilities of word processing to re-vise their writing organizationally and conceptually. We had an-ticipated that younger children would use word processing to explore print-speech relationships and to produce their own mes-sages by inventing spellings or copying words posted in the class-room. For several months, we saw little of these things happening. If our study had ended after those first few months, we would have concluded that word processing was not very useful for elementary school children. Teachers found that teaching word processing added an extra burden to an already too-full curricu-lum. The children were preoccupied with keyboarding issues, and although they liked working at the computer, it seemed to provide little educational benefit.

Within the next few months, however, we saw changes in every classroom and at every grade level. Most important, key-boarding ceased to be a major issue, and children began to concen-trate on composing, revising, and editing issues. Over the next few months, other changes occurred, and by June children were using word processing in ways that were very different from those we had initially observed. Teachers felt positive about the benefits of word processing, and all of them were eager to con-tinue with the computers for another year. During the second year of the study, similar phases of word processing use were ob-served.

Our research also demonstrates that it is premature to make global statements about the benefits of word processing for ele-mentary school writing programs. Rather, we need to describe the diversity of ways in which word processing is introduced and used in individual classrooms.

To understand this diversity, it is helpful to view word pro-cessing as something that is embedded within a complex web of school culture—the character of the community in which the school and school district are located and the values that operate in that community; the pyramid of relationships of teachers, prin-cipals, and district administrators and the formal and informal requirements and policies in force at each level of the pyramid; the assumptions and perceptions of individual teachers regarding effective teaching and human learning, the nature of language and literacy acquisition and development, and the specific needs and abilities of children in particular situations; and, perhaps most important, the personal and professional identities, goals, strengths, and concerns of individual teachers.

In many ways it seems odd to describe word processing in the classroom in relation to the personal identities of teachers or the social and political hierarchy of the school system. And yet, as this chapter has demonstrated, these factors played extremely significant parts in determining both how word processing was used and not used in particular classes and how successful teachers tended to be at integrating it into the curriculum. For this reason our research cannot suggest *the most effective way* to introduce and use word processing in the elementary classroom, but it can suggest useful lenses for exploring the roles of computers in various programs as well as identify some of the factors that have a part in shaping these roles.

IMPLICATIONS FOR SCHOOL POLICY

Especially for elementary schools, computer technology is still new. Often, teachers know little about what computers are, how they work, and how they can be used in curriculum. Many teachers remain uncertain about whether they even want computers in their classrooms. School districts, however, continue to develop and implement their computer curricula. Finally, our research suggests important implications for school computer policies in two closely related areas: staff development and classroom implementation.

Staff Development

Training teachers in computer curricula and/or introducing them to the hardware and software that a school district has purchased have typically been carried out in top-down fashion: Computers are purchased and installed in schools; software is provided; teachers attend workshops or inservice meetings at which the equipment is displayed and described; and teachers are required to use computers in the classroom. Unfortunately the results of staff development programs designed in this way are generally unsatisfactory: Because teachers are uncertain about what to do and how to do it, they simply do not use the computers provided or, if pressured to do so, they use them for very specific, circumscribed projects that are isolated from the rest of the curriculum and short term in duration. The training is inadequate and far too brief, and many staff development studies have demonstrated that top-down strategies do not have lasting effects.

Our research points to two of the most important reasons that this sort of staff development does not work and suggest some of the ingredients that would be necessary for effective teacher training in word processing. First, as we have argued, teachers' ways of using word processing in the classroom are closely related to their assumptions about teachers' roles in the culture of the school, effective teaching, children as learners, and the nature of language and literacy development. For this reason, it is essential that staff development programs allow time for teachers to sort out these assumptions and then to consider them in relation to the capabilities of word processing. Teachers need to consider, for example, what they expect children to learn and accomplish in their writing program over the course of a school year. They then need time both to thoroughly learn how to word process and to consider how and whether word processing can help them meet their goals for children's writing development. Even in school districts where some computer training is offered, teachers generally do not have the opportunity to learn thoroughly how to use software, let alone consider its use in relation to their teaching goals and assumptions for the year.

The second essential ingredient in staff development in word processing has to do with the roles teachers play. It is essential that teachers, themselves, have opportunities to direct their efforts to incorporating word processing into the curriculum. This is not a quick process. It unfolds over the course of weeks and months. It provides opportunities for teachers to make important decisions about the uses of word processing in their classrooms based on their beliefs about its appropriateness for the children with whom they work and for the goals of their writing programs. Staff development of this kind operates on two assumptions: (a) that teachers know more about their classrooms than outsiders do and (b) that insider knowledge is essential in making decisions about how and whether to integrate word processing into the curriculum. This is not to say that the advice and knowledge of computer and curriculum experts are not valued; rather, their expertise is not globally generalizable to all elementary school classrooms. Instead, it must be adapted and recreated by individual teachers.

Classroom Implementation

One of the most important things our study demonstrates is that the benefits of word processing are directly related to and derived from the writing programs that exist in various classrooms. Computer word processing will *not*, in and of itself, change or improve the nature of children's writing. Children will *not* revise their writing simply because word processing makes it easy to revise. Nor will they use early drafts to discover what they have to say simply because word processing allows for the easy refinement and rearrangement of brainstormed ideas. If these writing conceptions and strategies are not already within children's repertoires, word processing will not create them. If, however, these strategies are (or are coming to be) parts of children's writing, then word processing can enhance them and make it easier for children to use them within their writing.

Finally, our research indicates that teachers need help and support over the course of the school year (and even longer) during which they integrate word processing into their writing curriculum. This is not to suggest that it took teachers a year or longer to figure out how to word process or to get children started. It is to suggest, however, that as they work to integrate something new into their reading/language arts curriculum, teachers have many questions, concerns, and insights about their children's writing development. During the two years of our research, they had many opportunities to voice the issues that were important to them: They wrote dialogue journals with the researchers; they talked with researchers every time they came to observe; prompted by some of the questions researchers asked them, they began to ask some of those same questions of themselves; they began to reflect more on their own teaching practices; they participated in computers-and-writing workshops during both summers of the study; and they met monthly as a group to share their ideas with the researchers and with each other.

Certainly most school systems that implement word processing into their writing programs will not be involved in a research study where researchers provide support, mutual classroom inquiry, and expertise in computers and writing. But there are many other ways to provide these opportunities for teachers. And, as our research clearly indicates, there are many ways to encourage teachers to help each other do many of these things. The teachers who introduced word processing during the second year of our study, for example, learned a great deal from the experiences of the group that had begun the year before. Similarly, monthly meetings gave teachers the opportunity to hear about what others had been doing with word processing and gave them many ideas to try out in their own classrooms.

SUMMARY

This chapter began by reporting that educators are asking hard questions about how to incorporate computer technology into the existing curriculum in ways that make pedagogical and practical sense. It concludes by claiming that one of the best ways to answer these questions is to involve teachers in a process of inquiry about their own curriculum and the functions computers can serve within that curriculum.

REFERENCES

Bruce, B.; Michaels, S.; & Watson-Gegeo, K. (1985). How computers can change the writing process. *Language Arts, 62*(2), 143–149.

Calkins, L. (1983). *Lessons from a child: On the teaching and learning of writing*. Portsmouth, NH: Heinemann.

Calkins, L. (1986). *The art of teaching writing*. Portsmouth, NH: Heinemann.

Cioffi, G. (1984). Observing composing behaviors of primary age children: The interaction of oral and written language. In R. Beach & L. Bridwell (Eds.), *New directions in composition research* (pp. 171–190). New York: The Guilford Press.

Cochran-Smith, M. (1984). *The making of a reader*. Norwood, NJ: Ablex.

Edelsky, C. (1984, Spring). The content of language arts software: A criticism. *CRLA*, 8–11.

Edelsky, C., & Draper, K. (1983). *Reading/'reading'; writing/'writing'; text/'text'*. (Unpublished manuscript).

Erickson, F. (1986). Qualitative methods in research on teaching. In M. Witlrock (Ed.), *Handbook of research on teaching* (pp. 119–161). New York: AERA, Macmillan.

Geertz, C. (1983). *The interpretation of cultures*. New York: Basic Books, Inc.

Goodman, K. (1986). Basal readers: A call for action. *Language Arts, 63*(4), 358–363.

Goodman, K., & Goodman, Y. (no date). A whole-language comprehension-centered view of reading development. Manuscript. University of Arizona.

Graves, D. (1983). *Writing: Teachers and children at work.* Portsmouth, NH: Heinemann.

Green, J. (1983). Exploring classroom discourse: Linguistic perspectives on teaching–learning processes. *Educational Psychologist, 18,* 180–199.

Green, J. (1984, March). Computers, kids and writing: An interview with Donald Graves. *Classroom Computer Learning, 4*(8), 20-28.

Harste, J., & Burke, C. A new hypothesis for reading teacher research: Both teaching and learning of reading are theoretically based. In P. D. Pearson (Ed.), *Reading, theory, research, and practice.* 26th Yearbook of the National Reading Conference, St. Paul, MN: Mason Publishing Co.

Heath, S. (1984). Ethnography in education. Toward defining the essentials. In P. Gilmore & A. Glatthorn (Eds.), *Ethnography and education: Children in and out of school.* Philadelphia: University of Pennsylvania Press.

Hymes D. (1974). *Foundations of sociolinguistics.* Philadelphia: University of Pennsylvania Press.

Lytle, S., & Botel, M. (1988). Pennsylvania Comprehensive Communication Arts Plan (Rev. Ed.). Harrisburg, PA: Pennsylvania Department of Education.

Moffett, J. (1968). *Teaching the university of discourse.* Boston: Houghton Mifflin.

Rich, S. (1985). Restoring power to teachers: The impact of 'whole language'. *Language Arts, 62*(7), 717-724.

Smith, F. (1985). *Reading without nonsense.* New York: Teachers College Press.

Turkle, S. (1984). *The second self.* New York: Simon & Schuster.

Vygotsky, L. (1962). *Thought and language.* Cambridge, MA: The MIT Press.

5 Preparing the Classroom and the Children to Use Computers

RUTH J. KURTH
University of North Texas

Little has been written about the management of computers in the classroom; however, the research that has been done shows that the classroom teacher is the key ingredient in computer success in the classroom. Jungck (1987), for example, found that even though a computer literacy curriculum committee was actively functioning in a school, the individual teachers' attitudes toward computers influenced the use of computers more than any other factor. Unless teachers were interested in and knowledgeable about computers, there was little computer implementation at either the building or district level. Jungck further reported that even in schools where it was believed computers were used in a model way, computer use was not very great. In a similar study of computer use, Mathinos and Woodward (1987) found that the computer was used infrequently in many schools. These researchers reported that in a 13-week period only 40 percent of the students used a computer, and that almost half of that time was spent in gaming. It was also found that children were given very little direct instruction in computer use. When studying computer use in early childhood classrooms, Naymark and Plaisant (1986) found very little correlation between the early childhood curriculum taught each day and the material children were using on the computers. One of the explanations for this lack of computer utilization was that individual teachers were not provided with sufficient resources to develop their own computer literacy, which could then be translated into effective computer use in the classroom.

These dismal facts are reported here not to discourage teachers from experimenting with computers in the classroom;

rather, they are presented to underscore the importance of the role of the teacher in the use of classroom computers. The individual classroom teacher is the single most influential factor in the success or failure of computer programs in schools. This influence becomes even more crucial when the computer is used to teach writing in early childhood classrooms.

The goal of this chapter is to help teachers of young children introduce effective and efficient computer use in their classrooms. The introduction of the computer in a classroom affects the classroom curriculum, classroom management, and even room arrangement. All of these elements must be orchestrated by the classroom teacher if the computer is to be used effectively. Often, it is the difficulties presented by the management of these classroom elements that discourage or even intimidate teachers as they attempt to use computers to help young children learn to write.

The quality and quantity of computer use in a classroom depends primarily on the teacher's ability to integrate this use with existing curricula. It is the purpose of this chapter to discuss specific methods for the implementation of computers in the writing program in a classroom.

ORGANIZING THE CLASSROOM FOR EFFECTIVE COMPUTER USE

The integration of the computer into the classroom poses a definite problem in the organization of both classroom space and instructional time. One of the first questions that arises concerns the physical placement of computers in the school.

Placement of Computers Within the School

There has been much discussion among classroom teachers, computer teachers, and curriculum consultants concerning the most efficient placement of computers in schools. However, there is no definitive research that describes the most effective placement of computers. In the majority of secondary schools, computers have been placed in laboratories rather than in individual classrooms. Instruction in computing is often given by a computer specialist to entire classes at one time.

If, however, computers are to be used as an aid in an elementary writing program, their placement within individual classrooms is strongly recommended. This allows for more control of classroom variables by the teacher. If computers are placed within classrooms, children can use them whenever they wish, or the teacher can schedule their use in an efficient manner. If the writing program is to be an integral part of the school day, it is helpful for children to be able to use the word processor whenever time permits. Accessibility to the computer during most of the school day has been shown to be an effective means for increasing the amount of computer use by children (Kurth, 1987).

In certain instances, computers are shared between class-rooms and moved from room to room. While not ideal, this arrangement can result in an adequate writing program if the writing and prewriting activities described elsewhere in this volume are scheduled close to the time that the computers will be in the room. Valuable time is often lost when computers must be moved and rebooted several times during the day.

Even if computers are housed in a separate laboratory rather than in the early education classroom, it is still possible to have a quality writing program that utilizes computer word processing. If computers are housed in a laboratory, it becomes necessary to schedule class time in the laboratory and to teach the writing classes there. Because computer use will probably be limited if children have access to computers only during laboratory time, it will be necessary for much of the prewriting instruction and draft writing to be done in the classroom before the children go to the computer laboratory.

Placement of Computers Within the Classroom

If computers are to be located within individual classrooms, the placement of these machines becomes very important. Generally, placement is determined by the size of the room, the size of the class, the basic plan of the classroom, and the curricular uses that will be made of the computers. In general, it is important that the computers be placed in an easily accessible space that can be monitored by the teacher. If collaboration with other children in written projects is desired, computers must be placed where quiet discussions will not disturb the rest of the class. If many activities using editing groups are planned, it becomes necessary for the computers and printers to be placed in a space large enough to accommodate groups of two or three children working together.

It is generally not a good idea to have the computers in a secluded nook or corner, completely isolated from classroom activities. If the computers are too isolated from the main work areas of the room, it becomes difficult for children to view the computers as tools for writing.

It is also important that the computer monitors be placed at the right height for the children in the room. Computers placed at comfortable heights for adults often are not comfortable for small children. Because using a computer demands a great deal of both visual acuity and motor ability, the keyboards and monitors should be placed at heights suitable for young children.

Providing a Safe Computing Environment

It is also imperative to plan for safety of the children when placing computers and printers. Computers must be connected to electrical outlets with standard Underwriter Laboratory approved connections. Electric cords must be placed carefully in permanent locations not accessible to children. Computers and printers use a considerable number of cords and cables, which must be connected permanently. There is no place in a classroom for loose cords or cables. Young children should not be allowed to handle extension cords, plugs, cables, surge protectors, or outlets. I have often observed classrooms in which computer cables and cords were strewn haphazardly in the computer area. This has resulted in both injury to children and damage to equipment.

If computers are going to be moved from classroom to classroom, it is advisable to have a self-contained cart to which the computer is permanently attached, with all electrical outlets surge protected and covered. Then, only one cord from the cart needs to be plugged into the classroom outlet.

Caring for Computer Equipment

It is very important, and seems obvious, that adequate care must be taken to protect valuable computer equipment in the classroom. Computers are, for the most part, durable pieces of equipment. In general, they will last a long time in classrooms if a minimal amount of care and upkeep are given to them. Care must be taken to ensure that computer equipment is not dropped. If computers are moved often, the probability of dropping them increases. Therefore, stationary placement of the computer is generally perferable to movement from classroom to classroom or from place to place within the room.

Periodic cleaning of the exterior surfaces of computers, monitors, and printers with a mild non-scratch cleaner is also needed. Printer ribbons need to be changed and print wheels cleaned when necessary. Other maintenance that should be planned includes cleaning and adjusting disk drives.

ORGANIZING CLASSROOM TIME
TO INCORPORATE COMPUTER USE

Experience has shown that certain factors need to be taken into consideration to make working with computers beneficial and convenient. Research by Naymark and Plaisant (1986), Kurth and Kurth (1987), and Bradley (1982) has shown that preschool and primary-grade children can use the computer effectively as a pedagogical tool. However, these same researchers maintain that it is necessary to have a well-understood code of conduct regarding the use of computers. Naymark and Plaisant (1986) claim that without a classroom organization designed to regulate access to and time of use of the machines, there is a high risk of perpetuating or even increasing existing differences among children. However, because children are usually eager to use the computers, they will respect the code of conduct if they wish to be allowed to continue using the computers.

Scheduling when the computers will be used and who will use them is a major part of efficient classroom management when working with computers. The number of computers in the classroom will make a difference in how children's work on the computer is scheduled. One of the most advantageous ways to teach composition using word processing involves having at least two computers and one printer in the classroom. If children have access to a computer at all times during the day, scheduling can be done throughout the day. Access to a computer during all aspects of the writing process can greatly facilitate the work of children during composing. It is helpful for some children to use the computer while generating ideas and organizing the structure of their papers. However, if computer access is limited, it might be necessary for children to do some prewriting with paper and pencil before they get to the computer. In that case, they can probably use 15- to 20-minute blocks of time on the computer very efficiently. Experience has shown that a 20-minute block of time is adequate for most first- and second-grade children to work on a piece of writing if they have had prewriting guidance. The 15- to 20-minute period is often long enough to complete work and yet not too long for children's attention spans.

It is necessary to teach children that computer time is valuable and that they need to spend their time efficiently. Students can be taught to monitor themselves and to follow schedules. A small kitchen timer with a soft buzzer may help children maintain the established schedule. However, it is equally important to teach children to value other children's computer time. Often, when young students realize that the time at the keyboard is limited, they monitor each other and are more apt to stay on task. If children are collaborating, extra care must be taken to keep them on task.

If pupils have access to computers only in a laboratory, it will be necessary to schedule a language arts period during the computer period. Children can go to the laboratory after prewriting activities have been completed in the classroom. In these instances, it is necessary for the teacher to accompany the students in order to teach writing skills. Children can print copies of their writing efforts, which can be brought back to the classroom for collaborative efforts. Careful attention to scheduling computer use during the introductory phase will be well worth the extra effort in planning.

USING WORD PROCESSING IN
THE CLASSROOM WRITING PROGRAM

The most important ingredient in any writing program in the elementary school is the individual teacher. This does not mean that a teacher needs to be an expert in computers; rather, the teacher needs expertise in teaching writing. Just as giving children paper and pencil does not constitute a writing curriculum, neither does giving children a computer with a word processor. The computer is only a tool to make the writing process more efficient for young children.

The use of word processing can be very beneficial, however, in the development of a strong writing curriculum. As we have seen in Chapter 3, the ease of producing a printed copy helps students reach beyond the mechanics of writing and frees them to concentrate on form, content, purpose, and audience. Nevertheless, the most important ingredient in any composition program is a teacher who is knowledgeable about the composing process. Instruction in prewriting, organizational methods, draft writing, and revision, and provision for publishing student work are necessary parts of any composition program. The use of word processing cannot substitute for quality instruction in the entire writing process.

It is often helpful for the teacher to visualize the word processor as simply the vehicle by which students will write their stories; the heart of the writing program is detailed instruction in writing that is given systematically and carefully by the teacher. No computer can teach children to write; a word processor can merely simplify some of the more tedious tasks of writing such as hand printing the letters, recopying, and making multiple copies.

Modeling Computer Use

As shown in other areas of curriculum, the importance of the teacher's modeling behavior cannot be overlooked. If children are going to view the word processor as a valuable aid to efficient writing, it is helpful for them to see the teacher using the computer for word processing. If the teacher uses the word processor and printer to write notes to the children, to write notes to parents, and to carry out other daily writing tasks, the children will soon recognize that the teacher values the computer as a helpful aid for writing. When children see their teacher use the computer as a tool for writing memorandums, for drawing graphics, and for producing neat publishable copies of written work, they will gain a sense of the purpose and usefulness of the word processor before they are asked to use it themselves. Using the word processor, the teacher can demonstrate the ease of forming letters, of correcting writing errors, and of producing printed copies.

Modeling is a powerful force in the lives of young children, and they will soon pattern their attitudes toward the computer on those shown by the teacher. A teacher who is afraid of the computer or who does not value its usefulness will convey these feelings to the pupils. However, a teacher who is enthusiastic about the computer can have a highly positive effect on the children's attitudes toward word processing.

It is not necessary for the teacher to learn all the features of the word processing program that has been chosen for the classroom. Children can be taught to word process using only a few standard commands, which can be easily mastered in a short time, with some practice. Just as it is not necessary to completely understand the internal combustion engine of an automobile before one can drive a car efficiently and safely, so it is not necessary to understand the entire disk operating system of a computer before one can write effectively. Nor is it necessary for the teacher to be an expert in keyboarding; the teacher must only be able to model correct hand position for children to watch.

It is helpful to become familiar with the basic commands of the program before attempting to teach word processing to an entire classroom of children. Introductory modeling of the program for children can help the teacher establish a level of expertise with the program. Also, modeling of the program for children can give teachers confidence that they have mastered the basic commands of the program.

Selecting Appropriate Hardware for Word Processing

There are now many adequate brands from which to choose when selecting a computer for word processing in elementary schools. The only major requirement is that the computer have a memory large enough to handle the selected word processing program. If the word processing program uses speech synthesis, it is important that the computer be equipped with a compatible speech synthesizer. (There are many variations in quality of speech synthesizers. Although children can adapt well to synthesized speech of questionable quality, it is advisable to choose a synthesizer that has good sound quality; see Chapter 9.)

Choosing a monitor for word processing by young children is very important. The on screen characters must be relatively large and clear. Small print monitors or monitors with poor resolution make it very difficult for young children to read the text on the screen. A high quality monitor is more necessary when children are learning word processing than when they are using computer programs for drill and practice.

Access to a printer is also very helpful in a computer-assisted writing program. A letter quality or near letter quality printer helps children realize the importance of standard orthography in written communication and helps them develop a sense of audience as they print compositions to be shared with others. Because printer noise can be very intrusive in a classroom, printers that print with almost no sound are highly recommended. If this is not possible, printer boxes that muffle sound can be purchased.

Selecting Appropriate Software for Word Processing

The myriad of software available for classrooms sometimes overwhelms teachers, and they perceive learning about computer software to be a time-consuming and difficult task. The easiest way to learn is simply to use a program until one is familiar and comfortable with its purpose and functions. Just as no one person reads every book in the library, so it is not necessary for a classroom teacher to be familiar with every piece of computer software in the software library. For teaching writing, it is necessary to learn only one word processing program.

There are many adequate word processing programs on the software market today. Often, the choice of software has already been made by others, and the teacher must use the word processing program that has been adopted at the district or building level. In my experience, children can learn to use most word processing programs effectively if they are given systematic instruction.

A good composition program can be taught using only a very simple word processing program. It is more efficient if young children are taught only a few basic word processing commands. A powerful word processor with many advanced features is not necessary for young children who are just beginning to learn to write. Also, it appears to be helpful for small children if the screen is relatively clear. On screen menus and complicated data lines seem to confuse young children as they attempt to write.

One very desirable feature in a child's word processor is a prompt that reminds children to save their work before the program is exited or the diskette is removed. This feature ensures that valuable data will not be lost by forgetting to save it. Adding a simple graphics program allows children to illustrate their written material easily if they wish to do so. A spelling checker has also been shown to be a useful tool for children learning to write with the word processor (see Chapter 10).

Introducing Children to Start-Up Procedures

Very young children can be taught to handle diskettes in a short time. Modeling diskette use by the teacher is probably the best type of instruction. For young children, a small red dot seal placed on the top front side of the diskette will help them remember which way to insert the diskette in the machine. If they place their finger on the dot, and the dot is on the upper side of the diskette, children will usually be able to insert the diskette properly. Children need to be taught that diskettes must be stored carefully in their packets and that they cannot be bent, folded, or licked. It is important that diskettes never be stored near magnets or magnetized surfaces because these magnetic fields can destroy data stored on diskettes. Because telephones use magnetic fields, diskettes should not be placed near telephones. It is advisable to have a safe storage area near the computer for storing diskettes. Diskettes kept in children's desks often are ruined when they are crushed by other objects in the desk. Children can be easily taught that it is their responsibility to keep the diskettes in working order.

In my experience, it is generally easier to have the word processing program loaded on the computer before children are asked to write. This is advisable because loading programs is often time-consuming and wastes valuable computer use time. If the program is already loaded on the machine, the children can simply insert their own personal diskette and write and edit their stories.

Teaching Children to Use the Word Processing Software

If children are going to learn to use the word processor efficiently, instruction in its features must be provided by the teacher. There are certain basic word processing commands which need to be mastered before children can be successful at word processing. However, most young children can learn them easily if they are taught systematically. These commands include ENTER, simple cursor movement, SAVE, DELETE, RETRIEVE, PRINT, and, if a voice synthesizer is used, TALK. (Advanced features of word processing, such as moving blocked text, are best introduced only after children have had substantial practice using the word processor.)

The ENTER (or return) key is the instruction that tells the computer to perform the entered operation. In some programs, arrows allow free cursor movement through written text without disturbing it. The DELETE command tells the computer to erase whatever has been typed on the screen or saved to a diskette (care should be taken to use this command judiciously with respect to the latter). The SAVE command tells the computer to save whatever has been typed on the screen to the diskette. The RETRIEVE command allows material that has been saved on a diskette to be brought back to the screen for viewing, editing, or printing. The PRINT command allows the student to print material on paper. The TALK command allows the words written on the screen to be synthesized into oral sound.

When introducing young children to word processing, it is easier to practice writing using simple sentences, which the children copy. Because direct teaching of computer skills is advisable for this introduction, it is better if a small group of five or six children are taught at one time. After the demonstration, children can be assigned practice times. In most instances, it is helpful for the children to have had some keyboarding training before they attempt word processing. In the initial introduction, the ENTER command, the DELETE key, and the arrows can be explained. It is helpful to explain to children that the word *delete* simply means *erase*, and that this key will erase part of the text on the screen.

When children begin to practice entering text, it is advisable to have the teacher or an older student monitor the entries. Young children are sometimes easily frustrated, and close monitoring in the early stages is often helpful to avoid frustration.

The second introductory lesson on word processing should introduce children to the idea of saving, retrieving, and printing text. These procedures also need to be taught to children through direct instruction. Children need to understand the importance of remembering the names of files so they can retrieve them from the catalog/directory.

After these two introductory lessons have been taught, children are ready to begin using the computer as a tool in the language arts class. Now it becomes important that the teacher schedule prewriting activities so that children can begin to write stories using their newly learned skills. With careful introductory lessons, it is surprising how quickly even kindergarteners can learn to use the word processor. As before, for the very first attempts at writing their own stories at the computer, it is helpful if an aide or knowledgeable older student is available to help if problems arise. This assistance is necessary only for the first two or three practices; it is helpful in making a smooth transition to using the word processor. Students from the upper elementary grades are often willing to act as computer helpers.

Managing Editing Groups

An important incentive for both global and group editing is the ease with which finished copies, multiple copies, and revisions of compositions can be made. However, it is important that the process of group editing be taught to the children; this encourages them to think about the content of the material, rather than the simple mechanics of writing. It is also significant that teachers emphasize the revision function of editing groups. Teachers interested only in spelling and punctuation utilize word processing primarily for correcting errors and deprive children of an important step in the writing process.

Researchers such as Cohen and Riel (1986) have found that the use of word processing can foster group collaboration and group editing in writing. However, this collaborative writing does not occur naturally. A teacher needs to plan for these specific collaborative activities and schedule times for them. Even small children can work effectively in editing groups after the teacher has given them guidelines for working together. Codes of conduct during collaborative writing or editing must be clearly specified by the teacher. If children understand the collaborative tasks and are given clear directions as to the acceptable and unacceptable behavior, they can work well together.

One technique is to divide the editing group task into two specific parts—discussion of content and discussion of mechanics. Only when the children are satisfied with the content of the story is the correction of mechanical errors allowed. This technique helps children focus on the communicative aspect of the writing process, which is essential to all good writing.

Printing

One of the advantages of computer word processing is the fact that printed copies to share with others can be made easily. These copies can have the look of a professional document if the printer is a letter- or near letter-quality printer. This feature of the computer helps to give children the idea that in most instances the purpose of writing is to communicate with other people. For that reason, messages should be as legible as possible. The use of a letter-quality or near letter-quality printer enables children to print their work in a format that is worthy of their best ideas and that can be easily read by others. Thus, the use of word processing in composition makes it easier for children to learn the communicative aspects of writing.

Teachers, nevertheless, need to be aware that students generally find the printing process more fascinating than any other word processing activity. This is especially true if they have illustrated their stories with computer-produced graphics. Most children enjoy watching their own stories come from the printer. Printing, however, is the most expensive step in word processing. Paper and ribbons are costly and can be rapidly consumed by a roomful of eager young writers. Therefore, guidelines need to be given to children about the use of the printer.

In several writing projects in which first and second graders used word processing, I found it necessary to limit the amount of printing that children were allowed to do. A good general rule is that a child may make one copy of a story during each scheduled computer time. If editing groups are used, the teacher could suggest that printing be done only after the editing group and/or the teacher has read and approved the story on screen. If this is not feasible, children could print one copy of their stories for each member of the editing group.

If graphics such as those found in Print Shop or Print Master are used to illustrate stories, it is generally advisable for the teacher to approve these graphics before they are printed. This is because graphics generally are more expensive and more time-consuming to print than the short stories written by young children.

Printer noise during classes can be very distracting to children; often, it can be mitigated by a printer box that muffles the noise. If this is not possible, printing may have to be limited to special periods during the day when classes are not scheduled. It is also possible for the teacher to do all of the printing for the children outside of class, which is necessary if no classroom printer is available. Although this is not as advantageous as having a printer in the classroom, it can serve as motivation: Children come to school the next day eager to see their stories in print.

Maintaining Records

Writing teachers have long recognized the value of keeping a record of student writing to trace developmental progress. Word processing makes it especially easy to store copies of children's writing in a very small space. If each child uses one diskette for all stories, this diskette can become a personal record of writing progress. When parents attend progress conferences, the teacher can simply review the child's writing for them by retrieving the stories to the screen for their viewing. Making back-up copies of student disks at certain intervals is advisable to ensure that the record of children's progress will not be lost. Children can easily be taught that the proper care and storage of their diskettes is their individual responsibility. It is helpful to have a safe and convenient storage container near the computer so children can have easy access to their own diskettes.

Integrating the Computer
into the Classroom Curriculum

The computer is best used as an integral part of the curriculum. Polin (1987) noted that computer use often degenerates to isolated drill and practice activity that has no relevance to any curricular activity. Thus, it is not enough to teach children the word processing program and tell them to write stories whenever they wish to. If the computer is going to be used as a tool for improving writing skills, word processing activities must follow carefully structured lessons on prewriting, writing, rewriting, and editing activities, as described throughout this volume. Thus, children feel that using the computer is part of the ongoing curricular activity in the classroom; the computer becomes a useful educational tool.

In their classroom observations, Naymark and Plaisant (1986) found that computer work rapidly becomes tedious and cut off from the children's daily activity if the teacher does not provide for its linkage to other class activities. A word processing writing program can be used as a tool for eliminating some of the more tedious parts of writing for young children, such as letter formation, correcting, recopying, and revision. This type of instruction can make computer use a viable part of the curriculum, rather than the practice of isolated and seemingly irrelevant skills.

SUMMARY

The teacher is the key to the success of word processing in the writing curriculum. The use of word processing can be of great benefit to children because some of the more tedious tasks of writing are done by the computer. However, the integration of the computer into the classroom poses definite management problems for teachers. Classroom instruction, organization, and schedules must be adjusted. With careful preplanning of these management changes, the addition of word processing to the writing program can be exciting and profitable for both children and teacher.

REFERENCES

Bradley, V. (1982). Improving students' writing with microcomputers. *Language Arts, 59,* 732-743.

Cohen, M., & Riel, M. (1986, August). *Computer networks: Creating real audiences for students' writing.* Report #15 from the Interactive Technology Laboratory of the Center for Human Processing; University of California, San Diego.

Jungck, S. (1987, April). *A critical analysis of local curriculum development: The case of computer literacy.* Paper presented at the annual meeting of the American Educational Research Association, Washington, D. C.

Kurth, R. (1987, January). Using word processing to enhance revision strategies during student writing activities. *Educational Technology, XXVII,* 13-19.

Kurth, R., & Kurth, L. (1987, April). A comparison of writing instruction using word processing, word processing with voice synthesis, and no word processing in kindergarten and first grade. ERIC Document No. 283 196.

Mathinos, D., & Woodward, A. (1987, April). *The use of instructional computing in an elementary school: Removing those rose-colored glasses.* Paper presented at the annual meeting of the American Educational Research Association, Washington, D. C.

Naymark, J., & Plaisant, C. (1986). The computer and the pre-school child; the written language and play. *Computer Education, 10,* 167-174.

Polin, L. G. (1987, April). *Factors affecting the development and implementation of a computer based composition program.* Paper presented at the annual meeting of the American Educational Research Association, Washington, D. C.

Woodward, A., & Mathinos, D. (1987, April). *Microcomputer education in an elementary school: The rhetoric vs. reality of an innovation.* Paper presented at the annual meeting of the American Educational Research Association, Washington, D. C.

6 Language Experience as an Introduction to Word Processing

TERRY S. SALINGER
Educational Testing Service

The language experience approach (LEA) to reading instruction is a common supplement to more traditional reading and language arts methods in the primary grades. This chapter proposes that the LEA method, without detracting from its power for emerging reading, can be employed with the help of word processing to facilitate text production in the early years. As such, LEA can be used as an indirect but efficient model of composing behaviors that children will need if they are to take full advantage of word processing. In effect, teachers can at first become word processors themselves. In that role, they can help children gain insight into editing and revision, the aspects of composition that word processors most clearly enhance.

LANGUAGE EXPERIENCE: TRADITIONAL USES

The language experience approach has an august reputation. It has been stated that "beginning with language experience to teach children to read and write is like using a complete food to achieve good health rather than combining a number of incomplete ones" (Jewell & Zintz, 1986, p. 177). The completeness of LEA stems from its integration of all language systems—speaking, listening, writing, and reading—and its adaptability for most instructional situations. The basic concept of LEA is that whatever children say can be written down, and once statements are written down, the speakers themselves and others can read them. The transcription becomes the basal material for reading instruction. Because it reflects children's own ideas, the material is highly motivating and relevant to young readers.

In most traditional use of LEA with large or small groups, children dictate their ideas about a shared experience, such as a field trip, or about a stimulus probe, such as "Our Families." Teachers transcribe what children say, and teachers and children share the resulting story, which is often used for additional reading instruction. Transcription can take many forms. Teachers may use dialogue for each child's statement. Thus, for example, a LEA story might read:

> Joan said, We went to the zoo.
> Matt added, We saw lots of animals.
> I like the elephants because they were big, said Luis.

In a variation without scripted dialogue, teachers transcribe statements exactly as dictated or sometimes make minor changes so that the LEA text shows standard grammar and usage. Exact transcription helps children realize the connection between oral and written language. As discussed in Chapter 7 of this book, this method can be especially useful with children who have limited English proficiency, speak non-standard dialects, or code switch between two languages. In these instances, LEA transcription results in instructional material that sounds right to beginning readers whose oral language differs from that of basal reader series. Gradually, teachers may edit children's statements to demonstrate mainstream usage and provide a bridge between variant dialects and school language.

Because children often attempt to sound booklike or are overly attentive to syntax and word choices, dialogue and exact transcription can produce boring, repetitive stories. In their attempt to sound right, children may essentially edit naturalness and vitality from spontaneous speech. An alternative form of transcription, which will be discussed in detail below, is more dynamic in that teachers listen to what children suggest and selectively combine ideas to weave together a coherent story. However they are transcribed, LEA stories, which are frequently written on large chart tablets, can be saved and used for ongoing reading and sharing. Themes such as "Our Trips" or "How Our Plants Grow" may be compiled in one big book, or stories may be copied on smaller paper, bound together, and kept as library books.

The language experience approach can also be used individually, for example, when a teacher transcribes a sentence or two under a child's drawing. Further, LEA is employed when a teacher helps individual children compile word banks of significant, personal words. Children request words they would like to know and teachers write them on file cards. These cards become a core vocabulary which children review frequently, play with, swap, and use as a personal dictionary for their own story writing. Because children request words that they want to learn, the words are meaningful and easy to remember. Teachers help children generalize word-attack and word-building skills from this basic sight vocabulary and lead them toward independent decoding of unfamiliar words.

Whether LEA is used for group or individual instruction, children contribute to text production, that is, they generate ideas even if they do not transcribe them. The resulting material is meaningful in that it reflects children's experiences and ideas. Furthermore, the reading level of the resulting composition is appropriate because children have drawn from their own vocabularies and knowledge of grammar and usage. Children, unlike adults, rarely attempt to use words or sentence structures that they do not at least think they know. Additionally,

> the use of language experience is highly motivating to children. The use of personal words, like the use of one's name, is a highly satisfying experience. [Children] gain the same sense of self-esteem that adults do when seeing their own ideas in print; they are not only important to the person individually, but they are important enough to be preserved and shared with others. (Jewell & Zintz, 1986, p. 177)

The references at the end of this chapter list several sources of information about LEA.

USING THE POTENTIAL OF LEA FOR TEXT PRODUCTION

Many teachers limit LEA use to dictation, transcription, and reading of chart stories; compilations of word banks; and annotations on individuals' drawings or paintings. They do not capitalize on the potential of LEA to promote text production—the composing process in its fullest sense. Mere talk written down is not full text production. Researchers investigating children's mastery of composition usually describe the writing process in terms of several distinct steps (Graves, 1983). At the very least, composing involves these stages:

1. *Prewriting*: developing and organizing ideas, often through talk
2. *Drafting*: getting ideas down quickly
3. *Revising*: reworking drafts to make better; adding or deleting words and ideas; moving text around for better organization and flow
4. *Publishing*: preparing a finished, neat copy of a written work for sharing with others.

Experienced writers may go through several revisions before they are satisfied with a composition; beginners usually do not revise extensively but should at least be aware of the process.

The language experience approach can be used to model these stages if teachers listen to children's dictation, edit ideas, and transcribe selectively. Throughout LEA sessions, teachers can elicit suggestions for changes and revisions and demonstrate how easily proofreading marks can be used to edit an emerging story. As they weave children's dictation into text and elicit revisions, teachers are actually modeling behaviors that will be needed if a word processor is to be more than a typewriter and automated file folder. By moving from the role of scribe to that of editor, teachers engage children in an active process of structuring ideas into unified, interesting prose. In effect, teachers become word processors themselves. They demonstrate the hard decision-making processes involved in writing and then model how easy it can be to change an emerging draft. Children see that what can be said, can be written down, and what can be written down, can also be changed. This scenario, following a class trip to the zoo, is an example of this approach.

Teacher and first graders are seated in front of a chart tablet with "Our Big Book of Trips" on its cover. Teacher turns to a blank page.

TEACHER: Let's write a story about our trip. Ideas for a title?
CHILD 1:   The Zoo?
CHILD 2:   The Trip to the Zoo?
CHILD 3:   Our Trip to the Zoo?

TEACHER: Anyone else? No? Well, which title do you like?

CHILDREN: Our Trip to the Zoo.

TEACHER: Zoo starts with what letter?

CHILDREN: Z! [Teacher writes the title at the top.]

TEACHER: Ideas for our first sentence?

CHILD 1:   We went to the zoo.

CHILD 2:   We had a trip to the zoo.

CHILD 3:   We went to the zoo on May 15.

TEACHER: OK, here goes. Look at what I write: We took a trip to the zoo on May 15. Other ideas? What did we see *first*? [She emphasizes "first" to demonstrate that stories should be in sequence.]

CHILD 1:   We saw big elephants.

CHILD 2:   They were really huge and gray.

CHILD 3:   We had lunch.

TEACHER: Right. We saw elephants first; we had lunch much later and we'll write about that after we write about all the things we did before we ate. Watch what I write: We saw elephants. They were huge. Any comments?

CHILD 2:   They were r-r-r-really huge.

TEACHER: OK, you want to say really huge; this is what I can do. [She writes an arrow and inserts "really" above the line of print and rereads the sentences, pointing to each word.]

CHILD 3:   And they were gray too; put that in too.

CHILD 1:   And had big floppy ears. [Teacher crosses out the period and continues: "and gray and they had floppy ears." Then she inserts "big," over the line.]

TEACHER: Who will read what I wrote?

CHILD 3:   Our Trip to the Zoo. We saw elephants—first, oh, first isn't there, put it in. [Teacher makes the addition. Child continues:] We saw elephants first. They were really huge and gray and had big, floppy ears.

TEACHER: Good. Let's think about what we should write next.
        . . .

[After the entire story is written, children and teacher reread it and the teacher asks for suggestions for changes.]

TEACHER: Anyone want to add something or change a part?

CHILD 1:   We didn't say that the lion had a baby. Can we add that?

TEACHER: Sure. Who can read the sentences about the lion?

CHILD 2: We saw two lions. One was a female and one was a male. The male had a big mane of hair.

CHILD 3: We could add: The female was a mommy.

CHILD 2: We could say: There was a baby too.

TEACHER: Well?

CHILD 1: Write "and she had a baby." Put it before the part about the male.

TEACHER: OK, I think I know what you want. Watch and see if this is it. [She makes the additions and changes the structure of the original sentence.]

CHILD 1: Good. I'll read it: We saw two lions. One was a female, and she had a baby. One was a male, and he had a big mane of hair.

This kind of interaction shows children the complex task of transforming talk into text. Even preschoolers and kindergarteners gain insight from participation in these LEA sessions. They listen to each other and observe their teacher actually thinking about their ideas before transcribing.

Time spent sharing ideas is similar to the prewriting or organizing phase prior to actual writing: Ideas spin around in a writer's head until he or she finally puts them together for actual transcription. When teachers begin to write, children can recognize their own and others' ideas embedded within the written message. As the text emerges, children are encouraged to weigh possibilities and suggest and reject ideas and words. This, too, is like real writing. In this approach, teachers maintain control of the flow of a story, as in the interchange above where the teacher reminded a child that the story must go in sequence. This reflects the selection process in real writing in that writers must organize and sequence their ideas in accordance with the pattern required for the kind of writing they are doing. Teachers may make a brief written note about ideas that are presented out of sequence or may ask children to remember them and introduce them again later. This postponing of ideas will not be construed as rejection if teachers explain their purpose in sequencing a story in a particular way. If children present ideas that are totally inappropriate for a group story, teachers can use the same exclusion process, with the explanation that the suggestion is a good one for another story.

Asking for suggestions after a story is finished, even several days after initial transcription, gives young writers awareness of the progression from first draft to revision to final copy. If LEA transcription demonstrates the transition from talk to print, then editing and revising an LEA story show the transition from the first to the finished draft. In the editing and revising stage, children have more input because it is they who make suggestions for changes and additions. Teachers serve primarily as scribes unless they direct children's attention to a particular part of a story. After a story has been completed, the teacher may copy it over for group sharing or inclusion in a class book. Cleaning up an edited story in this way represents the publishing phase of the writing process, the step in which a story is made ready for the public.

Because the goal of LEA is to teach children about the writing and reading processes, teacher monitoring and control of ideas that are written down is highly instructive. The approach requires different levels of teacher and student involvement from those required by the traditional transcription method. Teachers have to think about what children say and make decisions about what to write in processing oral statements into coherent written text. Children, too, have to work hard because it is not enough to make a single statement, see it written down, and consider one's responsibility complete. Rather than being automatically transcribed, children's statements are edited, combined, and often restated. How ideas are actually recorded may be surprising, and new comments should make sense within the emerging text. Children are also given the opportunity to change their minds, to add new ideas, or to take out ones they do not like. For children, the whole process is almost like writing themselves—except that teachers do some of the mental work and all of the handwriting.

USING LEA TO INTRODUCE WORD PROCESSING

If teachers adopt the edit/transcribe/revise processes of the LEA to model the writing process and if their classrooms have a computer, logic would dictate using a word processor for LEA sessions. Word processors make it easy to compose, edit, restructure, and re-edit text and to produce clean copies for publication. Because revision is easy with word processors, writers tend to "take risks, to be more tentative about meaning for longer, to consider organization and word choices more freely than ever before" (Newman, 1984, p. 495). Using the word processor for LEA can reduce actual teacher effort, and computerized LEA sessions can

introduce word processing within a comfortable, meaningful context. Both individual and small group instruction lend themselves
to computerized LEA. Four cautions concerning the use of word
processing with LEA should be noted.

1. Children must be thoroughly familiar with revision as a
   natural strategy in composition; if they think that first
   drafts are final drafts or that revising means copying over,
   revision with a word processor will not make sense.
2. Children should be familiar with the computer, even if
   they have not worked with word processing before.
3. Teachers must remember that it may take time for children
   to master all the steps in using a word processor and that
   children may be fearful of losing their text in the computer.
4. Instruction at the computer should be conducted with individuals and with small groups so that everyone can see
   easily.

Introducing word processing to individual children will be discussed first.

Introducing Word Processing to Individual Children

A participatory demonstration is often effective in introducing
word processing within LEA. First, individual children should be
invited to the computer to dictate a story. Once they are familiar
with the procedure and interested in computers, most children are
willing to accommodate the teacher's invitation. The best approach is to sit a child on one's lap, invite him or her to dictate,
and merely type.

The child has a line-of-sight view of the teacher's hands, the
monitor, and the keyboard. The teacher may pause from time to
time to see what the child thinks will happen to the words: Will
they split at the ends of lines, wrap around, go to the next line?
Even the most sophisticated young computer user will be intrigued by type marching across the screen. If a story grows to a
size that causes the text to scroll, children are often convinced
that their words are lost forever in the computer. These simple
attributes of word processing become especially interesting when
it is the child's own words on the monitor.

As the story emerges, the child observes the monitor, the
teacher's hands, and his or her own words. The child may dictate

more than usual, merely to observe the monitor. The child can see the correction process, count the words, and point to the space between words. Revision should not be stressed during the introductory session. After a story is finished, the teacher saves the work in a file labeled with the writer's name. The child receives a printed copy as soon as possible and spends a few minutes re-reading the story. At this point, the child may want to make editorial changes or additions and should be encouraged to do so. Arrows, crossings out, and carets that are familiar in LEA chart stories can be used on these printed stories as well. The following shows a story dictated by a kindergartener and his requested changes.

> I played He Man. I gived some kids some popcorn. Timmy ran after me. I tried to get away from him. I had some very good fun. I never went against the wall. I'm glad that I didn't meet a snake over there. I'm glad that I'm at this school.

The child's story was transcribed verbatim, printed, and presented to him for reading and editing. He requested that the verb "gived" be changed to "gave" because the latter sounded better.

Individual children may want to begin typing their own stories at this point, and teachers must make a decision about timing. If independent composition is the ultimate goal, direct instruction in word processing should be given first. Having seen the magic of word processing through their LEA dictation, children will be receptive to small group instruction on word processing and anxious to try it themselves.

Introducing Word Processing to Small Groups

To introduce word processing to a small group of children, a teacher elicits a group story that will, ideally, fit on the screen in its entirety. Children familiar with LEA should be comfortable contributing ideas for this computerized story. If teachers make typing mistakes, they merely fix them and again point out the wrap around and other features of the word processor. The next step is for volunteers to read the story, count the words, find words of interest, and generally study the text. Suggestions for revision and additions come next, and the teacher may query children about how revision strategies familiar from LEA can be applied to the story on the monitor. "Just watch!" is the response. As the cursor moves over the screen and as words are inserted and deleted, children are fascinated—and more interested in the computer than in the revisions. (Marcus, 1987, described this interest in his finding that children often view this as writing with light.) Teachers should stress that stories should be saved, but may not want to overemphasize the mechanics of doing so at this point. Printing clean copies of the story makes the experience complete. Below, a group dictation is shown, which served this introductory purpose.

> Once there was a great big, gray and black and purple robot named Olga. She could do anything at all you wanted. She had two cousins named Paul and Georgie. They were all nice robots. They ruled the universe, and when aliens came, they fought. And the robots won!

Children in a second-grade class dictated this story during their first session with word processing. They collectively selected the theme of the robot, which they named Olga after one of their group members. Olga suggested that her cousins be included. After dictation, the children supplied the descriptive color words and suggested that the last sentence end with an exclamation point.

The group's second session at the computer provides more direct instruction. The teacher stresses the sequence of steps for loading the word processor and retrieving stories from storage, with special emphasis on the need to save stories after working on them. The teacher may make a chart of these steps to hang near the computer or may use LEA procedures to help students develop a "How to" file to save on a class disk. Figure 6.1 shows a sample file prepared for second graders. They referred to the file when they needed to review procedures for using the Bank Street Writer. Retrieving a story from storage may seem like magic when children have been used to games and Computer Assisted Instruction (CAI) that load directly: They themselves must do something more active to find the file and bring it to the screen. The first few times children write independently at the computer, they may forget to save their work. Then, when they go to retrieve it, their fears about lost files are confirmed. Careful instruction in the various steps of beginning and ending word processing sessions can avoid frustration.

Figure 6.1   Sample "How To" File of Procedures
for Using Bank Street Writer

1. Boot Bank Street Writer with label facing up.
2. Remove Bank Street Writer and insert your own or the class disk.
3. Press ESC to get to the EDIT MODE; then use one of the APPLE KEYS to get to the TRANSFER MODE.
4. Press RETURN to highlight RETRIEVE and indicate YES to get a catalog of the files on the disk.
5. Select the file you wish to use and retrieve it from memory.
6. Read the instructions in the MENU at the top of the screen and do what you are told.
7. You may print your work if you know how; follow the PRINT instructions carefully.

Note: This file was prepared as a reference for students using Bank Street Writer I. Directions for any word processor can be written and saved in a "how to" file. Students refer to the file to make sure they understand the procedures needed to get started or to continue their work with the word processor.

When a file is retrieved, the teacher and children reread the story and decide if it merits any revision (it may not be meaty enough to stand additional work). If revisions seem appropriate, the teacher models and explains cursor movement and other aspects of the word processor. If a new story is needed for demonstration, the teacher may elicit another dictation or retrieve a prepared file already saved on disk (Prepared EDIT files are discussed below). Teacher control at this point, as in traditional LEA, guarantees that all children see what is going on before they themselves are given responsibility for independent work. Children can try to make changes themselves or go from mode to mode, but they may be reluctant at first for fear of losing the text. The group can be encouraged to discuss the relative worth of suggested changes, a procedure familiar from LEA. This prepares young writers for working independently and in pairs at the word processor. Observations of children writing with computers have indicated that

> in "milling around" the computer . . . students read each other's writing and interacted over it. These interactions affected both the content and form of student writing. Similarly, peer interactions during writing on the computer, student access to other students' work stored in the computer . . . can affect students' understanding of purpose in writing, and their sense of audience. (Bruce, Michaels, & Watson-Gegeo, 1985, p. 145)

This kind of interaction ought to have begun in dictate/edit/transcribe sessions and should be encouraged to continue.

To provide additional practice with the mechanics of word processing, teachers can prepare EDIT files and save them on a class disk. Figure 6.2 shows a sample EDIT file. These files should contain stories that were written by class members and possibly old LEA stories. The material should be relatively interesting but contain clearly identifiable errors for students to correct. By write-protecting the diskette (that is, placing a label over the protect notch on the diskette) the teacher prevents the children from erasing the stories, and the children can edit and change at will. Working in pairs, students retrieve a practice file, make their changes, and print their revised story. Clearing the write-protected file erases their changes. Because the stories are already composed and typed, children can concentrate their energies on two facets of word processing: learning the word processor and revising. They do not have to think up a story, nor do they have to type one.

Figure 6.2   Sample EDIT File

EDITING PRACTICE

Directions: This file will give you some practice editing with Bank Street Writer. Your job is to read the story presented below, to find spelling errors, and to make changes. The only thing you have to change are words that are not spelled correctly, but you may add other ideas of your own if you want. *One Hint:* Tiape is spelled correctly. It is the name of an animal that is a cross between a TIGER and an APE. NOW SCROLL down until you see the story. To SCROLL DOWN, you must be in the EDIT MODE. Just hold the DOWN ARROW key down until you reach the story.

Tiape

Once upon a time I saw a Tiape. It ate a lot of bannannas. It was huge and ugle like a monstre, but he bacam my frend. And we walked, played, and saw funny movies, and most of all we wnt to the soo to see his familey. We are the best of frends, but one day, the zoo polyce captured him. I was mad and sad. I did'nt eat or play. I got lonly with out the cretur. I saw it in my mind, all blak and yello. I hope he is happy at the zoo.

Note: Students read the instructions and practice using the word processor to make changes in the text. This practice file was prepared for Bank Street Writer I.

Just as teacher transcription is an efficient way for children to produce neat, clean copies of their own LEA stories, revising these sample stories provides an efficient way for children to practice new skills. As they experiment, they test their ideas about revision, discuss them with a partner, possibly double check them with the teacher, and strengthen the skills modeled in LEA sessions. They will probably even add new material and produce longer stories. They are gaining confidence in the word processor and their ability to use it.

Transition to Independent Text Production

Early childhood educators introduce word processing to children because they believe that even young children can write success-fully. Widespread acceptance of this belief, while not as new as microcomputers and word processing, is still relatively recent. For many years, early childhood teachers found that

> the difficulties of handwriting and spelling tend[ed] to impede and delay [children's] genuine desire to produce written lan-guage for a purpose. Traditionally this difficulty [was] met by inserting a more manageable task—copying. . . . It was not until the advent of language-experience methods that any real attempt was made to satisfy children's aspirations to use the mysterious symbols of print to record personal meanings. (Holdaway, 1979, p. 36)

Researchers have found that children who have participated in strong LEA programs tend to move into independent, creative writing smoothly and confidently, especially if their teachers keep emerging spelling and handwriting in perspective.

The word processor is another tool for this growth, not a manageable task in itself but a means for managing the tasks involved in beginning composition. Because word processors lessen the psychomotor and memory demands on young writers, beginners can concentrate on the more satisfying aspects of com-position—producing stories and fixing them up through revi-sion—so long as they have an intuitive sense about the stages in the composing process. Here, clearly, is the connection with LEA. Teachers were previously scribes, releasing children from the manual chores of writing. They were also editors as they wove ideas together and recorded revisions. Word processors require children to take more control of the composing process, while freeing them from having to remember, visualize, and manually form the letters they need in order to express their thoughts. Because of the time and energy these physical tasks require, they may actually inhibit some young children from composing extensively. Word processors allow children to recognize letters and press corresponding keys, two tasks more efficient than writing by hand. Also, the technology itself is motivating (Phenix & Hannan, 1984) so children attend to their writing for extended periods of time. Because it is easy to change text, they do not view it as fixed and permanent, and tend to revise freely even if only at the surface level. In fact, changing text becomes almost a game. Revision necessitates moving the cursor, sometimes using the search and replace function, and generally playing with the computer. Young writers see their texts taking shape on the monitor as they manipulate words and phrases, confident that a clean copy of the new version can be readily produced. If their word processor has a spelling checker, they know they can clean up their work further. Additionally, the knowledge that weak or slow handwriting will not impede their ability to produce what Balajthy calls publishable work (see Chapter 10) motivates children to write more for public sharing.

SUMMARY

The language experience approach is motivating because it uses children's own ideas; it is safe because teachers write text down. The approach gives children a sense of themselves as authors and when used interactively demonstrates real text production. Word processing is motivating because it uses both children's ideas and the computer. Word processing frees children to write more and better at an earlier age as long as they understand the stages of the composing process and the special usefulness of the word processor in that process. The key to good writing and the real advantage of word processing are the same: revising initial drafts of written work. When LEA is used to model revising and then to introduce word processing strategies, children understand revision and quickly appreciate the value of word processing in their writing.

REFERENCES

Bruce, B.; Michaels, S.; & Watson-Gegeo, K. (1985). How computers can change the writing process. *Language Arts, 62,* 143–149.

Graves, D. H. (1983). *Writing: Teachers and children at work.* Portsmouth, NH: Heinemann.

Holdaway, D. (1979). *The foundations of literacy.* Portsmouth, NH: Heinemann.

Jewell, M. G., & Zintz, M. (1986). *Learning to read naturally.* Dubuque, IA: Kendall Hunt.

Marcus, S. (1987, February). *Computers and writing across the curriculum.* Texas Joint Council of Teachers of English Conference, Corpus Christi, TX.

Newman, J. M. (1984). Language, learning, and computers. *Language Arts, 61,* 494–497.

Phenix, J., & Hannan, E. (1984). Word processing in the grade one classroom. *Language Arts, 61,* 804–812.

Salinger, T. (1985). Kindergartners and word processing. In L. Gentile (Ed.), *Reading education in Texas,* Yearbook of the Texas International Reading Association, Vol. 1, 1–5.

Part III
WORD PROCESSING
WITH SPECIAL NEEDS CHILDREN

7 Word Processing in the English as a Second Language Classroom

MARY A. JOHNSON
University of Texas at Tyler

As we have seen in previous chapters, word processing appears to have a great deal of potential as a tool for facilitating the writing process. Thus far, however, emphasis has been on the utility of this tool for English proficient students. This chapter will focus on the contribution of the computer as communication facilitator for the early-elementary English as a Second Language (ESL) classroom. Specifically, it will focus the literacy needs of the growing ESL population, the use of the language experience approach (LEA) with ESL students, the computer as facilitator within LEA, and the advantages of using word processing with ESL students. Finally, attention will be given to utilizing word processing with limited English proficient (LEP) students and to considerations about choosing a word processing package for the ESL classroom.

Considerable research has been and is being conducted to study the effects of computer usage in the classroom. With the introduction of O.K. Moore's Talking Typewriter in 1963, the positive effects of technology on student attitudes and achievement have been recognized. However, there is a notable absence of research with regard to computer use by students in ESL classrooms. Limited access to compuer use by minority language students and the prerequisite reading skill required by a good deal of software are cited as possible reasons for this research void.

While, as we have seen, reports from teachers and students using word processing tend to be mostly positive (Daiute, 1985; Hope, Taylor, & Pusack, 1984; Johnson, 1986; Kleinman & Humphrey, 1982; Manion, 1985; and others cited throughout this volume), none have focused on the power of this tool for minority language students. In a recent study of this area (Johnson, 1986), I found significant differences between the writing of first- and second-grade LEP students who used word processing and a control group who used pencil and paper to write their stories. The LEP students who used word processing generally wrote longer stories, edited more frequently, revised more extensively, and collaborated more readily in their writing than did students who used pencil and paper.

The writing process is often especially complicated for young LEP students. First, they tend to construct their ideas in their first language; second, they strain to think of the English translation; and third, they struggle with the correct formation of the letters needed to form the words in writing. It is easy to see how their ideas get lost in the process of writing. Word processing has been shown to be a successful tool in helping these students get their ideas down before they are forgotten. It is helpful in allowing students to write without the tedium of trying to shape letters with a pencil. Students using word processing know that whatever is typed may be changed or deleted very easily at a later time, so effort is expended in recording ideas as they come rather than in worrying about syntax, spelling, or handwriting. Word processing also has the advantage of helping make what is written more readable. Because the print from word processing parallels that which they see in texts, students associate their writing with what they read in class. Word processing also allows students to generate multiple copies of their stories. Value is given to what they have written when copies are available for the class collection of stories, the teacher, parents, peers, or anyone with whom the students want to share. Usually, as each person is given a copy, the children read their stories aloud, and this provides extra practice in reading. Parents of LEP students are often impressed by the students' ability to produce a computer story, and praise from parents is another source of motivation for these students.

A look at the growth in the number of language minority students throughout the United States dictates the need for greatly expanded research on such uses of computers in the ESL classroom.

LITERACY NEEDS OF ESL STUDENTS

Students who are learning English as a second language are a large, growing segment of our school population. Thirty years ago, twenty-four of the largest school districts in the nation had

English-speaking majorities; by 1980, only two did. This dramatic growth of non-English-speaking students is further underscored by the fact that in 1980 there were more than 50,000 non-English-speaking or limited English proficient students attending schools where they were a majority of the student body. During the period 1976-1982, the number of language minority students increased by 27 percent, while the number of all other students declined by 13 percent. These trends appear to be continuing, so we may anticipate that nearly a quarter of all school-aged students will be language minority by 1990 (Bell, 1984). To bridge the gap between English-speaking students and language minority students, the total literacy needs of the latter group must be considered.

Academic difficulties are usually encountered to some degree by all children entering school; however, these difficulties may become severe for LEP students, depending on their ability to relate to the spoken and written English language at school. Muskowitz (1974) describes what happens to many LEP children when they attend school for the first time. These children come to school confident that their language will serve their needs, only to find that they possess a language that will be ignored for the purposes of oral and written communication. For LEP children the first five or six years spent learning their home language may seem wasted when they enter school. School not only teaches language; most of its teaching takes place by the use of language. Learning in school depends on the interaction with teachers, books, and peers, and these interactions are mediated by language—a language that is unfamiliar to LEP students. Because children's education is dependent on their ability to comprehend and express themselves in the school's language, the ESL teacher's task becomes one of finding ways to enrich the student's language and give purpose to its expression.

LANGUAGE EXPERIENCE APPROACH WITH ESL STUDENTS

As was suggested in Chapter 2, language is a social phenomenon. It is learned in a social setting that encourages speaking skills and is based on shared experiences. As young LEP students become more familiar with using English as a medium for communication, expressing their ideas in writing will help them to experience the relationship of the spoken word to print. Most LEP students are motivated to write (Gonzales, 1982), but are hindered in their efforts by a lack of experience and fluency in English. Therefore, the issue becomes one of addressing ways of tapping the students' potential by reducing their fear of unfamiliarity with English and the writing process. The creative ESL teacher finds many ways to do this; one approach, LEA (see Chapter 6), is described here since it has been shown to be especially appropriate for ESL students. The language experience approach has the potential to bridge the gaps between children's cultural background, language level, and ability to express ideas in writing.

The language experience approach is particularly useful with language minority students who speak a variant dialect or whose background makes it difficult for them to relate to basal readers. This approach is based on the interrelatedness of language and reading, with experiences of the learner as the hub from which communication radiates. In Figure 7.1 Hall (1978) indicates the interrelatedness of communication (p. 2).

LEA may sustain the students' "confidence and feeling of belonging during a period when less familiar meanings of English language usage leave them with a certain sense of alienation" (Holdaway, 1979, p. 194). The experience of here-and-now situations meets the students' need to find relevance in written English. Using prior experiences as well as exposure to new experiences, the ESL teacher can encourage students to express their ideas, record them, and read them.

Knowledge of the students' background is essential if the teacher plans to use prior experiences as a base for discussion and writing. Common experiences such as birthdays, holidays, favorite foods, wishes, and family will have meaning to all students regardless of their cultural background. How holidays are cele-

Figure 7.1   The Communication Sequence in the
                 Language Experience Approach

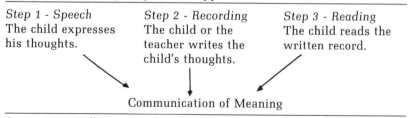

Step 1 - Speech	*Step 2 - Recording*	*Step 3 - Reading*
The child expresses	The child or the	The child reads the
his thoughts.	teacher writes the	written record.
	child's thoughts.	

Communication of Meaning

Source: M. A. Hall (1978). Reprinted by permission of the International Reading Association.

brated or which foods are eaten will differ among cultural groups, but the concept will be familiar. It is also important that LEP students be exposed to many new classroom experiences, the nature of which will be determined by the age of the students. As students have new experiences, they will have more to think about, more to say, and more to write. In this way, their reading and writing competencies improve in a speech-to-print direction as several language skills serve to reinforce one another.

Of crucial importance is the acceptance of children's existing language patterns (Hall, 1976; Polson & Dillner, 1976). When stories are dictated to the teacher, all of the text should be recorded with the students' vocabulary and syntax; however, standard spelling should be used. After hearing the story *Leo the Lop: Tail Two*, by S. Cosgrove (1984), a group of Spanish-speaking second graders dictated the story below to their ESL teacher.

LEO

Leo was sad and looked to the mirror. He was an ugly face
and he running away and the animals are in the forest.
There was a fire. Leo was running and save the animals.
The animals happy.

Error correction of ESL children's early attempts at language or writing has the immediate effect of putting the students on the defensive. It encourages a strategy in which the student tries to avoid mistakes, avoid difficult constructions, and focus less on meaning and more on form (Krashen, 1982). Rather, as students progress in their writing and gain confidence in their ability to express ideas, the ESL teacher encourages appropriate vocabulary, grammar, and syntax.

LANGUAGE EXPERIENCE WITH WORD PROCESSING

Stories using LEA have traditionally been recorded on charts by the teacher and with paper and pencil by students. The use of word processing as a tool for writing has been shown to have significant advantages over writing with pencil and paper for young language minority students (Johnson, 1986).

The paragraphs that follow describe how LEA is used with word processing to facilitate the development of LEP children's writing skills.

After the teacher has selected an appropriate language experience for the students to write about, a good deal of time is spent in talking about it. It is in the discussion and sharing of ideas that vocabulary and syntax develop. Depending on the age and language level of the students, the first LEA stories are dictated by the students to the ESL teacher. As the students share their ideas, the teacher types them into the computer. It is important that the computer be placed in such a way that the students can see the keyboard and watch the input process. In this way students become aware of keyboarding skills in an informal way. The teacher should encourage the students to feel free to revise their wording, change their sentence structure, add to their sentences, or delete what has been written. Students may need a good deal of encouragement to do this, because their previous experiences with pencil and paper may have discouraged major changes. When the story is complete and the students are satisfied, they should receive a hard copy of the story immediately; therefore, having access to a printer is imperative. The hard copy can be used in many ways to help the students improve their oral language, vocabulary, reading, and self-concept. A sense of pride in their work is noted as students search for their contribution to the story. In initial stories, it is helpful to indicate children's names with their comments; for example:

MYSTERY

Sergio thinks it is a cobra snake.
Roberto thinks it is a rabbit.
Ishmael thinks it is a octopus.
Miriam thinks it is a fish.
Giselda thinks it is a ghost.
It is a black, creepy bat!

New vocabulary words related to each story may be added to a group word bank and stored on disk. Copies of these words may also be given to students for purposes of vocabulary review.

When the students have enough vocabulary to begin writing individual stories, the teacher may wish to spend some time on keyboarding skills. Although young students do not seem to be frustrated by a lack of keyboarding skills (Bean & Hoffman, 1984; Daiute, 1985; Johnson, 1986), there are educational advantages for students, especially upper-primary students, who gain facility in keyboarding (Hoot, 1986). Even without formal keyboarding instruction, however, students gain a certain level of competence through informal observation of the teacher and through their own experimentation.

Along with keyboarding experiences, formal or informal, students need to know how to boot their individual disks, to retrieve the stories they wish to re-read or edit, and to save their stories. The age of the students will determine, to a great extent, their eagerness and ability to edit. Young students change words, erase, or add to their stories when the story is in progress. Rarely will younger students edit after they write "THE END." Older students, on the other hand, become quite adept at editing and frequently rework a finished product until it meets their satisfaction. Because the hard copy plays a significant role in the students' feeling of accomplishment, all students should be familiar with sending their text to the printer.

Student Progress

It is interesting to see the growth in vocabulary, syntax, and keyboarding skills as students continue to write stories using word processing. The following stories trace the development in writing skills of a second-grade LEP student, Sergio, over a period of about eight weeks. Sergio had participated in writing group stories for about five weeks prior to his writing these stories. The topics of the stories had been experienced and discussed in a group, and certain vocabulary words had been presented to the group. As Sergio wrote his stories, he was given additional help in spelling as he requested it.

FOOD

my favithe food is chile.My mothercooks.My fastes food.It tastesgood. I like moldo

TIME

Once upona time castal there was a king and aprin-cess.The unicorn gump upof the fence and the unicorm run and the princess got mad and the unicorn ruN awy.And in the End.

WOLF

I can see a wolf on Hallowen.And the wirch is flying and the monsteris mad. The fraKinstein is sleepy. and the vam-paire does't like the sun.dHaloween is scary. End.

DAVID-FISH

the fish does't got nos. The fish got sum gills the fish go
arand. The fish are friend The fish run fast. we have 3
fishes in are room and they are pretty. One is gold abnd
one is black abd one is orang. the balack is little and he
will get orange when he gros up big. The fish got scales
and they are ruf and they don't got no hands or feet but
they got fins. THE END

CAT

I wish I have a cat.
I call it Sam I like it. Sam wold catsh mice and play with
me to. I want a long tail and a big cat so he fight the cats
and win. I like Sam! THE END

RED

I am a red balloon. I see boys and girls. I like to fly up
high. I an go higher than the ther ballons go.My string is
very long and it is longer thaen the other strings. I have tag
and it got my name onit ther and I will get a letter if you
find me. Did you find me?

THE END

Word Bank Files

As students continue writing individual stories, their vocabulary
is likely to expand. The students will need to have a word bank
file on their individual disks to which they can add words. All of
the words entered into the student's word bank should be known
by the student and be spelled correctly. Therefore, the ESL
teacher will need to become involved in the selection of word
bank vocabulary. While the students are writing their stories, it is
helpful to have an index card available on which the teacher
writes the words the students request. After a story has been
written, the teacher may check to see if the student knows the
words on the card, and then the student can enter these into the
word bank file. There are any number of ways words can be
listed, but for young LEP students, I have found it helpful to list
the words according to the titles of their stories. The following is
the word bank file for a first-grade LEP student, Francisco (see
Figure 7.2). It was developed over a period of eight weeks during a

Figure 7.2 Francisco's Word Bank

NEW WORDS

BIRTHDAY	MYSTERY	tacos	note	weeds
party	ghost	peppers	find	chases
get	mask	stir	POPCORN	die
we	says	pan	kernels	air
present	frog	hot	popper	bigger
have	turtles	brother	oil	scare
cake	THE BAT	eat	bang	like
PETS	black	BALLOONS	shot	build
cow	long	red	steam	sand
moos	wings	blue	little	
bird	fly	yellow	salty	
flies	night	green	yummy	
goldfish	sleep	helium	white	
swims	cave	string	lots	
cat	ears	name	butter	
runs	teeth	sky	bumpy	
lamb	white	playground	FISH	
eats	rubber	wind	aquarium	
horse	bite	trees	oxygen	
plays	scared	lost	water	
rabbit	hang	caught	goldfish	
jumps	FOOD	Mexico	swims	
dog	pickles	grandmother	fins	
barks	like	free	gills	
like	green	clouds	tail	
play	Mom	ran	mouth	
funny	cooks	gone	sonar	

daily thirty-minute writing period. Before Francisco began typing a new story into the computer, he would retrieve his word bank file and run a hard copy of it. He could then use his word bank as a personal dictionary as he wrote the new story.

Word banks are a great source of help to LEP students. If a word is not in one student's word bank, it may be in another's, and this encourages students to work together. The word banks are also an excellent source for vocabulary review among the students. When they complete the writing of their stories, they can practice their words with each other. In this way, the students become familiar with new words that are in other students' word banks. Although this same process of keeping a word bank could be done using pencil and paper, there are advantages to keeping the words on disk: Additional words can be added easily to the list; the child always has a fresh copy of the words; the print is easy to read and resembles that in texts; and a second list can be printed for another student if two students are studying together.

Experimentation with Language

Limited English proficient students who write their stories using a word processor tend to experiment more with language than they do when writing stories with pencil and paper (Johnson, 1986). Because the computer allows the students to change or delete words with ease, students try a variety of words to express their ideas. This freedom is particularly important for LEP students who may be hesitant to express themselves in writing. There is a finality about writing with pencil and paper. Kleinman and Humphrey (1982) report that teachers of young children notice that the length of stories increases when attention is paid not to details but rather to expressing ideas and sequencing. This observation implies that the writer is in control and that changes will be made to enhance meaning. When students compose at the computer, they read and re-read their stories. Facial expressions denote concentration as they often read aloud what they have written and then make changes. This same kind of concentration is usually not apparent when students write with pencil and paper. When making changes in his story, for example, one first-grade LEP student remarked, "I love to write on the computer cuz the eraser (delete key) doesn't make holes in my paper." Children are concerned about neat papers, and the ability to try different words without losing the appearance of their papers encourages experimentation with language.

Collaborative Writing

Children who are learning English are eager to have someone help them express their ideas. Working in pairs or in groups of three offers young ESL students support in their efforts to write, and their stories tend to be considerably longer when they collaborate. Older ESL students usually prefer to work alone but will walk around, read what others are writing, and discuss the stories. Certain groups of students (for instance, Mexican children) may not be strongly competitive. These students may be more cooperative in a group activity than when singled out as individuals. Collaboration allows students to share ideas, test language, use each other's word banks for spelling help, edit together, and have fun working together to achieve a product. Using word processing encourages collaborative writing (Daiute, 1985; Grabe & Grabe, 1985; Johnson, 1986). Johnson (1986) compared the amount of collaboration among LEP students using pencil and paper with that among students using word processing and found that those who used word processing discussed and shared significantly more than those writing with pencils. The first story below was written by a second-grade Mexican girl, Maribel, when she worked alone. The second story was written by Maribel when she collaborated with two other first-grade LEP students.

FISH

The fish lif in the water and he swim all day.
He is pretty and he has fins. I like the fish I by one.

STAR

Once upon a time there was a beautiful goldfish named star.Star loved to swim in the little pond and to play with her freinds.One day star eatingf her lunch. All of a suden she saw a big giants foot coming from the top water but Star just look at the giants foot and began to swim away but the gian still fallo star just as star put along rope across the water.Giant put a hand in the water.Star was scare and began to fast to get away from the giant.The giant chass Star all over the water and then star was a flowr and she ran to it and hid by it and the giant cud not see her.She was saved.

Growth in Self-Esteem

According to Krashen (1982), several affective variables contribute to second language development in children: motivation, good self-image, and lack of anxiety. When efforts are made to motivate children, to help them be successful, and to teach them in a low anxiety atmosphere, they generally do better at learning a second language. Language is a trial-and-error process; it must be learned in an atmosphere that encourages effort, purpose, and experimentation. Observing first- and second-grade LEP students who had been using word processing for about three weeks, Johnson (1986) noticed that they exhibited a growing confidence in their ability to handle the hardware, to use the software, and to generate hard copies. Student comments such as: "I'll boot up all the disks today"; "My story is the best"; "I'm making copies for everybody!" indicate that the students felt good about what they were doing and were growing in competence.

A second-grade teacher who assumed that Roberto was unable to read was surprised when she found a story that he had written on the computer during a pull-out language arts class for LEP students. When she asked him if he could read it, he answered, "Yes, and I can read more." After the teacher had Roberto read his story to the class, she asked him if he could help teach the other students how to use the word processor in their classroom. He told her that he could and that there were four other Mexican children in her class who could "write on the computer." As a result of these children's ability to share a new aspect of computer technology with their peers, they began to interact more with the other students and showed more enthusiasm for second language learning.

WORD PROCESSING AND THE ESL TEACHER

Using the computer as a tool for writing does not introduce a new activity into the classroom; rather, writing is accomplished through a different medium (Kurland, 1983). Word processing programs are tools in the same way pencils, erasers, and typewriters are tools in an ESL classroom. However, the computer is a more versatile tool since it can store a student's text, retrieve it, allow revisions, and print it. The computer is a powerful tool for learning, but to assure that it is enabling and enriching to classroom instruction, Newman (1984) suggests a few crucial issues to be addressed:

1. What is the role of the computer in the total learning experience?
2. Does the software encourage the learner to take control of his or her learning?
3. Does the software facilitate a sharing of knowledge?
4. What is the role of the teacher in assisting the students to use word processing?

Teacher attitudes toward computers and their use is significant, because students will be influenced by their teacher's comments about computers and by the manner in which the teacher utilizes the computer. The ESL teacher needs to become familiar with the word processing package used so that she or he feels comfortable in helping students and can model its effectiveness for them.

A variety of word processing packages are available for students to use. Unique features such as built-in vocabulary, story starters, and graphics capability make different packages appropriate for different groups of students. In choosing a word processing package for the ESL classroom, the teacher may wish to consider the benefits of using one that encourages students to concentrate on writing their own stories, to use unlimited vocabulary, and to write without the distraction of graphics. A word processor such as Bank Street Writer encourages the generation of text rather than graphics. Students learning a second language appear to expend more effort on writing, at least in the initial stages, when graphics are not involved, As these students develop a more extensive vocabulary and become more confident in expressing their ideas in writing, word processors that include graphics and other creative features may be less distracting.

SUMMARY

There are significant numbers of LEP students in our schools today, and ESL teachers are faced with the task of helping them gain the level of literacy needed in our technological society. In this chapter we have looked at the use of word processing within LEA to help students express and share their ideas in a technological environment. Integrating word processing into the curriculum may help ESL students express their ideas more freely, collaborate with peers, experiment with language, edit and revise their writing, and develop a stronger self-concept.

REFERENCES

Bean, J., & Hoffman, R. A. (1984). Microcomputers in the schools. *Reading Improvement, 21*(1), 32-36.

Bell, T. H. (1984). The importance of language competence in education. *TESOL Newsletter*, 1-2.

Benderly, B. L. (1961). The multilingual mind. *Psychology Today*, 9-12.

Bradley, V. N. (1982). Improving students' writing with microcomputers. *Language Arts, 59*, 732-742.

Coburn, P.; Kelman, P.; Roberts, T.; Snyder, F. F.; Watt, D. H.; & Weiner, C. (1984). *Practical guide to computers in education.* Reading, MA: Addison-Wesley.

Cosgrove, S. (1984). *Leo the lop: Tail two.* Los Angeles: Price, Stern & Sloan.

Daiute, C. (1985). *Writing and computers.* Reading, MA: Addison-Wesley.

Gonzales, R. D. (1982). Teaching Mexican-American students to write: Capitalizing on culture. *English Journal, 71*(7), 20-24.

Grabe, M., & Grabe, C. (1985). The microcomputer and the language experience approach. *The Reading Teacher, 38*(6), 508-511.

Hall, M. A. (1976). *The language experience approach for the culturally disadvantaged.* Newark, DE: International Reading Association.

Hall, M. A. (1978). *The language experience approach for teaching reading: A research perspective.* Newark, DE: International Reading Association.

Hall, M. A. (1985). Focus on language experience learning and teaching. *Reading, 19*(1), 5-11.

Hersh, R. H. (1983). How to avoid becoming a nation of techno-peasants. *Phi Delta Kappan, 4*(9), 635-638.

Holdaway, D. (1979). *The foundations of literacy.* Sydney: Ashton Scholastic.

Hoot, J. (1985). Word processing in the kindergarten and primary grades. *Proceedings of the Fifth Annual TCEA State Conference* (pp. 433-435). Austin, TX: TCEA.

Hoot, J. (1986). Keyboarding instruction in the early grades: Must or mistake? *Childhood Education, 63*(2), 95-101.

Hope, G. R.; Taylor, H. F.; & Pusack, J. P. (1984). *Using computers in teaching foreign languages.* New York: Harcourt Brace Jovanovich.

Johnson, M. A. (1986). *Effects of using the computer as a tool for writing on the vocabulary, reading, and writing of first and second grade Spanish-speaking students.* Unpublished doctoral dissertation, Texas Woman's University.

Kleinman, G., & Humphrey, M. (1982). Word processing in the classroom. *Computer,* 96-99.

Krashen, S. D. (1982). *Principles and practices in second language acquisition.* Oxford: Pergamon Press.

Kurland, D. M. (1983). Software for the classroom: Issues in the design of effective software tools. (Technical Report No. 15) Montreal: AERA.

Lipkin, J. P. (1983). Equity in computer education. *Educational Leadership,* 26.

Manion, M. H. (1985). CAI modes of delivery and interaction: New perspectives for expanding applications. *Educational Technology, 25*-28.

Muskowitz, S. (1974). How should the culturally different child be taught to read? *Claremont Reading Conference Yearbook 38,* 75.

Newman, J. M. (1984). Online: Reading, writing, and computers. *Language Arts, 61,* 758-763.

Papert, S. (1980). *Mindstorms: Children, computers, and powerful ideas.* New York: Basic Books, Inc.

Polson, J. P., & Dillner, M. H. (1976). *Learning to teach reading in the elementary school: Utilizing a competency-based instructional system.* New York: Macmillan.

Wyatt, D. H. (1984). Computer-assisted teaching and testing of reading and listening. *Foreign Language Annals, 17*(4), 393-406.

8 Word Processing with Learning Disabled Children

CATHERINE COBB MOROCCO
Education Development Center, Inc.

SUSAN B. NEUMAN
Lowell University

The special education community has viewed the steady movement of computers into schools with both excitement and reservation. Computer technology offers enormous promise for children with mild to severe handicaps, yet it requires that teachers and specialists learn not only the technology itself but also how best to use it so that it can benefit individual children.

Word processing is one of the most promising of the new technologies for special needs children, particularly for those with learning disabilities. Despite normal intelligence, learning disabled (LD) students often struggle with writing. By the third grade many begin to slip behind their classmates in those learning areas that require writing skills. Their writing difficulties take many different forms. Some children are hampered by attentional problems, while others have problems with understanding directions, expressing a coherent sequence of ideas, and using correct grammar and spelling. Whatever the specific writing problems, LD children have one thing in common: frustration at not being able to express their ideas in writing.

Early reports describing the use of word processing with individual children suggested that word processing motivates reluctant writers, replaces illegible handwriting with clear print, and stimulates children to write and revise more. These promising reports motivated many administrators to purchase computers for resource rooms and to provide related staff development programs for remedial teachers. Because word processing programs are merely writing tools, however, even the most adventurous of teachers face many questions about how best to use them.

For the past two years, we have worked closely with resource room teachers and elementary school children, documenting how teachers use word processing and exploring approaches that we hypothesized would have the most benefit for students.* This chapter first describes guidelines for writing instruction and the features of word processors that can aid LD children in writing. We then describe three instructional approaches teachers use with word processing and how each approach might contribute to good writing instruction. Finally, we offer suggestions to teachers for classroom practice.

WRITING INSTRUCTION AND WORD PROCESSING

Extensive research over the past 10 years confirms that writing is a process that integrates thinking, social interaction and motor skills. Furthermore, for writing to be regarded as an important form of communication, writing instruction must be made meaningful to young students. Benchmark studies (Bereiter, 1980; Calkins, 1983; Freedman, 1985; Flower & Hayes 1981a,b; Graves, 1983; Langer & Applebee, 1987) converge on several important guidelines which together appear to foster good writing instruction.

> *Process*: Children need to spend time on actual writing activities, rather than studying grammar or isolated language elements.
> *Ownership*: Children need opportunities to find what they want to say, rather than complying with a teacher's topic or a specific writing agenda.
> *Collaboration*: Children need to learn appropriate listening and response strategies that help their peers' and their own writing. In working with their students, teachers need to place less emphasis on evaluating students' writing and more on supporting the children's own planning and idea generating.
> *Skills*: Students need to acquire a knowledge of the spelling, mechanics, and formatting conventions of their writing

*This project, carried out by the Education Development Center, was funded by the Office of Special Education and Rehabilitation Services, U.S. Office of Education.

community. Students master these by applying them to their own composing, after they have focused on what they want to say.

Procedures: Good instruction gives students procedures and structures that help them manage the complex demands of writing. They need opportunities to internalize those procedures and use them independently in a variety of contexts.

The challenge in our research has been to determine how word processors might improve writing instruction for LD children, who tend to find many of the above writing activities particularly difficult. These children often have problems with spelling and punctuation (Poteet, 1978; Hemereck, 1979; Poplin et al., 1980; Deno, Marston & Mirkin, 1982) and with some aspects of syntax, word usage and style (Poplin et al., 1980). They often lack the strategies that their normally achieving peers use in planning, transcribing, and reviewing their writing. This explains why LD children tend to have great difficulty in getting started with writing and run out of ideas quickly (Haynes et al., 1984; Loper, 1984; Thomas, 1984).

IMPORTANT WORD PROCESSING FEATURES

As part of our investigation, we identified the ways word processing was used in writing over two years, including observing children's reactions to the word processor used in writing activities. Two unique word processing features were found to be especially important—simplicity of revision and the interaction encouraged by word processing. These features, described below with examples from students in resource room settings, seem to make word processing a particularly useful writing tool for LD students.

Revision Features

Most of us are familiar with the revision features of word processors. Functions such as DELETE, INSERT, ADD, MOVE, COPY, and WRAP AROUND combine to make the process of changing text easier for children. We tend to assume that these revision features will have a strong impact on childrens' revision and editing processes. They may, but we found the most powerful impact of these features is on student productivity. The fact that students can make any kind of changes without having to rewrite the entire piece has a profound impact on their willingness to say everything they want to say in their writing.

Paul, for example, tended to write very little because his chronic spelling errors necessitated so many rewrites. His first story on the word processor was two pages long, and he was so excited about the length that he kept tabulating the lines. For students who struggle daily to write, the rewriting process can be agonizing. As a result, students with serious writing problems keep their texts as slim as they can get away with. Knowing that the computer will handle the rewriting encourages students to expand rather than limit their expression of ideas.

The wrap around, insert, delete, and movable text features make possible some procedures for generating and organizing ideas on the computer that would require much rewriting with paper and pencil. For example, children can use an outlining procedure by typing in the outline and then filling in text within the outline. They can use a procedure of writing the last line of a story first, then composing the text that precedes it. Equipped with Koala pad peripherals or integrated with a drawing tool (for example, LogoWriter), the word processor can facilitate the use of graphic organizer procedures to help students generate and organize ideas for writing.

A pitfall of the revision features is that they may stimulate premature editing. Students with a history of writing problems are anxious to be correct. Chronic misspellers tend to stop to examine each word. If, on top of this, teachers convey discomfort at seeing errors in print, students may not be able to focus on their ideas at all. Teachers sometimes feel that the word processor stimulates them to ask too much of students in the way of neat, correct format and to ask it too early in the writing process. When children focus on spelling, mechanics, and correct word choice in the midst of forming their ideas, they tend to lose their train of thought. Because errors are even more glaring on the monitor than on paper, it is tempting to ask students to correct their text when they need to be expanding and discovering their ideas.

Interactive Features

The interactive features of word processing are probably the most critical and useful for teachers working with LD children. A number of word processor features combine to support close interaction between teacher and students. The large print, for example, and the upright monitor make the text visible and easily accessible to others as it emerges. In addition, when students are encouraged to write group (collaborative) stories, writing on a word processor is more public than handwriting.

Some of the teachers in our study used these features to react to children's writing as an audience might during the writing process. In the example below, a young boy, Evan, is writing about a trip to a yearly family reunion in the South. The teacher walks by the monitor just as Evan is writing a story about how his grandmother's dog cured his asthma at their South Carolina reunion. She reads, "I took a plane down there and when I was down there I was playing with dinamite."

TEACHER: Dynamite! (Exaggerated horror)

EVAN: (Laughs) No! My grandmother's dog is named dynamite!

TEACHER: Whew! (Dramatically wipes her brow) Oh, I was worried. (Walks away)

EVAN: (Turns to observer to confide) I'll tell her who's dynamite . . . where it is.

OBSERVER: Well, I was sitting here getting a little worried too.

EVAN: (Next types "who is my Nana's dog.")

The open readability of his text enabled the teacher to point out the ambiguous "dynamite" reference. As a result of the above interaction, the session for that day resulted in the following text:

DINAMITE

Then in May I went to visit my nana and grand pa and aunt Kate and uncle Dan in South Carolina and I took a plane down there and when I was down there I was playing with dinamite who is my nana's dog and while I was playing with him and I had azma but I don't have it no more because the dog took it from me.

Evan's comment to the observer and his text revision indicated that he grasped the need to clarify his meaning to the reader. The public monitor enabled the teacher to catch the ambiguity and help him refine his thinking. Evan had the opportunity to experience his writing from another person's perspective, which led him to clarify his meaning.

As the example above suggests, the public, interactive character of word processing supported the teacher's efforts in individualizing writing instruction. When children get stuck, the teacher can see what has been written and can use any number of specific techniques to help generate revised thought processes. The teacher can, for example, easily prompt the child to expand the text by reading aloud what he or she has just written and asking a general question ("What else would you like to say?"); providing a specific direction for expansion ("Tell me more about his clothes"); or asking the child to clarify an ambiguous reference ("Are you talking about your father?"). Sometimes a child is prompted to add more text simply by hearing his or her own writing read aloud, as happened when a teacher read the student's sentence, "We are playing in the snow" aloud, and, as she finished it, the student added, "the wet, slushy snow."

The interactive features of the word processor enable the teacher to observe and immediately reinforce the child's content decisions, which would be less visible if the child were writing privately with paper and pencil. One teacher observed a student delete "deep red thick rugs" in a description of the Ritz and retype "red carpits." Because she could see the revision in process, the teacher stopped to read the sentence aloud and reinforce the child as a writer by stating, "You can change it because you're the author."

The readability and accessibility of the LD child's text on the word processor is also a powerful advantage over paper-and-pencil writing during instruction in spelling and mechanics. Both teacher and child can identify errors more readily, and the teacher can more easily monitor and also praise the child's editing efforts.

The interactional features create unique possibilities for collaboration, sharing, and assessing the child's progress. Yet, the word processor also makes the child's writing more vulnerable to criticism and evaluation. If the teacher has a strong agenda, children may have to work harder to maintain control over their writing. Our teachers reported that they tended to intervene more actively to make suggestions when a child was composing because the print was so visible.

In summary, a pencil is a private writing tool that the individual child uses to translate thoughts onto paper. Although a word processor also functions as an individual's writing tool, it creates a special kind of writing environment. It makes the child's writing more public. Teachers can more easily see what strategy a child is using at any particular moment and when a strategy has broken down. Other people can read the child's writing at the same time that the child is reading or writing it, and can make suggestions or react with their own related ideas and experiences. The computer makes the writing process more visible by bringing into sharp relief processes that are less apparent with paper and pencil.

This kind of writing environment can transform the writing experiences of LD children, provided it is used to reinforce their authorship role and to help them acquire writing strategies and skills needed in the mainstream classroom. Teachers in our study appreciated the status and equality that print gave their students; they valued the ease of collaboration that the writing tool promoted between teachers and students and among students. For children, the word processor represented freedom to make mistakes and change their minds without being penalized with re-writing.

THREE APPROACHES TO TEACHING WRITING

Word processors, therefore, can be used as a major resource for teachers, allowing them to provide strategies and new opportunities for writing instruction. But, as Kurth was careful to point out in Chapter 5, word processor features alone do not facilitate good writing. Rather, it is the teacher's approach that fosters the effective use of the computer. We found three major approaches that teachers used when working with their LD writers during composing:

- They collaborated substantively with the children in generating content for their writing.
- They provided students procedures or strategies that they could use themselves in generating ideas.
- They directly taught students skills or knowledge about writing rules and conventions.

Borrowing Bereiter's (1980) terms, we call these approaches substantive, procedural, and direct instruction.

Substantive Instruction

In substantive dialogues teachers and children talk about the content of the students' writing, what they have said, and what they can say next. The teacher and child generate topics and ideas together, decide which ideas should come first, or determine exactly what words to use. In the example below, the teacher thinks of topics or questions and the child supplies what is known about them.

TEACHER: Let's think of questions we could ask about snow.
STUDENT: It falls out of the sky.
TEACHER: Great. Write it down. What else?
STUDENT: It's slushy.
TEACHER: Fantastic, write it down. Great. How does it fall?
STUDENT: Sometimes slow, sometimes fast.
TEACHER: Fantastic.

The teacher's questions helped the child discover what is already known. With each question, the teacher helps the student take the content to the next level.

In another example, the student writes a few lines, then the teacher mirrors back the reader's excitement, prompting the student to write more.

STUDENT: [writes] "His mouth pulls down in a crooked line."
TEACHER: Wow! That is scary! I'd like to know more about him.

The teacher provides many different conversational supports to help students remember what they know. These include prompts, mirroring, praising, reading the students' work aloud, having the students read aloud, and having the students rehearse ideas. One assumption of these tutorial conversations is that LD students have a good deal of knowledge but need assistance in getting at that knowledge. In substantive instruction, the teacher takes part in the writing process, helping the child find what to write.

Substantive dialogue can help children who are particularly anxious and reluctant to begin to write. In the "snow" example above, it is likely that this was the only approach that could help this child realize that she had something to say in writing. It can also help children expand their ideas during composing when they come to the end of a train of thought and need help in getting started again.

The pitfall of the substantive approach is that it is highly teacher dependent. Further, it can shift ownership of the writing from the child to the teacher. If used too often, it can perpetuate LD students' feeling of learned helplessness, by making them feel that they are not in control of their own writing. Finally, a substantive dialogue is situation specific. A predominantly substantive approach does not provide children with tools to take into another writing situation where intensive collaboration is not available.

Procedural Instruction

In procedural dialogues, the teacher and child talk about a routine or procedure that the child can use for carrying out some aspect of the writing process. Usually it is a conversation about how to write, rather than what to write. In the example below, the teacher reminds the child of a self-questioning routine they have previously used to help the child stay on the topic.

> TEACHER: Remember what you stated in that first sentence. You've got to stick to that idea. Ask yourself, am I sticking to the idea that I presented in my first sentence?
> STUDENT: [echoes] Am I sticking to the idea that I started off with?

In another procedural conversation, a teacher reminded a student, Harry, of a strategy they had worked out for writing a character description. What is interesting here is that the student developed his own variation of the procedure.

Harry is at the computer to write a transformer character sketch. He types, "You can never count on Long Hall to carry out missions. Long Hall wants to be in control of the Devastator."

> TEACHER: [walks over] Remember that in a character sketch we should describe the inside as well as the outside.
> STUDENT: Yeah, I always describe the outside last.

Procedures may include ways to plan, organize, conference,

revise, and edit, or routines to help children put one aspect of the writing task aside so that they can focus on another one. For example, to help one student maintain fluent composing despite spelling problems, a teacher had him asterisk all words whose spelling he was not sure of and then go back to them when the draft was finished. These procedures help children focus on the composing process and allow them to shift to another aspect of writing when appropriate.

A procedural approach gives children strategies they can use in any writing situation. A memory strategy can help children recall what they already know about a topic. A self-questioning routine can help a child re-read a text for punctuation errors (When I read this aloud, where do I stop? Do I need a period there?). Once the strategy is learned, it can be applied to any context.

Direct Instruction

In direct instructional dialogues teachers transmit skills directly to students. These skills are related to good writing and knowledge of writing conventions, including spelling, rules for mechanics or word use, standards of well-formed writing, and formatting. In the dialogue below, the teacher is imparting a rule about double negatives.

> TEACHER: Okay, I want you to say this part of the sentence.
> STUDENT: [reads] I thought that I did not get no toys.
> TEACHER: Does that sound right? What's the word that's telling you that you couldn't get the toys?
> STUDENT: Didn't.
> TEACHER: Did not. Okay. What you did by putting the no here is tell the reader twice that you didn't get toys. You don't need to tell them twice because you already said it.
> STUDENT: I didn't get any toys.
> TEACHER: I'm proud of you.

In another example, a teacher is imparting information about effective leads in a report:

> TEACHER: Really, a good lead has three characteristics. It's punchy; you know you pay attention, you want to read more. Second, it's usually brief. You don't want the

reader to have to work through a long sentence and complex idea. Three, it tells just enough to hook you, but you want to read more. Got it? Now, you try some.

Teachers use a wide range of specific techniques in direct instruction—simple presentation, modeling, demonstration, role-playing. What makes the techniques direct is the intent to provide highly specific, delineated skills and information students need in order to write well.

Direct instruction is important in providing children the information, skills, and conventions about good writing of the larger writing community that they need in order to eventually participate fully in it. Direct instruction needs to be appropriately timed, however. Learning disabled students are particularly distracted by a request to attend to punctuation rules while they are in the process of generating ideas. Being asked to think about the form of what they are writing ("Is that a complete sentence?") shifts their attention from what they are trying to communicate. If timed appropriately, however, demonstrations of new writing skills can give students a concrete sense of mastery of writing.

WORD PROCESSING AND TEACHER APPROACHES TO WRITING

The revision and interactive features of the computer can clearly support all three teacher approaches. For example, though a simple word processing program does not teach strategies or procedures, the interactive features can support a procedural approach. Teachers can more easily observe when a child's writing process is breaking down. They, therefore, have natural opportunities to remind the child of procedures used previously or to provide the child with a structure or procedure to help the writing continue. The teacher watching Amy trying for several minutes to describe the inside of the Ritz tearoom suggested that she stop and draw a paper-and-pencil map showing where the door, the dessert tray, and the tea tables were located. With this structure in hand, Amy was able to continue her description independently.

Even though word processing can support all three approaches, we found that teachers used the substantive and direct instructional approaches far more than the procedural. One reason is that these approaches are more familiar to special education teachers. Procedural teaching techniques, which stress strategies rather than skills, are relatively new. In addition, the upright monitor, giving open access to children's writing, can sometimes encourage teachers to interact more frequently during the writing process. While this is clearly helpful to some children who are having difficulty writing, at times this type of interaction might be intrusive. There are times, for example, when children need to sit and think by themselves. We found that sometimes the empty screen phenomenon would lead overanxious teachers to help children generate ideas too early, leading them to compose before they were ready. Other times, the attractiveness of the revision features led teachers to expect a professional looking product when a draft would otherwise have been acceptable.

We have heard the idea voiced that children regard writing from the word processor as better than writing from paper and pencil. However, we would like to suggest that this is only partly true. The word processor does allow children to see work as a more professional looking product; however, we found that only in a limited number of cases did concern with the product over-whelm children's need for a sense of authorship and satisfaction during the writing process. If children focused on expressing their ideas during writing and received continual feedback that those ideas were valuable, the process was positive and they regarded the product highly. If, however, the process stressed multiple revisions, promotion of teacher content, or a focus on writing conventions, children tended to disengage from the writing, re-gardless of how the final product looked.

A Model of Writing Instruction

It is, therefore, important to determine when in the writing process each instructional approach is most suitable. Two models emerged from our analysis. One is an overview of the role each of the three basic instruction approaches can play in writing instruction with LD children (see Figure 8.1). The model connects the teacher's in-structional approach with the kinds of knowledge children need for writing, and with the general cycle of writing activity. Procedural instruction is critical throughout the writing cycle, because it pro-vides children with knowledge of how to plan, compose, review, edit, and even publish their writing. Substantive instruction is useful early in the writing cycle for an extremely reluctant writer and during writing once the children's own planning processes

Figure 8.1   Timing of Instructional Approaches with LD Writers

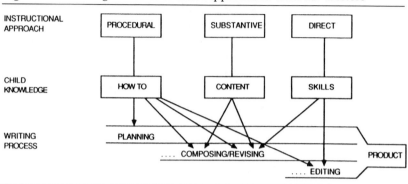

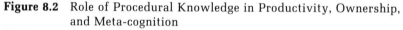

are underway. Direct instruction is most facilitative at the end of the cycle when the children have freely communicated their ideas and can focus on shaping the writing product in terms of tenets of good writing and formal rules of editing.

The second model portrays the specific linkages between procedural instruction and important student outcomes (see Figure 8.2). The model begins with the point at which students have a writing task. Because writing is always an act of inquiry, we

Figure 8.2   Role of Procedural Knowledge in Productivity, Ownership, and Meta-cognition

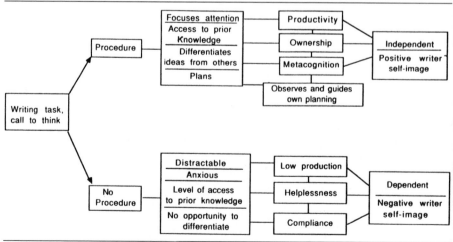

can think of it as a call to think. Students respond differently to that call, depending on their ability to bring planning, composing, and reviewing procedures to their writing process.

The top section of the model portrays the writing cycle of students with procedural knowledge of writing. A procedure focuses students' attention on the task, gives them access to what they already know, and makes them aware that they have knowledge and ideas separate from those of other people. A procedure or routine gives the students ways to integrate new information into the content of their writing.

As children remember what they know and generate ideas, they produce text and begin to own their writing. They notice and think about their own thinking and planning—a metacognitive awareness. When they begin to think about, choose, and manage their own writing, they have achieved some ability to carry out the complex task of writing independently. Finally, students see that they can generate ideas, manage their writing process, and begin to acquire a positive image of themselves as writers.

We represent the top section of the model as a cycle, since each increment in productivity, ownership, and metacognitive awareness gives children more ability to call on planning procedures with each new call to think and write.

The bottom section of the model represents the writing experience of students who are unable to draw on procedural knowledge when called to think about a writing task. Without a planning procedure the children are distractable and prone to anxiety; both those states block their access to their own substantive knowledge. Their inability to generate ideas means they write very little; it leads to a sense of helplessness and vulnerability to others' suggestions for what to write.

Cumulative experience of complying with others' ideas may lead students to a lack of ownership of the writing process and a negative image of themselves as writers. Because they lack knowledge of how to go about the writing process, each new writing task arouses the same pattern of anxiety and helplessness. Writing is a dead end process rather than a gradual development of communication abilities.

This model may help to fill a gap in current writing theory as it relates to writing-disabled children. We have needed a way to understand how the basic writing process breaks down for LD children and the kinds of help and interventions that could support them. By helping LD children to acquire the planning, organizing, reviewing, and revising strategies required to manage the writing process, we are giving them empowering tools, which can then be applied in any setting.

Suggestions for Teachers

The following suggestions, in the form of guidelines, follow from our analysis of using word processors to facilitate writing instruction with LD children.

1. *Identify each student's writing strengths and problems prior to having students work on the word processor.*

Two students referred to a teacher for help with writing may have opposite profiles: One student may have great strengths in generating ideas, vocabulary, and sentence structure but extremely poor spelling and mechanics skills; the other student's profile may be the reverse. These differences will dictate how the teacher might use word processing with them. Students whose major problems are not ideas or organization, but illegible handwriting, may have their problem essentially solved by writing on a computer. The teacher may want to arrange for them to be able to use the resource room to write assignments for social studies and science as well as for language arts. Students who are anxious about expressing their ideas may produce even less original text on the computer because they can so easily erase whatever they write. The teacher may want to help these students develop some confidence in their ideas before having them use this more public writing tool. Students who are highly creative may thrive on seeing their ideas reflected in professional print. Although the computer will tempt the teacher to intervene and give them suggestions, these students will need artistic control over their writing.

2. *Teach students machine skills at the beginning.*

Despite the particular character of their writing problems, most LD students can learn machine skills needed for word processing. However, unless they have regular keyboard practice, they are unlikely to acquire good typing habits—using all fingers and using the left hand on the left side of the keyboard and the right hand on the right side. They are likely to enjoy keyboarding drills and can manage keyboarding practice independently if the software has a simple format and gives them a way to track their own progress.

In a resource room setting, students can gradually acquire word processing skills such as retrieving, saving, and printing, since the teacher is available to help them manage the software. This means that students need to acquire only a few basic word processing skills (for example, inputting text, backward delete, and capitalization) in order to begin composing. They can gradually acquire intermediate and advanced keyboarding as more complex writing demands require them. Thus, students do not need to wait to begin real composing activities until they have had extensive experience with word processing. This situation is unlikely to be so in the computer lab, where the high ratio of children to adults would demand that students become independent on the machine so they can focus their attention on writing.

3. *Have students use the word processor for composing.*

Once students have acquired basic keyboarding skills and understand how to insert, delete, and capitalize text, the teacher should have them compose. Some people have been skeptical that LD students can create as well as edit on the computer. As a result, many early uses of word processing have focused on having students transcribe a handwritten draft into the computer and then edit and print it out. It is the revision/editing features of the computer that seem to make it such an appealing composing tool for LD children. The fact that they do not have erasure shavings to blow away and do not have to recopy stimulates many students to write more than they would with paper and pencil.

4. *If students are new to word processing, provide them alternatives to revising on the computer.*

Many LD students without prior word processing experience have difficulty using the word processor for revision when they first begin to write. Deletion and insertion require understanding the concept of adding and subtracting space, which is difficult for some students to grasp. Further, if they try to revise on the computer, they often tend to overdelete and lose track of their text. If, as an alternative, they make their revisions on hard copy first and then try to make them on-line, looking back and forth between hard copy and monitor, they tend to get confused and lose their place. Until students acquire revision skills, teachers can try the following strategies:

    a) A student author can be paired with a student typist; the typist manages the mechanical processes, and the author dictates what changes should be made. This works well if students are able to maintain their separate roles. If they begin to struggle for decision-making control over what changes should be made, the revision process will break down.

b) The teacher can work with the students, letting them take the author role while the teacher acts as typist. This allows the students to think with the teacher about what changes to make, while the teacher manages the mechanics of the revision process.

c) For students with extensive problems in mechanics and spelling, the teacher can make some corrections on the students' disks outside of class, to prevent the students from becoming discouraged with excessive editing, and to ensure that their final product has correct spelling. Some teachers feel this is intrusive on their students' writing; we found it appropriate for students who would become turned off with writing if they had to correct all of their spelling errors.

While on-line revision was difficult for many of the younger students to manage, a year's practice on the word processor was sufficient to develop the skills of inserting and deleting within text.

5. *Be wary of pushing students to edit before they have finished composing.*

Because word processors are designed for making changes, we are tempted to point out students' errors when the students are still thinking about what to say. Computers can make anxious students even more obsessive about their mistakes, if the teacher encourages them to focus on corrections too early. If students become overly focused on spelling or on how to say it, the teacher can have them put an asterisk next to an uncertain word or phrase and come back to it later.

6. *Respect students' need for control over the content of their writing.*

The accessibility of the child's writing makes the composing process less private and potentially less under the child's own control. On the other hand, where the child is able to maintain control over the content and direction of his or her writing, the public character of the computer stimulates considerable talk among students. The visibility of their ongoing composing process can give the teacher opportunities to reinforce and appreciate the child's writing process and to prompt further writing when the child seems to run out of ideas.

SUMMARY

The word processor can be used as a major resource for teachers working with LD children. As a powerful, new writing tool, it has the capacity to motivate children to write and to foster students' self-esteem as writers. But word processors alone will not produce good writers. It is the teacher and good instructional approaches that take into account the strengths and needs of LD students that will make the difference. In this respect, teachers who bring a working knowledge of the writing process can use the unique features of the word processor to further extend their repertoire of good writing strategies for children.

REFERENCES

Bereiter, C. (1980). Development in writing. In L. W. Gregg & E. R. Steinberg (Eds.), *Cognitive processes in writing* (pp. 73-93). Hillsdale, NJ: Erlbaum.

Calkins, L. (1983). *Lessons from a child: On the teaching and learning of writing.* Portsmouth, NH: Heinemann.

Calkins, L. (1986). *The art of teaching writing.* Portsmouth, NH: Heinemann.

Deno, S., Martson, S., & Mirkin, P. (1982). Valid measurement procedures for continuous evaluation of written expression. *Exceptional Children, 48*:363-370.

Flower, L. S., & Hayes, J. R. (1981a). Plans that guide the composing process. In C. H. Fredericksen & J. F. Dominic (Eds.), *Writing: The nature, development and teaching of written communication,* Vol. 2 (pp. 39-58). Hillsdale, NJ: Erlbaum.

Flower, L. S., & Hayes, J. R. (1981b). A cognitive process theory of writing. *College Composition and Communication, 32*:365-387.

Freedman, S. (1985). *The acquisition of written language: Response and revision.* Berkeley, CA: Ablex.

Graves, D. (1983). *Writing: Teachers and children at work.* Portsmouth, NH: Heinemann.

Haynes, J. A.; Kapinus, B. A.; Malouf, D.; & MacArthur, C. A. (1984).

Effect of computer-assisted instruction on disabled readers' meta-cognition and learning of new words. Technical Report No. 101. Institute for the Study of Exceptional Children and Youth. College Park, MD: University of Maryland.

Hemereck, L. A. (1979). Comparison of the written language of learning disabled and non-learning disabled elementary children using the *Inventory of Written Expression and Spelling.* (Unpublished manuscript, University of Kansas)

Langer, J. A., & Applebee, A. N. (1987). How writing shapes thinking. A study of teaching and learning. NCTE Research Report No. 22. Urbana, IL: National Council of Teachers of English.

Loper, A. B. (1984). Accuracy of learning disabled students' self-prediction of decoding. *Learning Disability Quarterly,* 7:172–178.

Poplin, M.; Gray, R.; Larsen, S.; Banikowski, A.; & Mehring, T. (1980). A comparison of components of written expression abilities in learning disabled and non-learning disabled students at three grade levels. *Learning Disability Quarterly,* 3:46–53.

Poteet, J. A. (1978). Characteristics of written expression of learning disabled and non-learning disabled elementary school students. (ERIC Document ED 158-830j) Muncie, IN: Ball State University.

Thomas, A. (1984). Microcomputer problem solving: Styles and strategies of LD and average achieving students. Paper presented at the annual meeting of the American Education Association, New Orleans.

Part IV

SUPPORT PROGRAMS
AND DEVELOPING ISSUES

9 Talking Word Processors for the Early Grades

TERESA J. ROSEGRANT
George Washington University

Young children have a better understanding of written language than adults often recognize. Children's natural awareness of and interest in written language is incorporated into their early efforts to use it meaningfully (Goodman & Goodman, 1979). Most beginners I have observed use their knowledge of the basic features of written language to "explore" writing. But the degree of independence and control that children seek in these initial explorations of written language is sometimes difficult to maintain given the requirements of writing.

Children's desire for autonomous learning can seemingly be accommodated through the use of a microcomputer (Papert, 1980). Yet my first experiences in using a simple word processor with young children suggested that more was needed from the technology to support sufficiently children's novice efforts at writing. A further extension of the microcomputer was needed to create an adequate developmental context that would enable young writers to continue their meaningful exploration of written text. As I watched children at computer keyboards, I puzzled over how to use this tool to facilitate young children's efforts as beginning writers.

This chapter includes a brief description of my efforts to develop a "talking" word processor, and a more lengthy account of the understandings I've gained from over five years of research and teaching children as they used that software.

DEVELOPMENT OF A TALKING WORD PROCESSOR

My work as an educational researcher enables me to spend many hours watching young children learn. Often these observations are truly a special time as I watch the enthusiasm children bring to new learning experiences. Some of their favorite times include early efforts to read and write. Children show a natural interest in written language. They seem to want to be a part of the people and places found in this new world of print. But in school the young child's romance with written language often ends too soon. The desire to read and write is increasingly altered by the many requirements for skill development in reading and writing. These skill requirements translate into a need for the child to get it or do it "right." This imposition of accuracy into their literacy activities is troublesome to most young learners I have observed. After several years of observation I began to wonder if there might be a way to sustain the young learner's romance with written language through the use of a microcomputer.

My initial vision of using the microcomputer to assist beginning writers led me to collaborate in 1981 with a talented engineer, Russell Cooper. Together we worked on a design for a talking word processor for young writers. The software was created by interfacing an Echo speech synthesizer that produced "speech-like" sounds with our version of a simple word processing program. This talking word processor was designed to provide children with a flexible means for exploring writing through the use of various forms of speech output from the Echo synthesizer. The software program provided a multi-sensory learning context that enabled young learners to focus on the meaning-centered functions of writing.

A talking word processor seemed helpful, for a number of reasons. The talking element of the software could give the child auditory output useful for understanding relationships and rules about how written language works. With the speech element, children would be able to construct understandings about what they had written, at a number of levels: morphologically (vowels and consonants in certain combinations create sounds), syntactically (words in certain combinations create meaning), and semantically (certain words communicate forms of meaning). The word processing element could provide the children a means for gaining access to, control over, and interaction with the many functions involved in reading and writing. The combination of these two elements meant that young students could learn without feeling pressured by a heavy skill requirement. The talking word processor could provide a meaningful support until such skills were mastered.

The program provided children a means for hearing their texts while they typed and as they reread them. While they composed text, they could hear every letter name as they pressed a letter key (or they could turn off this option) and they could hear each word pronounced as they pressed the spacebar (or they could turn off this option). After they had written some text, they could decide to listen to any part of the text, or to the entire text, as often as they pressed a command key to have the program read aloud either a sentence or the entire page of text. As the program read each word on the screen it highlighted that word. If the children heard something they decided to change, text editing was simplified with the various word processing features they now had within their command at the keyboard. Once changes were made, the young writers could listen to that part of the text again. Editing did not seem so difficult with the speech output to support the students' examination of their writing.

As I watched children use the early version of the software, I was impressed with their quick transition from typing single alphabet keys so they could hear letter names to listening to each word said aloud as they composed a letter to Grandma. It never seemed to occur to these beginners that they should spend their time learning the entire alphabet before trying to write. With the support provided by this tool, they naturally learned letter names while they composed text. This rather basic talking word processor indeed gave young writers independent access to written language within the supportive learning environment of the microcomputer.

Initial Research into Children's Use of the Software

In 1981, I set up a small lab at Arizona State University to study the effectiveness of the talking word processor as a learning tool. I was interested in determining whether the combined speech technology and word processing software was providing young and remedial beginners an alternative way to learn to write that would contribute to measurable progress. Each day in the lab we studied children and their parents as they used the software for writing.

Results of the first year of research indicated that children's improvements in beginning writing were related to their use of specific speech output features of the talking word processor

(Rosegrant, 1984a). The general conclusion of this research with beginning writers was that a talking word processor provided a different and effective means for learning to write, since children were able to use the speech output to support their own efforts when particular types of assistance were needed.

This one-year study led to new research questions as I sought to understand how children were actually using the talking word processor to gain support as learners. More focused and guided observations were needed to answer such questions. Accordingly, during the next four years, school-based labs were established for studying the various ways children used the talking word processor to become better writers. The results of this field work provided many examples of how children used the software to improve their understanding of written language and the fundamentals of writing (Rosegrant, 1984b, 1985). These observations also enabled me to examine the many ways teachers could adapt their writing instruction to include the use of this tool in classrooms and in writing labs. The core construct found in all of these observations involved the way the talking word processor was used as a form of scaffolding for beginning writing.

A Scaffold for Beginning Writing

The term *scaffolding* refers here to the temporary auditory, visual, and motor supports that are available to learners using the software. It was evident throughout the field observations that children used many forms of assistance within the program as a "scaffold" to support their beginning efforts at writing. With these supports, young writers were able to achieve a more meaningful use of language and to sustain a sense of competence. The types of assistance available to children were described as acknowledgment, feedback, and repetition (Rosegrant, 1984a). The program's design enabled each child to individually orchestrate the visual, auditory, and motor modalities to obtain whatever assistance was desired during a writing activity using the microcomputer.

The availability of these forms of assistance encouraged children sufficiently that a consistent strengthening of several essential language learning behaviors was evident. The young writers were found to have increased hypothesis-testing, risk-taking, focused participation, and persistence as they explored how written language functioned. Then, as they gained more skill and knowledge as writers, they were easily able to reduce the amount of support they received from the software. Like training wheels on a bicycle, the program's scaffolding helped children gain confidence, and then the supports were simply removed as the children's writing abilities developed.

Early Implementation
of This Promising Support Program

Despite these promising research results, I encountered much skepticism from other educators about the use of speech technology and the degree of educational benefit that could be derived from its implementation. I was not surprised at the time. Many factors worked against early acceptance of a talking word processor in primary grades in the early 1980s. During this period the Bank Street Writer was introduced into elementary schools for upper-grade students and while it did gain acceptance, its use was considerably limited by the small number of microcomputers in elementary schools. In addition, most of the microcomputers in schools were being used for Logo and/or BASIC instruction in order to provide the fundamentals of computer literacy. This left little time in the schedule for word processing. Given the difficulty that older students had gaining access to microcomputers for writing, it was not likely that a word processor for younger children in the primary grades would be quickly implemented.

The likelihood of educational implementation of talking word processors in primary grades was significantly enhanced by several developments beginning in 1984. Foremost was the introduction by International Business Machines Corporation (IBM) of two new software programs that used types of speech technology. The first was the Writing to Read program, which used digitized speech. IBM's aggressive marketing of the program gained public attention and shifted the focus of microcomputer use to kindergarten through third grade in the area of beginning literacy.

With much less fanfare, IBM released a second program, Listen to Learn (Rosegrant & Cooper, 1985) that same year. Listen to Learn was an IBM 128k version of our original Apple 48k talking text writer, with many additions and improvements. Field testing supported by IBM led us to incorporate many new features that were found helpful by young writers as they developed new skills. The testing, conducted in several urban and suburban sites, again showed the utility of the program for beginning writers (Rosegrant, 1984b). Unfortunately, IBM did not provide teacher documentation to share this information about the various uses for Listen to Learn. However, IBM's interest in both this program and Writing to Read encouraged a second look at the possible uses of speech-related software with primary-age children in the area of language arts.

This second look was augmented in 1985 by the impact of many speech-related products that were available from a wide range of sources. There was a significant increase in the number of software programs using some computer-generated speech, particularly in special education. At about the same time, several new talking toys met with success, while educational toys such as Speak and Spell continued to broaden their market. And a successful motion picture, "War Games," featured a talking computer. All of these happenings contributed to widening acceptance of technology-based speech.

One of the barriers against acceptance of speech-related software was the opposition of some educators to the "robotic" sounds of speech devices. Children, of course, accepted electronic speech more readily than adults and did not find it problematic, as evidenced by toddlers' use of the many Mattel See and Say products. Even young toddlers could use the less-than-perfect mechanical speech to learn new vocabulary words. Our own experience had been that children consistently preferred the computer to sound more like hardware and less like a person. Parents were also finding technology-based speech less offensive as they began to realize its advantages for young learners.

In 1986, Scholastic Inc. announced its new version of the Talking Text Writer (Rosegrant & Cooper, 1986), which was a major revision of our original Apple 48k version. Scholastic's entrance into speech software was important because its primary efforts are in English education. Scholastic also successfully sold the word processing programs Bank Street Writer and PFS Write in schools for use by intermediate-grade students and teachers. It was a logical extension for the company to offer a talking word processor for use in kindergarten through third grade.

These changes in perceptions and access to speech-related products have certainly advanced the use of talking word processors by young writers. As this acceptance has widened, educators have turned their attention to understanding the appropriate uses of talking word processors rather than debating their existence. This interest in implementation has led teachers to ask questions similar to those I asked as a researcher investigating this software's use as a scaffold for young writers. In particular, teachers often ask, "How can talking word processors be used effectively by beginning writers in primary-grade classroom settings?" The remainder of this chapter provides what I believe is a helpful conceptual framework for understanding the ways that talking word processors can be used to assist beginning writers.

FUNDAMENTALS OF COMPOSING AND REVISING

A clear and coherent conception of what a young writer is trying to learn to do is necessary if we are to assist the learner. The young writer must learn the fundamentals of the writing process—composing and revising text. I have isolated key elements of composing and revising skills that seem inherently difficult for young writers to acquire and yet are essential to learning how to write. These elements include having (a) an "inner voice" for constructing and editing the text subvocally, (b) a "critical ear" to hear and judge how the text sounds, (c) a sense of the requirements of the text, which goes beyond the needs of the writer and involves a "concern for the audience," (d) a repertoire of skills and strategies about features of written language that can be used to improve a text, and (e) a "careful eye" for meeting the conventions required of printed text for public presentation.

My experience with writing suggests that these five elements are often difficult for young learners to develop through entirely silent efforts occurring within inner speech. Various forms of external speech are needed to provide support for young writers as they build a working model for composing and revising. An "external voice" enables children to rely on their oral language abilities to make sense of the writing effort. A talking word processor provides various forms of speech output that can be used as an external voice to support the composing and revising efforts of young writers until they develop the fundamentals of writing (Rosegrant, 1986a).

Developing an "Inner Voice" for Writing

When a writer has full use of inner speech, the construction of text is largely an outcome of an internal discourse between the writer and what is written. Although an experienced writer may occasionally speak sentences aloud when drafting text, it is primarily an "inner voice" that is used to compose and revise text. Young children generally are not proficient in the use of this inner voice for composing and editing. They must rely on an external voice provided by the teacher, peers, or themselves to develop their ideas as writers. Children use what they hear from oral speech to foster a dialogue for writing. As that dialogue becomes increasingly subvocal, a "voice" is found completely functioning within inner speech.

Recognizing the importance of an external voice as a transition to an inner voice, teachers encourage beginning writers to use external speech to help them develop ideas for writing. Composing aloud is used to increase the flow of ideas in the initial draft. After some text has been written, it is often read by the child or to the child to provide a means for examining its meaning. This act of reading aloud creates a bit of mental distance, which enables the writer to listen for the fullness of expression and the flow of ideas. Listening to the text also provides a type of feedback that prompts writers to reflect on their writing for its adequacy at conveying their intended meaning.

Children use the speech output from a talking word processor as an external voice to read and re-read text during the composing and revising process. With the speech output from the synthesizer, writers listen to parts of or the entire text while composing to assist the initial drafting of an idea (production), to extend ideas within the text (extension), and to complete the logical or conceptual structure of the text (elaboration).

There are several features of a talking word processor that encourage beginners to use the speech output to obtain the oral feedback and repetition needed during this transition stage until they have fully developed an inner voice for writing. These features include enabling the learner to control how much text is spoken and how often it is spoken by the speech synthesizer, and allowing for easy implementation by requiring only a single keystroke to produce speech output.

The robotic speech of the Echo synthesizer has proven to be a particularly effective device for providing appropriate voiced feedback about what is literally written. The speech output provides a monotone pronunciation of the text, which is an excellent form of scaffolding for the learner. The advantage of monotone speech over a pattern that has more human-like qualities of inflection is that it conveys what the child needs to hear as it is written and revised instead of giving a complete oral interpretation of the text. The monotone speech allows the writer to provide "mental sounds" or qualities so the text is filled with his or her personal expression of ideas. Children begin by silently reading along with the speech synthesizer, but increasingly the text is read aloud with the expression needed to convey each child's own deeper meaning. This process is repeated many times with each text. As young writers read along with the synthesizer, expression from their own voices is added to give text the "feelings" that complete the meaning. Such an active use of external speech nurtures a rich sense of self-expression. Eventually the external voice used to read text aloud is replaced by an inner voice that is strengthened by this richly cultivated use of oral language.

Developing a "Critical Ear"

Of the five elements needed to become a good writer, I would argue that the most important for improving text is the writer's development of a critical ear. Young writers need to have the ability to "hear" whether a text sounds appropriate, if they are to make decisions about the use of written language. Developing a critical ear begins with consistent access to appropriate models, which enable young writers to hear how written language is used. Such auditory input forms an important foundation for the intuitive ability needed by writers to improve text.

The adequacy of a writer's auditory model is largely dependent on how often the writer receives input about written language and how much input is received. A critical ear is most successfully gained from acknowledging changes in text that sound better, from the redundancy created by the reading and re-reading of texts aloud, and from oral feedback provided by teachers and peers. Frequent listening to written text enables children to develop a "critical ear." Without sources of input, children are unlikely to develop the necessary sense of how text "sounds." The repeated experience of hearing sentences enables children to gain more sophisticated templates that create expectations about writing.

This notion of developing and using a critical ear describes the writer's use of auditory templates or structures to judge aspects of a text in a generalized manner as it is read aloud. The writer uses a critical ear as a means for deciding if a text "sounds all right." The judgments made about the text become an important form of feedback. This auditorily based sensibility about how text should sound is increasingly automatic as the process is repeated. It is similar to a native speaker's ability to judge the acceptability of spoken words. The speaker/listener knows how something should be said in order to be acceptable within his or her own dialect. What the listener hears is accepted or rejected based on the native speaker's sense of how things are "usually" said. Without this type of knowledge about spoken or written language, the speaker/writer would be required to judge each sentence without the helpful framework experience provides. Such a sentence-by-sentence evaluation would be an unreasonable mental burden and would certainly weaken the flow of ideas in either spoken or written expression. Instead, these auditory templates are used to guide children as composers and revisers toward an adequate use of written language.

As children compose at the keyboard, they are able to use the talking word processor to gain auditory feedback and repetition. Children begin to hear text as they are writing and to compare it with their existing auditory templates for its adequacy as written expression. The speech output can provide important support to the young writer, who can listen to initially drafted text to hear how it sounds. The speech output provides the writer immediate feedback while allowing for a spontaneous first draft.

The speech output is used by writers to listen to words as they type, then repeatedly listen to a line or paragraph aloud, and then add to the idea as they hear where to add more to their descriptions. This listening to text while composing provides the input for their critical ear, which is then used to judge whether the text is adequately conveying their desired expression. When the text does not meet the requirements for matching the templates of the critical ear, the young writer can choose to make adjustments or wait to revise the text at a later time.

Once a draft is written, children are often unable to judge the effectiveness of their ideas for revisions. They may judge that the text "doesn't sound right" but lack a means for comparing one or more versions of text revision. The speech output is used while revising to listen for problematic structures and unacceptable usage that can obstruct intended meaning and then provides the writer a means for evaluating probable revisions.

The speech output is used by writers to compare edited and unedited text, to determine the redundancy of vocabulary choices, to evaluate various reorganizations of an idea, to consider differ-

ent types of sentence arrangements, and to judge the completeness of an idea. The young writer can listen to the revisions and
select ones that meet the critical ear's criteria for acceptability.
This consistent effort to improve text may in turn lead to the
development of new or slightly altered templates, and so the
revisions actually provide a means for strengthening the critical
ear of the young writer.

Developing a Concern for the Audience

The early writing of children is often described as a form of self-
expression. The purpose of this type of writing is to tell about an
event, persons, or a happening in daily life. Initially, these expressive texts are a type of "running record" that literally represents
the child's recall of things that have occurred. Such remembering
is not always complete. Much is filled in mentally by the child
without realizing that the reader does not have the same view of
the experience. It is often assumed by the young writer that the
adult will "know what I mean," when in fact the adult cannot
sufficiently reconstruct an understanding of the event from the
child's written description. The young writer has not yet learned
how to consider the needs of the reader.

As children develop ways to analyze their writing, they begin
to understand that the reader needs more information about what
occurred in order to share in the experience. The young writer
begins to understand that these needs of the reader are required
elements of the text. Eventually, the young writer includes more
and more in the composition to help the reader construct an image
of what the writer has in mind. This shift toward making an effort
to more adequately share ideas involves a desire to communicate.
The writer is able to acknowledge and to incorporate this desire to
communicate if he or she can gain a distal response to the text.

An important goal of primary writing instruction involves
providing ways for young writers to gain a concern for their
audience. A variety of methods are used in the classroom to assist
beginning writers in developing a better sense of what the audience needs. During writing conferences the teacher asks questions to direct the writer's efforts. The adult also invites the child
to read the text aloud and listen for omissions. Editing groups are
sometimes formed so that the writer can listen to comments from
actual readers. Such techniques are attempts to create some psy-

chological distance between the writer and the text, so the writer can examine the text from the reader's perspective. This distance enables the writer to read the text for meaning instead of relying on personal experience to fill in the literal gaps.

Children use the speech output from a talking word processor to develop a better sense of their audience's needs. Mental distance from the text is more readily achieved as writers sit back and listen to parts of the text being read aloud by the program. The program enables children to control how much text is read aloud, the rate at which it is read, and how many times it is read. As children listen to parts of the text, they begin to recognize various omissions, substitutions, and confusions that make it difficult for their audience to gain the intended meaning. Once the audience's needs are revealed to the writer, the next stage of revising is much easier. Hearing that there are omissions, the young writer understands that more of his or her thoughts must be transferred onto the printed page. The speech output provides an easy means of gaining the mental distance to achieve a sense of what readers require.

Exploring Features of Written Language

To improve as writers, children need to form understandings of how the written system of language functions. They must begin to recognize how ideas take on form and structure through printed words. Young children can use their writing as an opportunity to explore the many elements of written English, including how language conforms to specific conventions (left to right, top to bottom, punctuation, spelling, and the use of grammar); performs many functions (informs, persuades, entertains, records, and requests); can be used in many forms (poetry, stories, letters, and reports); and involves many stylistic choices (many ways to say something, create humor, or create drama). These basic explorations of writing provide ways for children to develop expectations about features of written language. It is important for children to form their own hypotheses about how written language works and then test those hypotheses. However, hypothesis-testing is difficult to accomplish unless adequate repetition and timely feedback are available. Repetition and feedback within a writing activity allow children to construct a framework for testing their assumptions about written language. A talking word processor provides unlimited repetition and feedback throughout the writing activity for children to conduct their own experiments within the text. This provides young writers with a means for determining the relative success of hunches about sound, words, grammar, genre, or whatever else the writer seeks to pragmatically explore.

Repetition is particularly helpful to young writers as they attempt new skills and strategies. Repetition gives children sufficient opportunity to examine and construct understandings about specific features of written language. It also strengthens recall abilities that enable children to use language skills with increased fluency. It is difficult for the teacher, however, to know when to provide repetition and how much to provide during children's writing activities. Often, the adult provides too much or too little repetition and thus does not adequately support the child. With a talking word processor, children can control the amount of repetition they receive. They can practice and play with features within text, such as rhyme or alliteration, until they have successfully mastered the desired pattern. Children's playful explorations while using a talking word processor are filled with repetition as they listen to the structures they are examining within our writing system.

Children benefit from information about what they are doing, but the timing of feedback will often determine how helpful it is. Immediate feedback is most helpful, since it is given when the young writer has an opportunity to alter the approach taken. Children appear to transform feedback into further actions when it is readily available during their many experiments as writers. Feedback that is postponed is often interpreted as a form of criticism rather than support since it may leave little time for the writer to make any modifications or improvements.

A talking word processor enables children to listen to what they have proposed in a text and to evaluate a current assumption about written language. The auditory feedback can be used by young writers to explore features at all linguistic levels. By comparing two or more versions of the text auditorily, it is easy for students to keep one version of a paragraph and copy or change several others. Children can investigate structures, whether they pertain to text at the level of sound, semantics, or syntactics. These examinations of how language works foster improved usage as young writers develop insights about the nature of language in its written form. It is these insights that form the foundation for a repertoire of skills and strategies that can be used to improve a text.

Developing a Careful Eye

Once their text has been drafted, young writers must decide if it should be "published"—that is, printed and bound for use by readers in the classroom or school library. This decision to make writing available to a wider audience means that the writer must meet certain conventions of written language imposed on published works. Young authors must decide to examine their text with the more refined and detailed "look" that is required to uncover inappropriate or mistaken usages that all writers miss during earlier drafts. Finding these indiscretions within a text requires a "careful eye" as the writer checks and corrects the text. I have found that such scrutiny is accepted and even invited by children when publishing their work is the desired goal. Children can learn a great deal about writing by putting a careful eye to their drafted texts to prepare them for "publication."

Several features of a talking word processor are helpful in developing the young writer's careful eye. The software's highlighting of each word as it is spoken provides a strong auditory/ visual cue that prompts children to inspect each word for its appropriate use and spelling. Children are able to "hear" errors that are less obvious if one reads along silently without this cuing feature. The option within the software to have parts of the text re-read aloud enables the writer to listen carefully for and thereby locate dissonant text. This auditory repetition is helpful to young children whose ears are usually more skilled than their eyes at identifying problematic text. The writer, supported by the speech output, develops an understanding of the conventions of print for which the author is accountable. With this understanding of convention, the young writer becomes willing to scrutinize the text for its conceptual and structural defects.

When corrections are needed, the difficulty experienced by young writers in altering text to meet certain spelling, word choice, or structural requirements is greatly reduced by the use of the word processor. Children can rapidly make corrections and listen to the outcome. The various supports of a talking word processor make correcting inaccuracies less problematic. Young writers learn to respect the skillful use of a careful eye to craft their final products.

THE ROLE OF THE ADULT

Talking word processors provide children important support for their efforts as young writers. The forms of scaffolding they provide alter how children experience writing. This does not, however, remove the teacher from taking an active role in writing instruction, but it does change the nature of the adult's role within this learning context. The adult is asked to perform a new role that I would describe as a type of "key informant" to represent the broader community of writers. This role emerges as the adult is recognized by children as a helpful source of knowledge about how written language is used.

Implementing a talking word processor in a classroom writing program was not easy initially for many of the teachers I worked with, since the role of key informant required them to cultivate a different style of engaging young writers. Teachers reported to me that they initially felt awkward "just watching" children using the talking word processor, even though they thought it inappropriate to intrude. Fortunately, the adults were able to recognize the significance of their new role as key informant as children initiated interactions by asking a question or seeking an opinion. Once the young learners were engaged, the teachers tried to determine what form of assistance, if any, might help to gain new skills or insights into the process of writing. In many cases this meant encouraging children to make use of some feature of the talking word processor to gain a means for remaining autonomous. Over time, the adults responded to these requests without taking control of the children's learning.

The key informant role enables adults to engage in the learning context in many important ways. Adults maintained a degree of orchestration of the large context to ensure that children gained access to microcomputers and other materials needed to complete their writing. Teachers I observed frequently provided the following for young writers: a model of the behavior to be performed, support for the children's efforts, feedback on their efforts, acknowledgment of what they were trying to do, expansion on what they were trying to do, inquiry into what they understood or could do, information about what was occurring, accountability for task completion, responses to the children's requests, and purpose for the children's efforts. The significance of this support was found in children's need for daily interactions with teachers to assist these young writers in improving their drafts of texts.

These opportunities to discuss writing were facilitated by the open-ended context and the teachers' enthusiastic implementation of the talking word processor with their blossoming young writers.

SUMMARY

While there are many schooling practices that can provide young writers with a means for improving their skills and strategies, few approaches strengthen the other components of writing. Talking word processors are unique tools for supporting young writers as they develop an inner voice, a critical ear, a sense of audience, a careful eye, and a repertoire of skills and strategies for writing. Talking word processors provide young writers a new form of access to written language that fosters their autonomy as learners. And, in addition, children using them tell me that they make writing fun.

REFERENCES

Goodman, K. S., & Goodman, Y. M. (1979). Learning to read is natural. In L. B. Resnick & P. A. Weaver (Eds.), *Theory and practice of early reading.* Hillsdale, NJ: Erlbaum.

Papert, S. (1980). *Mind-storms: Children, computers, and powerful ideas.* New York: Basic Books, Inc.

Rosegrant, T. J. (1984a, February). Fostering progress in literacy development: Technology and social interaction. *Seminars in Speech and Language, 5*(1).

Rosegrant, T. J. (1984b). Talking word processors and beginning writing: A means for improving writing instruction. Report No. 4 (unpublished manuscript). IBM Corp., Boca Raton, FL.

Rosegrant, T. J. (1985, April). *Using the microcomputer to assist children in their efforts to acquire beginning literacy.* Paper presented at the meeting of the American Educational Research Association, Chicago.

Rosegrant, T. J. (1986a, April). *It doesn't sound right: The role of speech output as a primary form of feedback for beginning text revision.* Paper presented at the meeting of the American Educational Research Association, San Francisco.

Rosegrant, T. J. (1986b). Using the microcomputer as a scaffold for assisting beginning readers and writers. In J. L. Hoot (Ed.), *Computers in early childhood education: Issues and practices* (pp. 128-143). Engle-wood Cliffs, NJ: Prentice-Hall.

Rosegrant, T. J. & Cooper, R. (1985). Listen to learn. A software program published by IBM, Boca Raton, FL.

Rosegrant, T. J. & Cooper, R. (1986). Talking text writer. A software program published by Scholastic, Inc., New York.

10 Computer–Based Feedback for Editing in the Early Grades

ERNEST BALAJTHY
State University of New York at Geneseo

Advocates of the writing process approach to the teaching of writing often speak of a natural desire or primal need to write. They claim successful teaching of writing taps into these deeply felt internal motivations. Whether or not writers actually have such needs, the fact is that few students show indications of any primal need to revise and edit—to rewrite and refine their original drafts. "We live in a one-draft-only society," Calkins (1986) complained (p. 23).

Yet the revision stage is the keystone of the writing process. Without an appropriate student attitude toward revision, the writing process collapses. After completion of the first draft, peer and teacher conferencing and independent self-analysis of content and structure should be the focus of student attention. This revision is motivated in large part by the final goal of any writer: publication.

Editing is the crucial intermediate step between revision and publication. Teachers should clearly differentiate between the earlier revision steps, dealing with finalization of content (as discussed previously in this volume) and form, and the later mechanical step of editing. Editing is specifically designed to prepare a perfect version of the paper for publication. In order to qualify a writing for publication, spelling, grammar, usage, and punctuation ought to be reasonably correct (Graves, 1983).

With appropriate implementation strategies, and bearing in mind the limitations and difficulties involved in using computers with young children (Cuffaro, 1985), word processing can be used effectively with young children (Geisert, 1986; Seltzer, 1986; Smith, 1985). In addition to the well-researched beneficial effects of revision when students use word processing software, computers offer younger writers a valuable tool in the editing process, for several reasons (Balajthy, McKeveny, & Lacitignola, 1986–1987). For one, computers can perform text analysis at the word level, as in the identification of spelling errors. Since some limited amount of phrase and sentence processing can be carried out based on word-level analysis, computers can also perform indirect phrase and sentence analysis.

In addition, computers can make editing suggestions and decisions because many tasks in editing text are mechanical, requiring little knowledge of high-level artificial intelligence-based natural language processing. Research and development of computer systems that can actually understand natural language is still at a primitive stage (Balajthy, 1985, 1987). Nonetheless, programs without these artificial intelligence capabilities can perform useful text analysis.

WHAT ARE TEXT-ANALYSIS PROGRAMS?

Spelling checkers and text-analysis programs work in a word-by-word fashion to mechanically simulate proofreading. Spelling checkers are a simple form of computer-based analysis. With such a program, each word of the student's composition is isolated according to the simple process of breaking the document down into all letter groups separated from one another by spaces. These letter groups are then rearranged within the computer memory in alphabetical order for more efficient processing.

Each letter group in the document is compared with a dictionary, a master list of words stored on disk. The computer identifies those letter groups that do not match any word in the list. These possible misspellings, with suggested correct spellings, are then reported to the writer, who makes the final decision as to whether the document spelling should be changed.

Computer-based text analysis can be carried to a somewhat higher plane: the analysis of grammar, punctuation, and style. In such text-analysis programs (sometimes called grammar checkers, word choice checkers, and style analyzers), the on-disk dictionary contains lists of target words, phrases, and punctuation marks that are often misused by writers. For example, the distinction between *to*, *two*, and *too* is poorly recognized by many writers. A text-analysis program would identify each occurrence of these words as a possible error.

Computer-based text analysis is not sufficiently sophisticated to make decisions as to the accuracy of to/two/too usage in a sentence. To do so, the computer would have to understand natural language. The final decision as to usage, therefore, must remain the writer's. Each occurrence of to/two/too is displayed, in context, on the monitor. The usage rules are also displayed, typically with examples of correct and incorrect use of the words. As with spelling checkers, the writer makes the final decision as to whether the word should be changed.

Text-analysis programs may check commonly misused punctuation marks. Some, for example, check that all quotation marks occur in pairs. Others, such as the PROOFREADER OPTION in The Writing Adventure, go through the text to find each comma. The contextual sentence is displayed, along with several comma usage rules so that writers can check that one of the rules applies. Bureaucratic and vague words are also indicated in most text-analysis programs.

Text-analysis programs can provide other structured editing information. Ghost Writer, for example, gives a readability estimate of the text's difficulty level, based on the Fry graph. Its SENTENCE LENGTH ANALYZER graphs the length of each sentence. The PARAGRAPH OUTLINER prints the first and last sentence of each paragraph to facilitate the writer's examination of the text structure. The CLARITY CHECKER checks for overuse of "to be" verbs, nominalizations, and coordinating conjunctions.

Research and development of more and more sophisticated style-analysis programs is in progress. Among the better known research projects are Bell Laboratories' Writer's Workbench (Frase, 1987; Kiefer & Smith, 1983) and IBM's Epistle (Jensen & Heidorn, 1984). At the University of Pittsburgh's Learning Research and Development Center, theoretical work continues on identification of errors in natural language texts (Hull, Ball, Fox, Levin, & McCutchen, 1985).

ADVANTAGES OF TEXT-ANALYSIS PROGRAMS

The advantages of using text-analysis programs are described in the paragraphs that follow.

Efficient Proofreading

Much of the work involved in proofreading text is tedious and routine. A poor speller, for example, may be told by teachers to use a dictionary to check words that may be misspelled. In practical terms, however, this tedious task may encourage young children to become poor proofreaders. Rather than carefully checking each word, they learn to ignore possible misspellings so as to save themselves from the boredom of constant dictionary referral. A spelling checker can save enormous amounts of time by performing the checking and dictionary referral automatically and painlessly.

Similarly, in writing-process classrooms, a routine suggestion to students for encouraging editing is to use an editing checklist (Calkins, 1986; Graves, 1983). The editing checklist contains an individualized list of editing tasks to be carried out by the writer and checked off, item-by-item. For example, a student may have learned to differentiate to/two/too but does not yet automatically use the words correctly when writing an early draft. Therefore, use of to/two/too is one of the items on the checklist. After checking for that, the student goes on to the next item for another proofreading of the document. The tasks are carried out one at a time in order to avoid confusion from cognitive overload caused by trying to do too many things at once.

Each student's checklist must reflect his or her own particular progress in grammar and usage. Those editing tasks learned to the point of automaticity are deleted from the checklist. New tasks that can be carried out by students are added as the students learn them.

While checklists are an important part of the writing process, children are often poorly motivated to carry out this tedious procedure on their own. A computer-based text checker can make the step-by-step procedure much more efficient. Writers must still complete the necessary task of deciding whether to/two/too are used correctly, but the chore of laboring through the text to find each use of those words is carried out by the computer, and correction is simplified by using a word processor.

A crucial factor in students' adoption of effective, problem-by-problem proofreading is simple repetition. Teachers must enforce the policy of careful proofreading so that students repeatedly experience the effectiveness of the procedure. Only then will this technique become an automatic part of the student's writing process.

Text-analysis software serves as a model for this kind of proofreading. As students use the program, they see the technique in progress and learn its effectiveness. In this way, the computer-based proofreading can be a model for non-computer writing experiences (Daiute, 1983).

In The Writing Workshop, for example, one of the two style-analyzer disks, PROOFREADER, leads the writer or a peer reviewer through the text sentence-by-sentence. Comments can be inserted directly in the text for later referral for revising or editing. The STYLE subprogram simply asks the proofreader whether each sentence is written effectively and provides the opportunity to correct it. The FINAL CHECK subprogram encourages examination of each sentence for pronoun reference, sentence completeness, subject/verb agreement, and so on.

Risk-Free Feedback

Learning from computers involves little ego involvement on the part of younger children. Burg (1984) described one five-year-old student at work on the computer:

> Eric loves working with the computer! He trusts it. It doesn't laugh at him. It doesn't ask him to repeat. He can predict what it will do. It's safe. Eric speaks more often. . . . He gains confidence. Soon he may find it less risky to talk to peers. (p. 28)

Students are less likely to be cowed by a computer telling them about their errors than of their teachers or peers doing the same. By performing a preliminary computer-based analysis of the first draft, students can avoid some of the insecurities involved with showing their error-ridden drafts to teachers and peers.

Ease in Catching Typos

One of the most difficult tasks in proofreading is finding so-called typos that seem to disappear into the text and become invisible because of their minor nature. For example, some text-analysis programs check for double-typed words, where the typist has accidentally typed the same word twice. The Writing Workshop's

MECHANICS CHECKER disk finds sentences that begin with a lower case letter, and punctuation marks that are not followed by a space.

Model for Effective Conferencing

The peer conference is a crucial component of writing-process classrooms described in this volume. In a peer conference, student writers gather together to share their writings and to obtain and give advice.

While the sophistication of computer-based text analysis is limited, certain stylistic suggestions can be made by the computer. As the computer makes these suggestions to student writers, they learn how to make such suggestions to others. In this way, children learn to provide feedback more effectively to other writers and thus enhance the success of writing conferences.

Help for Poorer Writers

The shame involved in having one's writing weaknesses exposed repeatedly to one's peers is a real difficulty. Teachers must diligently work to establish adequate peer relationships and attitudes. Poorer writers can otherwise come to see writing time as punitive.

The use of computers to analyze text gives these poorer writers a greater sense of security as they share their creations with the teacher and with other children. They can face the writing conference with at least some sense of assurance that errors have been identified and corrected.

Early Success

Use of a computer to provide feedback yields early success in writing. As children receive instruction in a particular writing subskill, they are immediately given a computer-guided application of that subskill to their own writing. After learning the to/ two/too differentiation, for example, students can be guided to successful use of the words through carefully constructed text-analysis feedback.

In addition, young children can receive automatic feedback on spelling so that their written creations look more like carefully finished products. This early success instills a sense of pride in one's writings and may lead to increased enthusiasm for writing.

Greater Attention for Higher-Level Tasks

The use of a computer for dealing with lower-level proofreading tasks frees the students and teacher for attention to higher-level analysis. In the non-computer-based version of writing process, teachers try to focus writers' attention on higher-level issues such as completeness, clarity, organization, and coherence. Students are urged to put editing last on their list of tasks so that earlier stages of writing can be devoted to higher-level issues. While this strategy of enforced ignoring is generally effective, there can be no doubt that editing problems present a constant distraction from higher-level thinking.

Similarly, the teacher is often sidetracked by low-level editing issues at inappropriate points too early in the process. Writing-process teachers train themselves to ignore spelling and grammar errors when they conference with children who are still at the first draft or revising stages. Yet it is difficult to ignore these lower-level problems in a massively misspelled draft. A poorly spelled text sends automatic signals to the reader that make attention to the ideas difficult. A quick preliminary computer-based analysis of the first draft can help direct teacher and peer feedback to higher-level issues.

Teacher-Time Effectiveness

Some writing-process teachers believe that red-penciling of compositions before publication deprives students of a sense of ownership of their papers. These teachers avoid final correcting of student papers. Many other teachers, however, work with the children to give detailed feedback so that the published versions of the papers are perfect. These teachers believe that they can maintain a sense of student ownership and obtain even greater student pride in the creations by providing the necessary proofreading help.

Correcting final drafts, however, is notoriously time-consuming for teachers. One reason writing-process advocates have dictated against the procedure is that teacher attention is more effective when given earlier in the writing process than when given later (Graves, 1976), and the time necessary to correct final drafts takes away from the teacher's ability to pay attention to earlier drafts.

By providing detailed feedback on low-level matters, the computer can help students correct many errors before the paper reaches the final draft status. As a result, less teacher-time is necessary for correction at the later stage.

Developing a Sense of Ownership

Some teachers may fear that computer-based feedback on text will decrease children's sense of ownership of writings, that in some sense students will think of the final draft as created more by the computer than by themselves. Since ownership of writing is a key prerequisite to establishment of a sense of pride and accomplishment in publication, this might be considered a fatal flaw in plans to use computers for text analysis.

In reality, however, computer-based feedback takes no more away from children's sense of ownership than does feedback from peers and teachers in conferences (Sommers, 1982). The computer simply gives advice. The actual changes must be made by the child. Even in situations where the computer makes "automatic" physical changes in text, as when it replaces a misspelled word with the correct version drawn from the disk-based dictionary, the writer is in control. The child must first command the computer before it makes any changes.

Children quickly come to see that the computer can make no intelligent decisions itself. The bulk of analysis and the choice as to whether to make changes or not rests on the writer. The computer only identifies potential problems and offers advice.

Writing-process philosophy is based on the assumption that young writers function essentially in the same way that professional writers function (Emig, 1971). There is no doubt that text-analysis programs are becoming a natural part of professional writing, as word processing became a central tool in professional writing in the early 1980s. Teachers should lead children to the realization that text-analysis programs, like word processors, are simply tools to be used.

USING TEXT-ANALYSIS PROGRAMS IN THE CLASSROOM

Teachers should consider several aspects of text analyzers before using them in the classroom.

Preliminary and Final Editing

As noted above, computer-based text analysis fits neatly into the editing stage of the writing process, between revision and final publication. Depending on circumstances, however, teachers may advise some students to use text-analysis programs early in the process. While advocates of writing process often advise delaying editing, this linear view of writing is a simplification of the process. Revising and editing naturally occur at all stages in the writing process. Writing is not linear; rather, it is a complex interaction of recursive, embedded activities (Flower & Hayes, 1981).

Some children face great difficulties in sharing their written products with other students because of the poor mechanical quality of early drafts. While the peer-conferencing situation should be encouraging and supportive, and microcomputers can provide an impetus for young children to share discoveries and help their peers (Ziajko, 1983), this ideal is not always achieved in classrooms. Mockery of poor mechanical ability in writing can be subtle and can turn writing into a negative experience to be avoided.

Children who face the insecurities caused by lack of mechanical competence may wish to carry out an initial text analysis of their drafts prior to peer- and teacher-revision conferencing. While later changes will require a second text analysis prior to publication, this first analysis can greatly increase the child's confidence as he or she gives the initial draft to others for their responses and advice.

The second text analysis will be repetitive of the first. For example, every occurrence of to/two/too will be checked again, regardless of whether it was found to be correct in the first analysis. To avoid too much repetition, the student may decide to check only certain aspects of grammar in a first draft rather than referencing the full repertoire of the program's target rules. Perhaps the student will be satisfied with limiting the preliminary check to spelling and saving the more time-consuming grammar and style checking for later in the process.

Direct Instruction in Appropriate Use

Preliminary research has indicated a tendency of children to misuse spelling and text analyzers in a variety of ways. Moore (1983) has warned teachers: "As students of language, we should recognize the limits of any analysis based on surface features of a text. Style and substance, once distinguished, are not easily reunited" (p. 7). These problems can be overcome by simply informing students and teaching them correct applications.

For example, one valuable tool available in some analysis programs is a traditional readability index or a variation of one, such as a read-out of average sentence length. The PROOFREADER disk in The Writing Workshop provides a bar graph and word count of sentence length in each paragraph and in the paper as a whole. Writer's Helper asks students to estimate the grade level of their audience, performs a Fogg readability check, then reports on the match between estimated audience level and level of the text. If, for example, the readability level is two or more years below the estimate, the following message is displayed on the monitor screen:

> You seem to be writing below your audience. You may want to run the sentence graph to see if most of your sentences are short and choppy. Maybe you should combine a few. Also check your vocabulary. Are you using vague, one-syllable words like "nice" and "lots"? Use more specific words to rise to the level of your audience.

Many writers are tempted to misuse the readability indices available on text analyzers by simply chopping long sentences in half and replacing difficult with easier words, or vice versa. These cosmetic changes may not actually make text easier to read unless they are carried out with care and consideration for the reader. Also, students may place too much faith in spelling checkers. Misspelled homonyms, such as *read* and *red*, will still slip through unless close, personal proofreading is carried out by the student. Deciding whether to replace terms flagged by text analyzers is especially difficult. Coke (1982) has warned that words suggested by analyzers as replacements are often less specific or more confusing than the original terms.

Arranging Scope and Sequence

Children cannot be expected to make editing decisions that require a degree of expertise that is beyond their training. Decisions regarding use of to/two/too, for example, cannot be made unless students have an understanding of the parts of the sentence.

Teachers must choose software that fits appropriately into the scope and sequence of skill development in their classrooms. This can be done in two ways. First, teachers can choose text-analysis programs that are designed for the level of their students. A program designed for adults, such as Sensible Grammar, may be appropriate for secondary students. Its use in the early-elementary grades, however, would create confusion. Second, teachers can modify some text-analysis programs to deal only with the skills appropriate to their students. In The Writing Adventure, for example, the proofreading component of the program offers writers the opportunity to choose the targets for proofreading. If teachers do not want children to deal with complex rules for use of commas, they can instruct the children not to choose the proofreading option that analyzes punctuation skills.

Future developments in text-analysis programs for children may allow for greater personalization of the software. Teachers will be able to specify analysis procedures to be carried out and individualize those specifications to meet each child's needs.

Transfer of Text–Analysis Learning

Initial criticism of text-analysis programs indicated some concern that students would use the programs as a crutch to avoid learning. Computer checking of spelling, for example, might communicate to students that studying spelling words is unimportant. Such criticisms have been muted, however, as many teachers have long since come to realize the importance of computers as tools to augment the intellect (Englebert & English, 1968). The computer learning environment has brought about significant changes in the way teachers think about education. Changes in the teaching of arithmetic and mathematics, created by the introduction of the ubiquitous electronic calculators, have paved the way for similar changes in language arts education. As Schwartz (1983) has noted, "Computer aids can help us guide our students, with 'trainer wheels' at first if need be, but ultimately leading toward independent thought and language choices for more effective communication" (pp. 15-16).

In addition, teachers have generally recognized the power of incidental learning in the context of meaningful writing experiences. This recognition has been enhanced by long-standing evidence that direct instruction in some facets of writing subskills, especially grammar, has been ineffective (Braddock, Lloyd-Jones, & Schoerr, 1963).

Computer-based text analysis enhances incidental learning in several ways. Children are directed to analysis of problem areas in their own papers, providing motivation for learning and a sense of need. After all, they see their mistakes made evident for them. Those mistakes that are especially prevalent in their own writing are identified again and again by the computer, allowing for frequent exposure to the teaching principles involved. After seeing the word *independence* misspelled for the fifth time in a composition, a student will recognize the need to take time to learn to spell it correctly. When every use of to/two/too requires that the child work through the rules presented on the monitor screen, those rules are learned through simple repetition.

The point of computer-based feedback, then, is not to make children dependent, but rather to provide children with the ability necessary for future work (Schwartz, 1984). Kiefer and Smith's (1983) research indicated that writers provided feedback from Bell Laboratories' text-analysis software, Writer's Workbench, applied computer learning to non-computer-based writing. Frase and Diel (1986) have reported similar successful use of Writer's Workbench with older public school students.

Traditional red-penciling of compositions provides some of the same feedback, but in a much less effective fashion. Problems are identified for children, but too frequently the children are not led to do anything about those problems. Computer-based text analysis requires that children respond, first by making final decisions about possible changes and then by commanding the computer to make the changes or making the changes themselves.

Focus for Peer and Cross-Age Tutoring

The complex cognitive processing required by text-analysis programs dealing with usage, style, and grammar lends itself to peer and cross-age tutoring. Teachers can use these computer activities to combine the interactive benefits of computer-based instruction with the equally well-researched benefits of having children teach one another (Frase & Schwartz, 1975; Johnson, Maruyama, Johnson, Nelson, & Skon, 1981).

Peer tutoring is a widely used method for providing greater individualization of instruction. It is based on the philosophy that "he who teaches others teaches himself." Research on peer tutoring indicates that the tutors learn as much as, if not more than, the tutees (Hassinger & Via, 1969; King, 1982; Melaragno, 1976). Peer tutoring also improves self-concept (Mason, 1976) and attitude toward school (Kokovich & Matthews, 1971).

Microcomputer-based instructional techniques eliminate some of the need for training of peer tutors (Balajthy, 1986). Interaction among children can make clear the rationale behind decisions to change or not to change text. Better writers are provided the opportunity to analyze and explain their writing processes, and poorer writers are given in-depth explanations by their tutors, not simply the often-too-brief explanatory messages available on the monitor screen.

EVALUATING AND CHOOSING TEXT-ANALYSIS SOFTWARE

Teachers should evaluate carefully the different types of text analyzers before choosing software for classroom use.

Spelling Checkers

Spelling checkers can be evaluated according to two major characteristics: power of analysis and user-friendliness (see Figure 10.1). Power of analysis simply refers to the number of words stored in the spelling checker's on-disk dictionary. The more words included in the dictionary, the less likelihood there is that a large number of correctly spelled words will be reported as possible misspellings after an analysis of a child's composition. This is more of a problem with older learners than with younger ones. Younger learners tend to use common words in their composi-

Figure 10.1   Evaluation Criteria for Spelling Checkers

1. Number of words in on-disk dictionary: _____

2. Number of words that users can add to supplemental dictionary: _____

3. Number of steps involved in using spelling checker to analyze and correct composition: _____

tions; such words are ordinarily contained in even smaller on-disk dictionary lists. Spelling checkers designed for students are listed at the end of this chapter, and a detailed comparison of spelling checkers for adults and children can be found in Eiser (1986).

Every spelling checker allows expansion of the original on-disk dictionary. Users can add a limited number of words to the dictionary. For example, if students are writing compositions about their home town, the town's name can be added to the dictionary so that the spelling checker will recognize it as a correct spelling. The more words that can be added to the supplemental dictionary list, the more conveniently this facility can be used.

User-friendliness can be estimated in a simple, direct way. The teacher can use the spelling checker to analyze a composition, listing each step needed to use the spelling checker for analyzing the composition and for making necessary changes, and counting the number of steps needed. The more steps, the less user-friendly the software is likely to be.

Text Analyzers

Text analyzers are far more complex than spelling checkers, and as a result their evaluation is more involved (see Figure 10.2). Text analyzers designed for children are listed at the end of this chapter, and a detailed comparison of text analyzers designed for adults can be found in Raskin (1986).*

Inclusive appropriateness of analyses: Teachers should develop a list of the kinds of errors they want the software to locate. For example, they might want the software to identify uses of to/two/too, as well as to locate split infinitives. A sample student composition that contains two examples of each type of error can be constructed and checked to make sure that the software identifies all occurrences.

---

*Two popular and fairly easy-to-use text-analysis software packages designed for adults are: Sensible Grammar, by Sensible Software, 210 South Woodward, Suite 229, Birmingham, MI 48011, and RightWriter, by Decisionware, 2033 Wood Street, Suite 218, Sarasota, FL 33577.

Figure 10.2   Evaluation Criteria for Text Analyzers

1. Evaluation of inclusive appropriateness:

2. Evaluation of exclusive appropriateness:

3. Number of steps involved in using text-analysis program to analyze and correct composition: _____

4. Adequacy of explanations:

5. Readability level of explanations: _____

FEATURES AND PERFORMANCE:

  I. *General Features*
        Suggests alternatives for errors
        Allows marking of text
        Permits addition of customized words and phrases
        Allows on-the-spot correction

 II. *Typing, Punctuation, and Capitalization*
        Run-on sentences
        Capitalization errors
        Incorrect number of blank spaces between words and sentences
        Double-typed words

III. *Style and Grammar*
        Split infinitives
        Homonyms
        Wordiness
        Vague words
        Gender specificity
        Often-confused words
        Common redundancies
        Clichés
        Awkward phrases
        Archaic terms
        Passive voice

IV. *Indicators*
        Readability measure
        Sentence structure and length
        Paragraph length
        Word-frequency counts
        Percentage of prepositional phrases
        Percentage of passive constructions
        Outliner feature

Exclusive appropriateness of analyses: Teachers should develop a list of errors they do not wish the software to locate. For example, they might decide that the stylistic device of avoiding passive sentences in favor of active sentences is a skill too advanced for the class. Two examples of each error desired to be excluded from analysis can be included in the sample student composition described above. Then the composition can be checked to see whether the software identifies the occurrences.

User-friendliness: As with the spelling checkers, teachers can count the number of steps necessary to analyze a composition and to make corrections.

Adequacy of explanations: Teachers should evaluate the screen pages that explain errors and how to correct them. Is enough information provided to the students so that they can make good decisions? Are examples given of both incorrect and correct usage? Are the explanations written clearly and at the appropriate readability levels?

Systematic feedback: Frase et al. (1981) suggested that text-analysis software publishers provide more systematic feedback for increased instructional benefits. No existing style analyzer systematically sequences presentation of feedback and explanations. Instead, possible errors are presented in the order in which they occur in the text. A systematic, sequential form of feedback, in which, for example, all the to/two/too occurrences are presented to the child at the same time, could be an important feature in classroom text analyzers of the future.

Thesaurus Software

One final type of text-analysis software that is increasingly available is the thesaurus program. Presently these are available in software designed primarily for adult use. For example, Student WordPerfect, a word processor designed for use with older students, has a thesaurus program.

In the Student WordPerfect version for use on the IBM-PC, when the writer is using the word processor and wants to find a synonym for a specific word, an on-line list of possibilities can be provided almost immediately. If a replacement for *blunder* is desired, for example, in the sentence, "To blunder is human, to acquit sublime," the writer moves the cursor to *blunder*. Then the

THESAURUS disk is inserted in the disk drive, and command keys are pressed. The contextual sentence appears at the top of the screen, and a list of synonyms at the bottom, as follows:

```
blunder  (n)
    1    A   .error
         B   gaffe
         C   impropriety
         D   .mistake

blunder  (v)
    2    E   botch
         F   bungle
         G   .fumble
```

Words preceded by dots can in turn be referenced for additional synonyms, with a simple command listed at the bottom of the screen. Another command, followed by the appropriate letter from the list, will automatically replace blunder in the text with any of the listed words chosen.

Although at one time thesaurus programs were more awkward to use than a printed thesaurus, increased computer memory capabilities and integration of the programs into the word processing system have greatly improved their usefulness. Use of a thesaurus can easily lead to stilted writing and incorrectly used words by students who try to replace familiar words with unfamiliar ones. Traditionally, however, teachers have found that, used with constraint, the thesaurus can be a valuable reference tool.

SUMMARY

Computer-based feedback programs are being increasingly used in classrooms at all levels. Like word processors, these tools can minimize the tedious and routine tasks involved in the writing process and thereby provide greater opportunities for focusing on the content of writing. These programs, when used with competent teachers, are beginning to show a great deal of promise in facilitating writing as a communication process.

SOFTWARE DESIGNED FOR STUDENTS

Spelling Checkers

Bank Street Speller

Apple II-series, Commodore, IBM–PC

Scholastic, Inc., PO Box 7501, 2931 E. McCarty Street, Jefferson City, MO 65102

This program operates only with Bank Street Writer. Bank Street Writer III has a built-in spelling checker.

MECC Speller

Apple II-series

Minnesota Educational Computing Corporation, 3490 Lexington Avenue North, St. Paul, MN 55126

Student WordPerfect

IBM–PC

Chambers International Corporation, 5499 North Federal Highway, Suite A, Boca Raton, FL 33431

This version of WordPerfect contains the functions most often required by students, including a spelling checker and a thesaurus.

The Writing Workshop

Apple II-series

Milliken Computer Software, 1100 Research Boulevard, PO Box 21579, St. Louis, MO 63132

The Spelling Checker disk can be used only with Milliken's Word Processor.

Text Analyzers

Ghost Writer

Apple II-series

Minnesota Educational Computing Corporation, 3490 Lexington Avenue North, St. Paul, MN 55126

This program provides a variety of analysis subprograms, including the Fry readability, homonym checker, vocabulary analyzer, paragraph outliner, clarity checker, and sentence length analyzer.

Writing Adventure

Apple II-series

DLM, One DLM Park, Allen, TX 75002

This structured creative writing program includes story starter ideas for writing a fantasy adventure story, as well as a word processing component. The text analyzer is for use only with this program. It cannot be used with files from other word processors.

The Writing Workshop

Apple II-series

Milliken Computer Software, 1100 Research Boulevard, PO Box 21579, St. Louis, MO 63132

The Proofreader and Mechanics Checker disks can be used only with Milliken's Word Processor. This set contains the most comprehensive collection of support programs for classroom word processing on the market to date.

REFERENCES

Balajthy, E. (1985). Artificial intelligence and the teaching of reading and writing by computers. *Journal of Reading, 29,* 23-33.

Balajthy, E. (1986). *Microcomputers in reading and language arts.* Englewood Cliffs, NJ: Prentice-Hall.

Balajthy, E. (1987). Implications of artificial intelligence research for human–computer interaction in reading instruction. In D. Reinking (Ed.), *Reading and computers: Issues for theory and practice* (pp. 40-54). New York: Teachers College Press.

Balajthy, E.; McKeveny, R.; & Lacitignola, L. (1986-1987). Microcomputers and the improvement of revision skills. *The Computing Teacher, 29,* 27-30.

Braddock, R.; Lloyd-Jones, R.; & Schoerr, L. (1963). *Research in written composition.* Urbana, IL: National Council of Teachers of English.

Burg, K. (1984). The microcomputer in the kindergarten. *Young Children, 39*(3), 28-33.

Calkins, L. M. (1986). *The art of teaching writing.* Portsmouth, NH: Heinemann.

Coke, E. U. (1982). Computer aids for writing text. In D. H. Jonassen (Ed.), *The technology of text: Principles for structuring, designing, and displaying text* (pp. 390-397). Englewood Cliffs, NJ: Educational Technology Publications.

Cuffaro, H. K. (1985). Microcomputers in education: Why is earlier better? In D. Sloan (Ed.), *The computer in education: A critical perspective* (pp. 21-30). New York: Teachers College Press.

Daiute, C. A. (1983). The computer as stylus and audience. *College Composition and Communication, 34,* 134-145.

Eiser, L. (1986). I luv to rite. *Classroom Computer Learning, 7*(3), 50-58.

Emig, J. (1971). *The composing processes of twelfth graders.* Urbana, IL: National Council of Teachers of English.

Englebert, D. C., & English, W. K. (1968). A research center for augmenting human intellect. *Joint Computer Conference, 33,* 395-410.

Flower, L., & Hayes, J. R. (1981). A cognitive process theory of writing. *College Composition and Communication, 32,* 365-387.

Frase, L. T. (1987). Computer analysis of written materials. In D. Reinking (Ed.), *Reading and computers: Issues for theory and practice* (pp. 76-96). New York: Teachers College Press.

Frase, L. T., & Diel, M. (1986). UNIX Writer's Workbench: Software for streamlined communication. *T.H.E. Journal, 14*(3), 74-78.

Frase, L. T.; Macdonald, N. H.; Gingrich, P. S.; Keenan, S. A.; & Collymore, J. L. (1981). Computer aids for text assessment and writing instruction. *National Society for Programmed Instruction Journal, 20*(9), 21-24.

Frase, L. T., & Schwartz, B. J. (1975). Effect of question production and answering on prose recall. *Journal of Educational Psychology, 67*(5), 628-635.

Geisert, G. (1986). Byte size: A new tool for the toolbox. *Early Years, 16*(5), 22-23.

Grabe, M., & Grabe, C. (1985). The microcomputer and the language experience approach. *The Reading Teacher, 38*(6), 508-511.

Graves, D. H. (1976). Let's get rid of the welfare mess in the teaching of writing. *Language Arts, 53*(6), 645-651.

Graves, D. H. (1983). *Writing: Teachers and children at work.* Portsmouth, NH: Heinemann.

Hassinger, J., & Via, M. (1969). How much does a tutor learn through teaching reading? *Journal of Secondary Education, 44*(1), 42-44.

Hull, G.; Ball, C.; Fox, J. L.; Levin, L.; & McCutchen, D. (1985). *Computer detection of errors in natural language texts: Some research on pattern matching.* Paper presented at the meeting of the American Educational Research Association, Chicago.

Jensen, K., & Heidorn, G. E. (1984). First aid to authors: The IBM Epistle text-critiquing system. *Digest of Papers: Compcon 84, 28th IEEE Computer Society International Conference.* Los Alamitos, CA: IEEE Computer Society Press.

Johnson, D. W.; Maruyama, G.; Johnson, R.; Nelson, D.; & Skon, L. (1981).

Effects of cooperative, competitive, and individualistic goal structures on achievement: A meta-analysis. *Psychological Bulletin,
89*(1), 47-62.

Kiefer, K. E., & Smith, C. R. (1983). Textual analysis with computers:
Tests of Bell Laboratories' computer software. *Research in the
Teaching of English, 17*(3), 201-214.

King, R. T. (1982). Learning from a PAL. *The Reading Teacher, 36*(6), 682-
685.

Kokovich, A., & Matthews, G. (1971). Reading and the self-concept.
National Elementary Principal, 50(3), 53-54.

Mason, B. (1976). The effect of university student tutors on the self-
concepts of elementary school pupils. Unpublished dissertation,
Louisiana State University, Baton Rouge.

Melaragno, R. J. (1976). *Tutoring with students.* Englewood Cliffs, NJ:
Educational Technology Publications.

Moore, D. (1983). *What should computers do in the writing center?* Paper
presented at the Midwest Writing Centers Conference, Iowa City, IA
(ERIC Document Reproduction No. ED 248 521)

Raskin, R. (1986). The quest for style. *PC Magazine, 5*(10), 187-193.

Schwartz, H. J. (1983). *Computer aids for individualizing writing instruction throughout the writing process.* Paper presented at the Conference on College Composition and Communication, Detroit, MI. (ERIC
Document Reproduction No. ED 245 225)

Schwartz, H. J. (1984). Teaching writing with computer aids. *College English, 46*(3), 239-247.

Seltzer, C. (1986). The word processor—A magical tool for kindergarten
writers. *Early Years, 16*(4), 51-52.

Smith, N. J. (1985). The word processing approach to language experience. *Reading Teacher, 38*(6), 556-559.

Sommers, N. (1982). Responding to student writing. *College Composition
and Communication, 33*(2), 148-156.

Ziajko, A. (1983). Microcomputers in early childhood education? *Young
Children, 38*(5), 61-67.

11 Keyboarding in the Writing Process: Concerns and Issues

JAMES L. HOOT
State University of New York
at Buffalo

Previous chapters explored the potential of word processing as a tool for improving writing. At present, this potential appears limited by a child's skill with the primary computer input device—the keyboard. In his discussion of the importance of keyboarding skill, Troutner (1983, pp. 47–48) suggests, "There is no doubt that learning to type at an early age removes one of the stumbling blocks young students find when attempting to use computers."

While it seems that improved keyboarding skill would enhance the writing process, current keyboarding proposals and instructional practices raise a number of questions and issues for early childhood professionals. This chapter explores keyboarding as an emerging written form, current keyboarding proposals, research on keyboarding, curricular issues for professionals, and a look to the future.

KEYBOARDING AS A FORM OF PRODUCING PRINT

A couple of years ago, I viewed a popular television program featuring a teacher whose primary-grade children regularly won national awards for penmanship. While accolades were heaped on this educator for creating impeccable young handwriters, I could not help but wonder what elements of the curriculum (e g., writing as a communication process) were sacrificed in pursuit of such a goal. This issue is especially important when one considers the likelihood of twenty-first-century career options for impeccable handwriters. Before exploring issues associated with keyboarding as an emerging form of writing, it may be helpful to consider instruction in traditional written forms.

Although research is far from consistent concerning the most effective mode for teaching forms of written communications, the tradition of teaching manuscript to beginning writers has had widespread acceptance. (It should be noted, however, that at the beginning of this century, schoolchildren wrote exclusively in cursive [Wenzel, 1977]). Throughout our country, kindergarten and early-primary-grade children can be observed participating in activities designed to improve speed and quality of manuscript production. Just as children begin to develop enough facility to break into meaningful communication through manuscript, cursive writing is introduced.

Proponents of cursive writing (for example, Early et al., 1976) justify the effort devoted to this additional production form by asserting that cursive is easier to learn and more efficient, allows for more individuality, and is more accepted in the business world. Others (for example, Wenzel, 1977; Western, 1977) raise serious questions about the necessity of teaching cursive at all. While data concerning the relative effectiveness of these methods is far from consistent, the manuscript to cursive instructional sequence is now firmly entrenched in our educational system. Entrenchment alone, however, is hardly a justifiable reason for devoting precious instructional time to these activities. Furthermore, by preserving, without a research base, this manuscript to cursive progression in a computer age, we may be, as Papert (1980) suggested, "digging ourselves into an anachronism by preserving practices that have no rational basis beyond their historical roots in an earlier period of technological and theoretical development" (p. 33).

Today, increasing pressures are being placed on teachers of young children to include instruction in yet another character production form—keyboarding. Knapp (1986) suggests:

> The fact is, using a computer keyboard will very likely become the standard method for writing text in schools, homes, and businesses. Consequently, learning keyboarding skills will soon be recognized as a necessary basic skill in education. The sooner we accept this, the better our kids will fare. (p. 26)

When one considers the increasing technological demands that will be the legacy of the children we now teach, reasonable instruction in this skill appears productive.

It is my view that learning forms of character production (manuscript, cursive, and keyboarding) is good or bad only to the extent that such forms assist children in becoming more efficient conveyors of written meaning. While any of the above forms may assist in communicating written meaning, continued teaching of progressively different written forms at the expense of the ever-present goal of improving writing content is likely to be counter-productive. Unless we approach this issue with considerable thought, we are likely to have future generations of beautiful manuscript/cursive writers and highly efficient typists who are unable to produce meaning effectively through print. To ensure that communication is the primary focus of rapidly emerging keyboarding programs, a number of issues and concerns should be explored.

KEYBOARDING INSTRUCTION: DEVELOPING PROPOSALS

In response to the rapid increase of computers in elementary classrooms, nearly every school district in the country has had to deal with questions involving the teaching of keyboarding in the earlier grades. Keyboarding is perceived as a means of enabling users to more efficiently profit from interaction with computers. Rapidly developing proposals, however, are likely to result in the teaching of keyboarding primarily as a skill to be refined rather than a vehicle to promote immediate and meaningful writing experiences. Consider the following:

> For kindergarten through grade 3 where students' input is generally numbers and one-word responses, achievement of 20 words a minute with accuracy could be considered adequate. . . . Most students should be able to achieve this rate in four or five weeks. (Kisner, 1984, p. 22)

Clearly, proposals such as the above are armed with a great deal more enthusiasm than sense of developmental appropriateness. In light of our discussion, one might ask, "Are children who can type 20 words per minute better conveyors of meaning than those who do not type as skillfully?" Since this fundamental question has not been sufficiently addressed in the literature, proposals such as this can result in a great deal of frustration and actually dissuade developing writers. Nevertheless, unquestioning educators are currently establishing curricular objectives based on such proposals. One entire school system, for example, established a curricular goal of the achievement of 30 words per minute for kindergarten children. While research concerning keyboarding norms is nonexistent, a likely result, at best, of this 30 w.p.m. mandate is the creation of frustrated non-writers. In addition, many teachers of young children could not achieve such a speed (even in four or five weeks, as proposed above). To set unrealistic keyboarding objectives without a research base raises many questions for thinking educators.

Perhaps even more serious than the rapidly expanding proposals for unrealistic word-per-minute goals are those suggesting "how" typing instruction should be undertaken. Rauch and Yanke (1982), for example, note:

> They [children] positively *are* doing it! First-graders and kindergartners are indeed shamelessly hunting and pecking their way through various microcomputer programs. Furthermore, they are oblivious to the fact that business educators consider this technique inexcusable. . . . Unfortunately, these "little people" have *little* knowledge about correct keyboarding techniques and their importance. As business educators, we must realize the eventuality of such early beginning and the implications for us when these youngsters reach *our* keyboarding classrooms. (p. 19)

Again, one has to inquire whether students using what the above authors refer to as correct keyboarding techniques are indeed better writers (written communicators) than those using the more common hunt and peck method. Since some of the most prolific writers I know employ the latter approach, and since a research void exists in this area, the wisdom of this plea for employing correct keyboarding techniques with younger children is pedagogically suspect. Furthermore, in light of the current progress with voice-entry devices, which preclude the need for keyboards altogether, it is unlikely that today's youngsters will ever be in the keyboarding classes referred to above.

RESEARCH ON KEYBOARDING
IN THE EARLY GRADES

Even prior to the onslaught of computers into our classrooms during the 1970s, researchers explored the relative benefits of typing over manuscript or cursive writing. Wood and Freeman (1932), for example, conducted an extensive study of 15,000 students and found that typing had a highly motivational effect. Specifically, students who typed achieved higher scores in all subjects than students who did not type. Another important aspect of this investigation that was of particular interest to educators was that typing did not have a negative effect on handwriting ability.

Positive results were also reported by Rowe (1959). After only a short typing course, third- and fourth-grade students in his sample increased four months in reading comprehension and seven months in vocabulary improvement compared with a control group that lost ground in these areas.

Oksendahl (1972) reported on a statewide project designed to introduce typing to 50,000 elementary students in Hawaii. An especially noteworthy aspect of this investigation was that 91 percent of the children chose to learn typing.

Campbell (1973) conducted a study with two groups of special needs children using handwriting and hunt and peck approaches to respond to questions. Typing groups demonstrated significantly greater gains in reading. Campbell went on to postulate possible reasons for the superiority of the typing group by saying that (a) it is much easier for someone with limited psychomotor abilities to press a single key than to laboriously create letter shapes; (b) the hunt and peck approach encourages learners to pay more attention to details of print required for word recognition; and (c) typing is less stressful than handwriting.

Thus, research to date suggests that typing appears to be a highly motivational and effective medium for use in language arts programs. If anything, the above results are likely to be underrated because these early studies were conducted using manual typewriters rather than computer keyboards. Keys on the electronic computer keyboard no longer jam due to unsteady, inexperienced fingers. Also, the return key does not have to be hit at the end of each line. These features make computer keyboarding likely to result in even greater language gains.

KEYBOARDING IN THE CURRICULUM

Up to this point, we have explored the need for teaching keyboarding skills to very young children. We now focus on specific
concerns and issues teachers must address in the achievement of
this goal. Because of the dearth of research data regarding the
issue of computer keyboarding in the early years, the comments
that follow are meant for consideration and discussion rather
than as dogma.

Keyboarding Goals

Mention of the word *keyboarding* is likely to bring back memories
of sitting in front of a typewriter engaging in seemingly endless
repetitions of FJDKSLA, and other related drills designed to produce a high degree of proficiency with the keyboard. The typewriters at which we sat are now obsolete. We now live in a world
where the biggest typing error we can make is using a typewriter
instead of a computer.

Because of the tremendously enhanced capabilities of
computers compared with typewriters, traditional approaches to
typewriting may require instructional changes. School officials
approaching the keyboarding issue are now beginning to point out
differences between keyboarding and typing. Keyboarding is beginning to be seen primarily as a process of learning to use the
alphabetic, numeric, symbol, and function keys of a computer.
Typewriting, on the other hand, emphasizes the development of
speed and accuracy in keyboarding skills. Moreover, typewriting
entails the application of emerging skills in producing a quality
product. Other differences between keyboarding and typewriting
are described in the opening section of a keyboarding document
under development by the Bureau of Curriculum Development of
the University of the State of New York/State Education Department (1986), as follows:

> *Keyboarding*
> 1. Familiarization with alphabetic keyboard using correct fin-
>   gering, posture, and hand position.
> 2. Emphasis on practice of fast motions fitted together with the
>   pupil's best rate, without forcing.
> 3. Familiarization with simple horizontal centering, simple lim-
>   ited tabulations; friendly letters, stories.

4. Familiarization with numeric row and/or keypad.
5. Emphasis on correct fingering.
6. Emphasis on input; obtaining and communicating information.
7. Errors are corrected by backspace and replace.
8. Emphasis on input of initial thoughts.

Typing
1. Higher degree of proficiency with the alphabetic keyboard using correct fingering, posture, and hand position.
2. Emphasis on forcing speed with accuracy coming later as speed is cut back.
3. Formatting includes sophisticated horizontal and vertical centering; sophisticated tabulations; keying on ruled lines; proofreader symbols; interoffice memos; business letters.
4. Developed skill with numeric row or keypad.
5. Developed touch typing skill without watching fingers.
6. Emphasis on output; producing documents (hard copy) in final form.
7. Errors are corrected by use of lift-off mechanism or correction materials.
8. Emphasis on output of final product. (University of the State of New York, State Education Department, 1986, p. 2)

If keyboarding and typewriting are not the same, as the above listing suggests, perhaps instructional keyboarding goals should differ somewhat from those of traditional typewriting classes. Taking into account the differences noted above, keyboarding classes should focus more on *familiarization* (especially in the early grades when children are just learning letters) than on a high degree of proficiency; more on *developing a comfortable/ functional rate of speed* than on forcing speed; and more on the *inputting of ideas* into the computer than on creating a final product.

Despite the above differences, a great deal of controversy exists in the development of keyboarding curricula. Consider the typewriting emphasis on speed rather than the pupil's most comfortable rate. Speed is certainly an important goal in keyboarding instruction. If, for example, it takes a child longer to search for the appropriate alphabetic key than to scribble the desired character with a conventional pencil, little is gained. With keyboard facility, however, a child's ideas can be more quickly recorded and later massaged into more meaningful form using a word processor.

A practical problem of the speed issue for teachers is "How many words per minute should we expect for very young children?" As previously noted, Kisner (1984) suggests that a goal of 20 words per minute, with accuracy, is appropriate for kindergarten through Grade 3; and 25 words per minute is appropriate for Grades 4-6. Wetzel (1985), on the other hand, suggests that an appropriate goal for children is a typing speed equivalent to that suggested by handwriting norms and that students who can type 10 g.w.p.m. can make effective use of programs such as word processing packages. (G.w.p.m. is calculated by dividing the total keystrokes by five for each minute, without adjustment for errors.) While waiting for research to determine the relative benefits of the speed versus the best rate approach, caution appears to be especially productive. Although some children thrive in an environment designed to increase speed, others become quite frustrated and can build up an aversion to the computer because of speed-oriented programs.

When Should Keyboarding Be Taught?

Great diversity exists concerning the issue of when keyboarding should begin. Cameron (1986) proposes that "formal keyboarding lessons should begin in grade three" (p. 10). Kisner (1984) recommends that keyboarding be taught prior to the grade level in which students begin using computers for academic work. Further, a developing State Department of Education keyboarding document recommends that students should be provided instruction in keyboarding techniques "at the grade level in which they are first expected to use electronic keyboards in learning situations requiring efficient input, retrieval, and manipulation of words, symbols, and data" (The University of the State of New York/State Education Department, 1986, p. 2). Still others, such as Casad (1969), suggest that "typewriting is the logical sequence following the teaching of writing. It is not only a useful tool in itself, but it is of definite value in learning all phases of the language arts" (p. 150). It should be kept in mind that Casad's remarks preceded the widespread use of computers in the schools and the development of word processing packages for children who are just breaking into print. Now that writing is being taught with computers, waiting until handwriting is somewhat perfected may make less sense. Finally, in recognition of the importance of keyboarding as children begin writing, Knapp (1986) recommends

that teachers begin teaching keyboarding "as soon as we introduce kids to word processing" (p. 26).

As can be seen from the above proposals, the literature is of
little help in determining the optimal time to introduce keyboarding. Since neither recourse to child development theory nor research has been used in the development of existing proposals,
rigid mandates should not be implemented without a great deal of
caution.

How Should Keyboarding Be Taught?

The teaching of keyboarding to young children now runs the
gamut from free or informal approaches to forced or formalized
instruction. A more informal approach is described by Rubens,
Poole, and Hoot (1984), who developed a computer play center
designed to provide a non-threatening setting for pre-primary
keyboard exploration. This center provides a wide variety of
computer and electric typewriting keyboards for children to explore during free-activity periods.

Similarly, in an ethnographic study of five kindergarten children, Hines (1984) presents a delightful view of children learning
keyboarding skills in an informal environment without teacher
intervention.

> Students used a variety of approaches to typing on the keyboard
> of the computer. Jonathan was the only participant who used his
> thumb in typing. All students relied on their index and third
> fingers to do most of the typing. Alexandra and Danielle used
> those fingers on both hands (usually one at a time) to type
> commands. Alexandra used her fourth finger at times to press
> the keys, and Danielle used her fifth when she was playing the
> preskill games. Danielle remarked, "I use my pinkie for L when I
> only need to push one." Students typed with their second and
> third fingers with considerable facility and accuracy. The speed
> of their typing improved during the study (12 weeks).
>
> Andrea was the most creative in inventing new approaches
> to pushing the keys. She rolled her knuckles over them. She
> bounced her thumb off the space bar. She typed with her second
> and third fingers simultaneously (two fingers per key). Her most
> unusual approach was bending her fingers backward with the
> left hand and flipping them to hit the keys. She made many
> typing errors because her methods were not very accurate.
>
> In contrast, Alexandra and Billy were very conservative in

their approach to typing. They both typed slowly and tried to avoid making errors. They pushed each key precisely. They were usually deliberate, careful typists. (pp. 118–119)

Informal approaches to keyboard exploration are often supplemented by the use of keyboard game software products. These programs are designed to develop keyboard familiarity as well as provide more standard touch-typing experiences. Among these programs are Orange Cherry Software's Working With the Alphabet, Spinnaker's Kids On Keys, Aquarius's Alphabet Authors, and Bertamax Inc.'s Alpha Letter Drop. Such programs are designed to teach keyboard character location in largely non-competitive non-violent formats.

In addition to the above informal, game-type software, entire keyboarding curriculum programs, including software programs, student workbooks and materials, and accompanying teacher materials, are currently available for very young children. One example of a more formalized curriculum is Computergarten (Ainsa, 1985). According to the author of this program,

> *Computergarten* incorporates the development of basic early childhood skills into a motivational computer awareness program. Gross-motor skills are sharpened as children hop, jump, crawl, and fly on a giant keyboard on the floor. Active body movement, animal stories, fingerplays, and rhythms entice young children to learn numbers, letters, and directions. They quickly become familiar with the location of keys on the keyboard. This knowledge easily transfers to fine-motor activities provided in the *Computergarten* work activities provided in the *Computergarten* workbook (Ainsa, 1985, p. 3)

The above program combines software with activities common to most preschools. This introductory program is followed by a more structured program entitled Rainbow Keyboarding (Scholastic, Inc.) designed to refine beginning skills.

Sunkel and Cooper (1982) suggest that "in this computer age, all students need a touch-system for keyboarding" (p. 18). Likewise, Kisner (1984) states that "the objective on initial instruction in keyboarding for students at the elementary level should be mastery of the keyboard, by touch" (p. 22). In response to such comments, a growing number of more formal programs designed to teach standard touch typing (as opposed to hunt and peck) are readily available. Touch-typing software programs such as McGraw-Hill's SmarType are gaining popularity in even the primary grades. This program teaches standard touch-typing skills in 15- to 20-minute segments that are completed solely at the computer without additional teacher instruction. Unlike some programs, SmarType requires no special training with computers for either children or teachers.

Unlike SmarType, a number of older computer keyboarding tutorials such as MasterType and Type Attack use videogame shoot-'em-up formats to teach typing. With such programs, children become planetary defenders fighting off deadly invaders by typing appropriate characters. Since relatively little emphasis is placed on correct fingering, students are likely to improve speed with the fingers they are most comfortable with—the index fingers. Furthermore, while these programs are highly motivational and often effective in increasing speed, few are designed to move children into meaningful print. In addition, some teachers question the use of competitive/violent formats used by such programs.

Still another approach that is rapidly gaining interest is the traditional touch-typing instructor approach. This method grew out of the traditional typing classes previously popular in high school business programs. Instruction centers on correct finger position, practice with specified letter combinations, and, most important, speed. Given differences between keyboarding and typing, as previously noted, such an approach, by itself, may be a detriment to the writing process.

A final approach that is beginning to gain popularity is a combination of standard fingering instruction (generally taught in a computer lab setting) and supplemental exercises, provided by in-class computer typing tutors, for use during free moments. This combination, in conjunction with a teaching emphasis on the immediate use of skills in meaningful writing experiences, appears to be a useful approach.

As with the issue of when keyboarding instruction should begin, the question of how it should be taught is fraught with uncertainty. Because computers have been in early childhood classrooms for a relatively short period of time and because research regarding the relative merits of formal versus informal methods is moot, caution again appears to be reasonable advice for knowledgeable educators.

Who Should Teach Keyboarding?

In recognition of the importance of teaching keyboarding skills to children at all levels, many state departments of education are now mandating that such instruction be provided in all public schools. An additional problem that arises here is who should teach keyboarding skills?

Cameron (1986) suggests that three approaches currently exist regarding who should teach keyboarding:

> (a) A business instructor working in a team situation with the regular classroom teacher; (b) a business teacher with elementary training working along with the class; or (c) the regular classroom teacher, having been trained by the district, working alone with their class. (p. 10)

Kisner (1984) echoes Cameron's proposal that business educators should be the primary teachers of keyboarding at all levels. She states:

> Business teachers are currently the only group with the background preparation for teaching keyboarding. They have studied the psychology and methods for teaching psychomotor skills and have been applying those methods to teaching the typewriter keyboard. (p. 21)

While business educators may have the most experience in teaching business applications typewriting courses, they are unlikely to be as trained as classroom teachers in responding to the unique needs and interests of very young children. Furthermore, they are unlikely to be as skilled as classroom teachers in teaching writing, as defined in this volume. Since the goals of keyboarding are different from those of typewriting in their emphasis on more rapid movement into meaningful writing, Cameron's third proposal—that keyboarding be taught by regular classroom teachers trained in keyboarding techniques—may be the most appropriate approach to teaching this increasingly important skill.

Where Does Keyboarding Fit into the Curriculum?

While controversy exists concerning who should teach keyboarding, there appears to be unanimity in the feeling that keyboarding should be integrated into the language arts curriculum. Balajthy (1986), for example, states:

> If teachers are to be justified in using valuable instructional time to teach formal typing skills to their elementary students, these skills must be integrated with meaningful language activities far more thoroughly than in most earlier applications. Rather than using language development as a rationalization for the teaching of typing, typing should be used as one method for the teaching of language skills. . . . The key to integrating typing skills with language arts is the rapid movement from emphasis upon the motor tasks involved in finger movement to the use of meaningful language. (p. 198)

While most agree that keyboarding belongs in the time period designated for language arts, few recommend how such a program might actually fit into an already crowded school day. One approach to such integration is to teach more formal keyboarding skills during some of the time traditionally devoted to manuscript and cursive. Addy and Wylie (1973) found that handwriting instruction is formally taught in 34 percent of all kindergarten classes (11-20 minutes daily). In light of the increasing importance of keyboarding as an emerging form of print production, it may be beneficial to devote perhaps 40 to 60 percent of that time to keyboarding practice and the remaining time to traditional manuscript or cursive exercises. This approach, combined with typing tutor activities in free moments, is likely to enable children to become relatively proficient with the keyboard in a short period of time. Additional activities likely to enhance keyboard facility might include using word processors to type poems, stories, and spelling words; copy material from favorite books; or create original compositions.

SUMMARY

At present, the potential impact of word processing on the writing abilities of children is limited by keyboard facility. In light of increasing pressures on teachers to create computer-literate students, keyboarding appears to be too important a skill to leave to chance. Yet, as explored in this chapter, numerous questions concerning the integration of keyboarding instruction into the curriculum remain. Until much-needed research concerning keyboarding issues is undertaken, caution should be employed by responsible educators in responding to keyboarding mandates. Furthermore, unless early childhood educators are adamant that the writing process does not become subserviant to various forms of letter production, keyboarding is likely to become an end in itself rather than a means to improved communicative abilities. Proposals for the introduction of standard touch typing in the earlier grades are guiding curricula in increasing numbers of early childhood facilities. How we deal with these proposals is becoming increasingly important as we consider the impact that word processing may have in the educational lives of our children.

REFERENCES

Addy, P., & Wylie, R. (1973). The right way to write. *Childhood Education, 49*, 253–254.

Ainsa, T. (1985). *Computergarten.* New York: Scholastic.

Balajthy, E. (1986). *Microcomputers in reading and language arts.* Englewood Cliffs, NJ: Prentice-Hall.

Cameron, J. (1986). Keyboarding in the elementary school. *Computers in Education, 3*(7), 8–10.

Campbell, D. (1973). Typewriting contrasted with handwriting: A circumvention study of learning-disabled children. *The Journal of Special Education 7*(2), 155–167.

Casad, K. H. (1969). From keyboard to formal manuscripts in 27 hours. *The Journal of Business Education, 44*(6), 149–150.

Early, G. H.; Nelson, D.; Kleber, D.; Treegoob, M.; Huffman, E., & Cass, C. (1976). Cursive handwriting, reading, and spelling achievement. *Academic Therapy, XII,* 67–74.

Hines, S. (1984). *A qualitative analysis of the computer programming abilities and thought processes of five-year-old children.* Unpublished doctoral dissertation, North Texas State University, Denton, TX.

Kisner, E. (1984). Keyboarding—A must in tomorrow's world. *The Computing Teacher, 11*(6), 21–22.

Knapp, L. (1986). *The word processor and the writing teacher.* Englewood Cliffs, NJ: Prentice-Hall.

Oksendahl, W. (1972). Keyboard literacy for Hawaii's primary children. *Educational Horizons, 51*(4), 20–25.

Papert, S. (1980). *Mind-Storms: Children, computers, and powerful ideas.* New York: Basic Books, Inc.

Rauch, V., & Yanke, P. (1982). Keyboarding in the kindergarten—Is it elementary? *Business Education Forum, 37*(3), 19–20.

Rowe, J. L. (1959). Readin', TYPIN', and 'rithmetic. *Business Education World*, *39*(4), 9–12.

Rubens, T.; Poole, J.; & Hoot, J. (1984). Introducing microcomputers to micro-learners through play. *Day Care and Early Education*, *11*(3), 29–31.

Sunkel, M. J., & Cooper, M. (1982). Typewriting: Teaching touch keyboarding on computer terminals. *Business Education Forum*, *37*(1), 18–21.

Troutner, J. (1983). The issue of teaching typing. *Educational Computer*, *3*(7), 47–48.

The University of the State of New York/State Education Department (1986). *Developing keyboarding skills to support elementary language arts program*. Albany, NY: State Education Department, Bureau of Curriculum Development.

Voorhis, T. G. (1931). *The relative merits of cursive and manuscript writing*. New York: Teachers College Press.

Walmsley, S. (1980). What elementary teachers know about writing. *Language Arts*, *57*(3), 730–734.

Wenzel, E. (1977). *Research summary: Basic handwriting and spelling*. A paper presented at the annual meeting of the International Reading Association.

Western, R. D. (1977). The case against cursive script. *Elementary School Journal*, *78*(4), 1–3.

Wetzel, K. (1985). Keyboarding skills: Elementary, my dear teacher? *The Computing Teacher*, *12*, (9), 15–19.

Wood, B., & Freeman, R. (1932). *An experimental study of the educational influences of the typewriter in the elementary school classroom*. New York: Macmillan.

12 Computer Writing Programs: Linking Research with Practice

CAROLYN L. PIAZZA
Florida State University

Preceding chapters in this volume have shown that the word processor is rapidly becoming an important writing tool for teachers and students in the early elementary grades. Surveys suggest that, in addition to word processors, teachers also want complete computer packages that can be used along with their basic curriculum (Mazer, 1984). Although integrated computer writing packages are just appearing on the market, they already have widespread appeal. As computers become an integral part of many classrooms, teachers and administrators face the new challenge of identifying and selecting quality computer software packages that will complement their ideas about young children's writing processes and classroom writing instruction.

This chapter reviews two of the more widely used computer writing packages for younger children, Quill and Writing to Read, and explores the relationships between specific aspects of each computer program and recent research on the writing process. Although Quill and Writing to Read may be analyzed in many ways, this discussion compares each program's components with research on the natural behaviors of language learners, the meanings children give to writing, the nature of learning tasks, the writing strategies children use, and the contexts in which children learn to write. The chapter is divided into three major sections. The first section summarizes major findings from writing research and outlines effective writing practices that build on this process research. The second and third sections describe Quill and Writing to Read. Each of these two sections includes an overall description of the program and compares its key features with research on writing. A summary of each program appears in the Appendix to this chapter. The list of references at the end of the chapter provides further information on the two programs and on relevant research.

RESEARCH INTO PRACTICE

Writing process research explored throughout this volume can serve as an important framework for assessing the effectiveness of computer writing programs. The summary framework in this chapter for assessing the effectiveness of two specific computer programs, Quill and Writing to Read, includes a review of four major findings from writing research and a set of suggested practices that builds on this research.

The first major finding from research on the composing process is that writing is first and foremost a conceptual act that starts with the construction of meaning, not with a set of abstract skills or isolated elements of language. The act of writing is a process of "selecting, combining, arranging, and developing ideas in effective sentences, paragraphs, and . . . longer units of discourse" (NCTE Standards, 1979). It includes all preparatory efforts from the point of intention to write, as well as planning and organizing thoughts, generating and monitoring ideas for composing, and re-seeing and reshaping ideas based on feedback. This process, recursive in nature, places primary emphasis on the sequences and meanings of children's actions in learning to write and on the problem-solving strategies children use to gain control of language. A program that defines writing as a process would include the following program elements:

- Writing tasks that allow children to concentrate on the meaning aspects of writing before attending to sound/symbol relations
- Instruction that is devoted to all aspects of the writing process: generating ideas, drafting, revising, and editing
- Opportunities for children to do extended prose in which they recognize how context—topic, purpose, audience—influences the structure and use of language
- Instruction that emphasizes the writer's strategies for composing (that is, how children select ideas, rehearse ideas, encode, revise, and elaborate on meaning)

The second major finding of writing process research considers that the function of writing is related to the demands of the social situation. In other words, not only do social events and face-to-face interactions play an important role in the kind of writing that takes place in classrooms, but the communicative tasks and the text itself also place constraints on how speakers communicate to readers. A program that defines writing as a social process includes the following program elements:

- Opportunities for students to write for a variety of audiences in order to learn that approaches vary as audiences vary
- Opportunities for students to write in many forms (for example, essays, notes, summaries, poems, letters, stories, reports, scripts, journals)
- Opportunities for children to write for a wide range of purposes (for example, to inform, to persuade, to express oneself, to explore, to clarify thinking)
- Classroom learning environments that allow children to observe how written language functions in natural everyday settings (that is, to build social relationships, to get things done, to organize and communicate ideas, to express personal feelings)

The third major finding of writing process research emphasizes the role of oral language in writing. Several researchers have suggested that emergent writing is "as much an oral activity as a written one" (Dyson & Genishi, 1982, p. 126). For the very young writer, talk provides a natural entry into writing and can be used to accompany, reinforce, and supplement actions (Vygotsky, 1978). Talk to self as well as social interaction with others can mediate the writer's process and interpretation of text. In other words, as individuals construct meaning through interaction during or after writing, they learn how meanings are negotiated, gain a sense of audience, and learn how speech is translated into print. A program that defines writing as a linguistic process would include the following program elements:

- Opportunities for children to use language for various social purposes during writing—asking others how to spell words, asking other questions, telling others about writing, sharing writing

- Opportunities for children to use talk throughout the writing process (that is, for rehearsing ideas, formulating messages, encoding, re-reading, responding to writing, and elaborating messages)

The fourth major finding of writing process research considers written language development. Writing development is gradual and moves from global, undifferentiated concepts and meanings to more differentiated and distinct meanings (Clay, 1975; DeFord, 1979; Ferreiro & Teberosky, 1983; Langer, 1986). Children expect print to be meaningful and to serve various functions (Harste, Burke, & Woodward, 1982). As problem-solvers, children generate hypotheses, test them, and refine them on the basis of feedback. They engage in rule-governed behaviors and rely on context for meaning. A program that defines writing as growth and development includes the following program elements:

- Opportunities for children to make connections between talk and print, using their own rule systems (for example, invented spelling)
- Instruction that emphasizes children's problem-solving strategies for developing concepts of print and meaning (for example, the process of decentering; directionality)
- Opportunities for children to use their own resources for writing (for example, interaction with others, oral language, print environment)

These four findings of research and suggested writing practices can serve as the criteria for assessing the effectiveness of programs such as Quill and Writing to Read. As we shall see, if we use these criteria, Quill more closely reflects recent process research than does Writing to Read.

The next section reviews the Quill program and examines its overall goals. References selected from the program's manual are used to outline program features and to compare them with recent research on young children's writing.

QUILL

The Quill program, designed by researchers at Bolt, Beranek and Newman Laboratories, Inc., and the Network Educational Research Organization Inc., is available through D. C. Heath and Company. It is a set of microcomputer programs designed for children in Grades 3 and above. Quill is intended to supplement the language arts curriculum and encourage the use of writing across the curriculum. Its goals are to (1) teach students to prewrite, draft, and revise; (2) provide practice in various types of writing; and (3) create an environment that motivates students to write. To accomplish these goals, Quill uses four separate but closely linked computer program components: The Planner, The Library, The Mailbag, and The Writer's Assistant. These components encompass the prewriting/planning, composing/drafting, revising/editing, and publishing stages of the writing process.

The Planner helps children to select topics and generate information before they write and teaches them to reflect on and revise information afterward. A list of questions helps students develop critical thinking and focus on content, purpose, and audience. To use The Planner, a student follows a set of procedures for obtaining a menu. The menu presents options, including key words, title/author entries, and entry numbers. If the student types the option "key words," a set of Planner titles, such as story, report, science, food, newspaper, appears on the screen. After a student selects a Planner title, the screen presents a list of topics, questions, or ideas to help the student organize and write notes. For example, if a student chose the title "report," the following topics might appear (as listed in Bruce & Rubin's 1984 Quill Manual, p. 20):

Experimenter
Purpose
Date
Hypotheses
Apparatus
Method
Procedure
Results
Conclusion
Discussion

The student would then use this list as an organizer for gathering information for the report. If a student selected the title "Review of one's favorite restaurant," for example, the following questions might be asked (p. 22):

What is the name of the restaurant?
Where is it located?
On a scale of 1 to 10, how would you rate the restaurant,
and would you go back again?
Who owns it?
What kinds of foods are served there?
What is the specialty?
How is the service?

These questions would help the student focus on the content to include in the review. (In addition to the form planner described above, Quill also provides an option for students to create their own planner.)

The Library, a data base management system, stores pieces of writing that children have written and provides a repository of reading material for them to use and share. Its features encourage children to write for their peers, share meanings, and use new resources. To use The Library, students select the library option from the menu just as they did with The Planner. Library skills associated with indexing and accessing information by key words, title/author, or entry numbers help students summarize main points, relate titles and texts, and organize information for reading and writing. With The Library, children can read and use various models of written work as resources for their own writing. Children can also add new information and build on information already in the system.

The Mailbag allows children to communicate with real audiences and to discover different purposes for writing. An electronic mail system encourages them to seek information, announce and share ideas, entertain, and persuade. Through these activities, students discover how their words affect an audience and learn to revise messages so that they are more accurate. In retrieving information from The Mailbag, students may decide to (a) see mail written to them, (b) see mail that a group sends to them, or (c) view the public bulletin board. The mail appears on the screen when the student types in the keyword or entry. Just as with the Planner and Library texts, mail can be viewed on the screen or printed out by a printer.

The Writer's Assistant, a child-oriented text editor, permits children to type and revise text for The Planner, The Library, or The Mailbag. With as few as six basic commands, or as many as nineteen commands, students can add, delete, or rearrange words, sentences, and whole sections of their writing. This feature helps students experiment with new ideas and perspectives and improve their work without having to recopy the entire composition. When students have completed their writing, they can print out a final version to share with others. Children share their writing more easily when they have a product that is neat and easy to read.

If students want to create or modify Planner or Library programs or Mailbag messages, they can use The Writer's Assistant to draft their ideas or to add, delete, substitute, and change information. To index new programs, children must follow Quill's coding procedures. For a Mailbag message, senders give the message a title and specify their name. To enter new Library or Planner programs into the system, children must code the information by key words, by title/author, or by entry number. Although some of these procedures may sound complicated, the program is generally easy to use and allows students to see, use, create, and modify information depending on their purposes for writing. Proponents of Quill believe that the program provides tools for writing and a learning environment in which children can accomplish challenging, meaningful writing activities. These activities are meant to (1) emphasize the teaching and learning of writing as a process; and (2) encourage students to develop purposes for writing and a sense of audience. The following sections consider each of these features and compare them to research on children's writing.

Feature One:
Emphasizes Writing as a Process

Quill helps both teachers and students approach writing as a process. The Quill Manual (Bruce & Rubin, 1984) states:

> Quill is a set of microcomputer programs that use the computer's capabilities to help teachers teach writing. (p. 4)

> Quill meshes the technological capability of the microcomputer with a writing process approach to language arts. (p. 6)

Quill's components and the ways they are to be used reflect a particular orientation toward writing: (a) Writing is a process; and (b) this process is recursive. To provide a process approach, the program components focus on the different stages of writing (pre-writing, drafting, feedback, revision, editing, publication) and include process-oriented activities like brainstorming, note-taking, reading and re-reading, sharing, and multiple revisions. Because all of the components are interchangeable and flexible, children can select and use different approaches to writing and problem-solving. For example, if students want to generate ideas for writing or rewriting, they can (a) use The Planner's set of questions and topic prompts; (b) read other students' work in The Library; or (c) experiment with written ideas using The Writer's Assistant. If they want to organize their ideas, they can use the note-taking function of The Planner, the indexing scheme of The Library, or the composing and revising commands of The Writer's Assistant. With the teacher's help, students can also use The Planner and The Writer's Assistant to write for different purposes and audiences. For example, writing a report and writing a message are different tasks that require different strategies. Quill's components are flexible enough to be used for both types of writing.

The intended audience will also influence how a student uses the Quill components. If a student discovers that a reader does not understand or is misinterpreting a message in The Mailbag, he or she can use The Writer's Assistant or The Planner to clarify and refine the message.

Related Research. Over the past 20 years, research on writing has provided useful information on the nature of the writing process and on the multiple strategies that writers use (for reviews of the writing process, see Cooper & Odell, 1978; Hillocks, 1986; Humes, 1983; Krashen, 1984; Petrosky & Bartholomae, 1986). Rather than concentrating on mechanics and exact wording, skilled writers plan, re-read, and revise for the purpose of clarifying ideas to an audience (Perl, 1979; Sommers, 1980; Stallard, 1974). Quill components parallel this process by blending and overlapping different stages of writing within one program and across the set of programs. The program's designers recognize that good writers do not take a linear approach, but instead continually interrupt their writing to plan, revise, and reformulate their work. Used separately and together, the Quill components encourage writing practices that are supported by this research.

Research on individual differences show that some writers plan by mentally rehearsing ideas, others discover ideas by writing drafts, and still others first ask themselves questions about their topic (Emig, 1971; Graves, 1975). The purposes of the writing may also require different skills and strategies (Kinneavy, 1971; Moffett, 1983). For example, a letter differs from a story not only in genre, but in diction, syntax, organization, and the writing strategies used (Applebee, 1986).

Individual approaches, task requirements, and the writing context all interact. Research on the social and educational influences of writing indicate that the context or the environment for writing influences the type and function of the writing produced (Florio & Clark, 1982; Gundlach, McLane, Stott, & McNamee, 1985). Environments in which children interact give them purposes and meanings for writing (Leichter, 1984; Taylor, 1983). The designers of Quill have considered this and similar research in developing the program's components. Two of Quill's components, The Library and The Mailbag, allow children to write for real audiences and to discover a variety of purposes for writing. These components, combined with The Planner and The Writer's Assistant, use the microcomputer's capacities to support a process approach to writing. By effectively combining technology with this approach, Quill considers all of the elements in the writing process: the writer, the text, the task, and the context.

Feature Two:
Helps Establish Purposes and Develop Audience Awareness

Quill stresses the importance of a communicative environment in which students develop purposes for writing and become aware of different audiences. The Quill Manual (Bruce & Rubin, 1984) states:

> Computers can create a unique environment that gives students a purpose in writing. (p. 5)

> Quill creates a unique environment in which students are encouraged to write for their peers as well as the teacher. (p. 27)

The Quill programs are based on the perception that writing is a process of expressing and communicating one's intentions to a real audience. The writing that children store in The Library becomes a portfolio of childhood experiences, facts, and different points of view that students can enjoy and use as a basis for more writing. Children can add information or take an existing topic and develop it for a new purpose or from a different perspective. For example, children may write a composition on a topic such as mice in which they share a personal experience, entertain others, or report factual information. When students use The Mailbag to send and receive messages, they become aware that the primary purpose of written language is communication with others. By sending and receiving electronic mail, students become sensitive to others' interests, understandings, and expectations for writing. Readers' responses help children decide whether they should revise their messages. By experiencing reader reactions, children can learn to adjust their topic, tone, style, and amount of detail to match their audience's needs and expectations.

Related Research. Research suggests that purpose and audience are the two most important considerations in writing (Kinneavy, 1971). Recent research on children's writing suggests that young children use writing for multiple purposes (Cochran-Smith, 1984; Dyson, 1983; Dyson, 1984; Florio & Clark, 1982; Taylor, 1983) and consider audience reactions long before they learn to encode and decode words (Lamme & Childers, 1983; Piazza & Tomlinson, 1985). As early as kindergarten, children can interact and communicate with readers in meaningful ways (Nystrand & Himley, 1984). Research also points out the need for teachers to reinforce the concept of writing as communication and to create situations in which audiences of peers receive and respond to children's writing. Giving and receiving feedback can help children shape and develop their writing (Petrosky, 1982) and understand different readers' perspectives (Calkins, 1983; Sowers, 1985). Teachers who require children to write in different formats help them learn to adjust their style, vocabulary, and sentence structure to the type of writing they are producing.

The Quill program encourages students to function as good writers do. It provides a creative learning environment in which children write for a variety of purposes and consider others, rather than themselves, as their primary audience.

WRITING TO READ

The Writing to Read System, distributed by International Business Machines Corporation (IBM) and created by John Henry Martin, is a computer-based instructional program designed to develop reading and writing skills of kindergarten and first-grade children. The system includes the Writing to Read computer program, work journals, commercial games and activities, listening libraries, and writing/typing activities. With these components, it combines all of the language arts in a single instructional period and provides materials and methods that reinforce linkages among reading, writing, speaking, and listening. Proponents of the Writing to Read System state that it (1) develops reading and writing skills by building on children's natural language growth; and (2) increases opportunities for teachers to interact with children. During a one-hour session, children participate in three or more different activities at several work stations in what is called the Writing to Read Center.

At the computer station, children select one of the interactive computer programs that teach particular sound-symbol correlations. Children working in pairs use instructional diskettes that present the 42 phonemes used in English. The program introduces 30 key words and phonemes in 10 self-paced cycles with interactive reinforcement. Each lesson begins when the color monitor shows a picture that stands for the word being introduced. For example, for cat, the first word taught, a picture of a cat appears along with the word *cat* at the top of the screen. The computer says "This is a cat" and then directs the children to say and type the three sounds (/c/a/t/) that make up the word. The picture of the cat then reappears and the children are directed to say *cat*. This process is repeated twice (once for each child in the pair), and then the children type the word. If a student hesitates too long, the computer repeats the directive, "type cat."

In the next learning episode for the word *cat*, the picture screen is bordered by a number of phonemes. One by one, the letters that make the word *cat* fall into place in the middle of the screen as children chant, clap, and stamp their feet in response to this reinforcement of the word *cat*. Following this activity, students complete the first three words in the cycle (cat, dog, fish) and then do a task completion exercise called the mastery test. Those who successfully complete the test go on to a "make words" computer lesson (described below) in which they substitute graphemes to make new words. For example, "cat" becomes "fat," "dog" becomes "fog," and "fish" becomes "dish." Silly sentences such as "Can a fish ride in a wagon?" and computer games like "Cat and Mouse" and "Turtle and Rabbit" also extend the cycle lessons.

At the work journal station, children practice computer words and phonemes in study books called work journals. The first page of each set of cycle lessons is an audio lesson. Children listen to audio cassette instructions and say and write words and their sound symbols in the work journal. Then, on their own, the children complete a word practice page and phoneme practice page for each word in the cycle. When the children have finished these practice pages, they do a work journal mastery test. If children are having difficulty with cycle words, they can return to the computer lesson for more practice and review. For children who have begun to master the phonetic alphabet, the journal provides a printed version of the make words activity. Also included are cumulative review pages, empty pages on which children may draw or write the words they are learning, and progress letters to parents. A reference guide to phonemes appears on the inside back cover. On the back, a progress chart allows the children to record end-of-lesson results.

At the "make words" station, children use commercial games and manipulatives such as beads, clay, and wooden letters to help them learn the phonetic alphabet. While the computer program, work journals, and games allow the students to practice words and sound symbols, the listening libraries and writing/typing activities help them apply what they have learned to reading and writing.

The listening library station reinforces conventions and reading practices associated with text. Children listen and follow along with stories on audio cassettes and read children's classics. The slow pace of the stories helps children recognize words and match speech with written language. During these activities, the children get to read what others have written and develop an appreciation for literature.

At the writing/typing stations, children write words, sentences, and stories either at the writing table or at the computer. The children may choose from paper of all sizes, shapes, and colors and from a variety of writing tools (crayons, pencils, chalk, magic markers, IBM selectric typewriters, and word processors). Working independently or with the teacher and other students, children progress through six writing stages: (a) cycle word writing; (b) new word writing; (c) phrase/sentence writing; (d) simple story writing; (e) intermediate story writing; and (f) advanced story writing. At each stage, teachers are given directions on how they can assist the learners.

The following sections relate the program's features to research on young children's language and literacy development. The first section, which discusses the program's efforts to build on children's natural language growth, focuses on the Writing to Read computer lessons, the prototype for instruction in the work journals, reinforcement games, and writing activities. The second section discusses the entire system and the opportunities it provides teachers to help children learn to read and write.

Feature One:
Builds on Oral Language Skills

The Writing to Read computer program develops reading and writing skills by building on oral language skills. It defines "building on the natural language growth of children" almost exclusively in terms of children's acquisition of spoken vocabulary. The Writing to Read Manual (Martin, 1984) states:

> Writing to Read builds on students' natural language development. (section 1, p. 6)

> The Writing to Read computer instructional materials provide a dependable and consistent approach to the presentation of the phonemes of English speech to young students. (section 6, p. 4)

> Children learn better if the material is organized to invite them to think—to find the logical order in their growing understanding. (section 1, p. 10)

> The Writing to Read System provides an uncluttered consistent phonemic spelling system for students to use. (section 1, p. 4)

Highlighting the fact that children have a vocabulary of over 2,000 words before they enter school, the Writing to Read program defines extending children's lexical knowledge as converting sounds that are already known to sounds that can be written. To learn phonological, syntactic, and semantic structures of language, children systematically practice key words and phonemes. The program's self-paced cycles introduce sounds to be combined into words, and words to be combined into sentences. This graduated presentation is based on the view that children's written language learning develops as a logical series of skills. The program developers believe that in order for children to put thoughts on paper, they need an uncluttered, simplified way of encoding words and combining them into sentences. The program takes this same approach with spelling. Instead of requiring children to use conventional spelling or invent their own spellings, the program introduces a simplified phonemic alphabet much like the pronunciation key in standard dictionaries. Proponents of the program believe that the phonemic alphabet helps children add any word they can say to their written vocabularies.

In learning these phonemic spellings and basic language structures, children respond to auditory and visual stimuli in consistent and predictable ways. For example, the computer's voice synthesizer directs children to repeat sounds and words. Children also type letters and chant, clap, or stamp their feet to the sounds they hear. With such responses, "children use their individual perceptual learning styles to acquire the alphabetic principle for writing words, sentences, and stories" (Writing to Read Manual [Martin, 1984], section 6, p. 3). According to the program designers, this approach to learning the alphabetic principle provides a risk-free environment in which children's correct responses to computer demands are always encouraged. For example, if a student does not respond quickly enough or types an incorrect letter, the computer voice repeats the direction until the child makes the correct response.

Related Research. Recent research on young children's writing has seriously questioned the belief that instructional programs should isolate and teach linguistic structures and phonemic spellings before they permit children to use these structures in writing. As their language develops, children learn linguistic structures and phonemic spellings by experimenting and taking risks in real communicative situations (Bissex, 1980; Clay, 1975; Ferreiro & Teberosky, 1983; Goodman, 1986; Goodman, 1984; King, 1980; Langer, 1986; Lindfors, 1980; Smith, 1973). Children use environmental, situational, linguistic, and cultural cues to help them generate hypotheses about language structure and approximate the adult language system (Harste, Burke, & Woodward, 1982). Instead of encouraging risk-taking and experimentation, the Writing to Read program takes language out of context and limits the cues children can use to interpret meaning.

The program's approach also departs substantially from what we are discovering about young children's writing processes. The Writing to Read program presents a linear view of writing that proceeds from words to phrases to stories. Research has shown, however, that students become concerned about using letters and words when they attempt to write complete messages (Clay, 1975; DeFord, 1979; Halliday, 1975). Instead of mastering language in a fixed sequence like the ones in most of the Writing to Read tasks, children simultaneously work at multiple levels. Whether they use single letters or words to represent objects or create messages, they focus on meaning, not on a progression from word to sentence to story. In the process of learning to write, they intermingle their learning of letters, words, and word groups (Clay, 1975). Teachers who use the Writing to Read computer system must resolve the methodological and philosophical discrepancies between the proposed benefits of the Writing to Read program and research on children's learning to write.

Meaningful writing tasks give children as much control over the task as possible and help them understand how graphics and meanings interconnect during writing (Smith, 1973). Writing tasks such as recording and organizing information, expressing feelings, and narrating actions and events teach children to assess the importance of variables that compete for attention such as spelling, syntax, coherence, and meaning (Jacobs, 1985). Unfortunately, the Writing to Read activities do not permit children to initiate and control all aspects of the writing process. Effective activities would allow students to discover a subject, create meaning, construct syntax, connect discourse, spell words, and combine these structures in a meaningful context.

In its approach to spelling, Writing to Read may also reflect adult perceptions of how children learn to spell, rather than reflecting research. For example, simplified tasks for spelling that use adult phonemic systems may interfere with a child's developing system of meanings. A phonemic spelling system like the one used in the Writing to Read computer program is based on an adult logic of encoding words rather than on a child's development of rule systems and strategies. Researchers have suggested that children need only five or six sound–symbol relationships (usually consonants) to write (Graves, 1983; Read, 1975). Thus, children's invented spelling may be far less cluttered than the elaborate scheme of phonemic spellings taught in the Writing to Read program.

In the Writing to Read computer approach, the role of oral language is limited to encoding words, repeating sounds, and reciting words in response to a voice synthesizer or auditory and visual stimuli. Researchers have observed that children use oral language during writing to talk about meaningful graphics, ask others for help, elaborate on the meaning of their work, and share their work with others (Dyson, 1983; Lamme & Childers, 1983; Piazza & Tomlinson, 1985). These numerous and diverse uses of oral language during writing provide children "with both meaning and the systematic means for getting meaning on paper" (Dyson, 1983, p. 17). Computer programs that limit or restrict children's use of oral language skills and separate language from meaningful contexts are not well supported by research.

The Writing to Read's approach provides positive, corrective feedback to children, but not if they generate their own hypotheses about written language, make errors that show growth and risk-taking, or use information they have to correct themselves (Harste, Burke, & Woodward, 1982). Rather than using children's rule systems as a basis for activities, the program stresses error-free drill performances of adult rule systems. While features of the Writing to Read System allow students to progress in certain types of learning, research on children's natural language and literacy learning does not support the program's approach to writing. Because the program is central to instruction at the work journal station, the make words station, and the writing/typing stations, teachers who use the program may want to consider adding supplementary activities that are supported by recent research.

Feature Two:
Increases Teacher–Student Interaction

The manual for the Writing to Read System (Martin, 1984) suggests that the program offers teachers new options for enhancing classroom management. The Manual states:

> Since the computer and the other components provide much of the instruction, your role (classroom teacher) is elevated to that of educational manager of the Writing to Read System. . . . Your role as manager, rather than as teacher of every new item of learning, provides several attractive new options that enhance your effectiveness. (pp. 2-4)

Because the computer provides direct instruction, teachers are able to explore new roles as managers, diagnosticians, facilitators, and coaches. As manager, the teacher orients children to the computer, demonstrates the proper use of materials and equipment, and plans a schedule for individual and group instruction. In this role, the teacher helps students learn everything they need to know about the system, including how to prepare for class each day, how to select a partner to work at the computer, and how to select language arts activities at the center. Students also learn how to begin and end work activities, how to seek help, and how to work with a partner.

As diagnostician, the teacher reviews the students' mastery tests, assesses children's strengths and weaknesses, and routes the children to particular activities. With the teacher's help, children learn to keep records of their progress and to begin selecting activities in the center. As facilitator and coach, the teacher helps children apply their phonemic learning in the work journals, in word-making games, and in free writing exercises. During free writing, when children write letters, words, phrases, or stories, the teacher asks questions and provides feedback. Although the program materials suggest ways that teachers may facilitate the organization of the program, assist children in the use of program materials, and help children with their lessons, they do not address the content of the program and how this content affects a teacher's options.

Related Research. Research has shown that writing develops "through a process in which the writer imagines the audience, sets goals, develops ideas, produces notes, drafts, revises text, and edits to meet the audience's expectations" (Commission on Composition, 1986). Thus, to become a manager, a teacher would have to organize writing activities that allow children to practice one or more of these activities. For example, to help children develop a sense of audience, a teacher might simply ask the children, "Whom is the writing for?" and create opportunities for the children to write for different audiences. A teacher might also set up forums in which children share their writing with their peers.

Research shows that by interacting with teachers, children learn to negotiate meanings, exchange points of view, and discover functions of reading and writing (Dyson, 1983; Lamme & Childers, 1983; Green & Wallat, 1979; McDermott, 1977). The teacher should try to learn which strategies the students use for writing and which resources they rely on to discover and explain ideas. Through such interactions with children, teachers socialize their students to literacy and provide writing strategies necessary for using print. For example, a teacher can help children learn which information to focus on, which knowledge is relevant to the creation or interpretation of text, and how to use this knowledge in relevant and appropriate ways (Cochran-Smith, 1984; Heath, 1983). Teachers may also model prewriting strategies such as brainstorming, note-taking, and reading. In individual conferences, they can help students revise and edit their writing. During the conferences, teachers may ask questions focusing on the processes that particular children use (Graves, 1983). For example, a teacher might try to find out which strategies a child uses to spell a word, clarify information, or reorganize text.

Acting as diagnostician, a teacher using the Writing to Read program can go beyond computer-generated evaluation. If the instruction includes student writing samples, journals, and writer's notes, the teacher can then chart and build on student knowledge and skills about writing, examine students' drafts, and prepare students to experiment with new forms of writing (Piazza & Wallat, 1987).

SUMMARY

This chapter has considered the application of research to two different, yet very widely used, computer writing programs, Quill and Writing to Read. Key features of each program were compared with general research on writing and with research on the process young children use to communicate information. The Quill program teaches students that writing is a process, that it is recursive in nature, and that it serves different functions. It also allows children to write for real audiences and get feedback and review.

The Writing to Read program, on the other hand, emphasizes encoding and decoding before children put thoughts on paper. It stresses a linear view of writing and imposes a phonemic alphabet for children to use in their writing. Although both programs incorporate computer technology into English/language arts instruction, provide an organizational structure for the teaching and learning of writing, address broad language and literacy goals, and result in positive student learning outcomes, only the Quill program appears to mesh computer technology with research on children's writing. If computer technology is to have an impact on children's writing, program developers will need to consider writing process research in designing future computer packages for classroom writing instruction.

APPENDIX:
PROGRAM DESCRIPTIONS

The Quill Program

The Quill program, designed by researchers at Bolt, Beranek and Newman Laboratories and by the Network Educational Research Organization, is available through D. C. Heath and Company. It is an integrated set of microcomputer programs that provide the tools and the environment for learning to write. The package includes (1) a Quill master disk that contains The Planner, The Library, The Mailbag, and The Writer's Assistant (text editor); and (2) a utility disk for creating Planners, Library Entries, and Mailbag disks. A teacher's guide describes the program components and gives step-by-step directions for operating the program. A section in the guide called The Cookbook provides teachers with 20 detailed lesson plans for introducing Quill to students.

QUILL PRODUCT DESCRIPTION

Hardware: Apple II+ (with 64k) or Apple IIe computer; printer; 2 disk drives; 80-column card; green screen monitor
Software: Quill master disk and Quill utility disk
Support Literature: Teacher's guide; laminated card of Writer's Assistant commands
Price: $150.00
Publisher: DCH Educational Software, D. C. Heath and Company, 125 Spring Street, Lexington, MA 02173

The Writing to Read Program

The Writing to Read System, distributed by IBM and created by John Henry Martin, is a computer-based instructional program designed to develop reading and writing skills of kindergarten and first-grade children. The system includes computer programs, work journals, games and activities, listening libraries, and word processing activities.

The program is accompanied by a comprehensive teaching manual that describes the system materials, provides operating guidelines, outlines teacher and student roles, and includes supplementary language development activities.

WRITING TO READ PRODUCT DESCRIPTION

Hardware: 6 IBM PC jr. computers; 1 IBM printer; Computer color displays and speech attachments; 5 cassette players (needed but not purchased through IBM); 16 headphones (needed but not purchased through IBM)

Software & Materials: Word processing software for each computer; 1 set of listening library cassette tapes; 3 sets of instructional cassette tapes; 3 sets of Writing to Read diskettes; 120 sets of student work journals (one set of 10 work journals per student); 1 set of children's books (printed versions of listening libraries—needed but not purchased through IBM); 1 make words game; 1 Bingo game; 120 work journal sleeve cases (optional); and miscellaneous supplies like crayons, scissors, paste, and paper (needed but not purchased through IBM)

Support Literature: 6 teacher's manuals

Price: Approximately $11,500.00 for IBM products (includes all products except those listed as "optional")

Publisher: International Business Machines Corporation, 4111 Northside Parkway, Atlanta, GA 30327

REFERENCES

Applebee, A. (1986). Problems in process approaches: Toward a reconceptualization of process instruction. In A. Petrosky & D. Bartholomae (Eds.), *The teaching of writing: 85th yearbook of the National Society for the Study of Education* (pp. 95–113). Chicago: The University of Chicago Press.

Bissex, G. (1980). *GNYS AT WRK: A child learns to write and read.* Cambridge, MA: Harvard University Press.

Bruce, B., & Rubin, A. (1984). *Quill.* Lexington, MA: D. C. Heath.

Calkins, L. M. (1983). *Lessons from a child: On the teaching and learning of writing.* Exeter, NH: Heinemann.

Clay, M. (1975). *What did I write?* Exeter, NH: Heinemann.

Cochran-Smith, M. (1984). *The making of a reader.* Norwood, NJ: Ablex.

Commission on Composition. (1986). *Teaching composition: A position statement.* Urbana, IL: National Council of Teachers of English.

Cooper, C. R., & Odell, L. (Eds.). (1978). *Research on composing: Points of departure.* Urbana, IL: National Council of Teachers of English.

DeFord, D. (1979). Young children and their writing. *Theory into Practice, 19,* 157–162.

Dyson, A. H. (1983). The role of oral language in early writing processes. *Research in the Teaching of English, 17,* 1–30.

Dyson, A. H. (1984). Learning to write/learning to do school: Emergent writers' interpretations of school literacy tasks. *Research in the Teaching of English, 18,* 233–264.

Dyson, A. H., & Genishi, C. (1982). Whatta ya tryin' to write? Writing as an interactive process. *Language Arts, 59,* 126–132.

Emig, J. (1971). *The composing processes of twelfth graders.* Urbana, IL: National Council of Teachers of English.

Ferreiro, E., & Teberosky, A. (1983). *Literacy before schooling.* Exeter, NH: Heinemann.

Florio, S., & Clark, C. M. (1982). The functions of writing in the elementary classroom. *Research in the Teaching of English, 16,* 115–130.

Genishi, C., & Dyson, A. H. (1984). *Language assessment in the early years.* Norwood, NJ: Ablex.

Goodman, K. S. (1986). *What's whole in whole language?* Portsmouth, NH: Heinemann.

Goodman, Y. (1984). The development of initial literacy. In H. Goelman, A. Oberg, & F. Smith (Eds.), *Awakening to literacy* (pp. 102–109). Exeter, NH: Heinemann.

Graves, D. H. (1975). An examination of the writing processes of seven-year-old children. *Research in the Teaching of English, 9,* 227–241.

Graves, D. H. (1983). *Writing: Teachers and children at work.* Exeter, NH: Heinemann.

Green, J., & Wallat, C. (1979). What is an instructional context? An exploratory analysis of conversational shifts over time. In O. Garnica & M. King (Eds.), *Language, children and society.* New York: Pergamon Press.

Gundlach, R.; McLane, J. B.; Stott, F. M.; & McNamee, G. D. (1985). The social foundations of children's early writing development. In M. Farr (Ed.), *Advances in writing research, Vol. 1: Children's early writing development* (pp. 1–58). Norwood, NJ: Ablex.

Halliday, M. A. K. (1975). *Learning how to mean.* London: Edward Arnold Ltd.

Harste, J. C.; Burke, C. L.; & Woodward, V. A. (1982). Children's language and world: Initial encounters with print. In J. A. Langer & M. Trika Smith-Burke (Eds.), *Reader meets author/bridging the gap* (pp. 105–131). Newark, DE: International Reading Association.

Heath, S. B. (1983). *Ways with words: Language, life and work in communities and classrooms.* Cambridge, MA: Cambridge University Press.

Hillocks, G. (1986). *Research on written composition: New directions for teaching.* Urbana, IL: ERIC Clearinghouse on Reading and Communication Skills.

Humes, A. (1983). Research on the composing process. *Review of Educational Research, 53,* 201-216.

Jacobs, S. E. (1985). The development of children's writing. *Written Communication, 2,* 414-433.

King, M. L. (1980). Learning how to mean in written language. *Theory into Practice, 19,* 163-169.

Kinneavy, J. L. (1971). *A theory of discourse.* Englewood Cliffs, NJ: Prentice-Hall.

Krashen, S. (1984). *Writing: Research, theory and applications.* Oxford: Pergamon Press.

Lamme, L. L., & Childers, N. M. (1983). The composing processes of three young children. *Research in the Teaching of English, 17,* 31-50.

Langer, J. A. (1986). *Children reading and writing: Structures and strategies.* Norwood, NJ: Ablex.

Leichter, H. (1984). Families as environments for literacy. In H. Goelman, A. Oberg, & F. Smith (Eds.), *Awakening to literacy* (pp. 38-50). Exeter, NH: Heinemann.

Lindfors, J. (1980). *Children's language and learning.* Englewood Cliffs, NJ: Prentice-Hall.

Martin, J. H. (1984). *Writing to read* (computer program). Atlanta, GA: International Business Corporation.

Mazer Corporation. (1984). *Trends '83: The school microcomputer market.* Dayton, OH: Mazer Corporation.

McDermott, R. P. (1977). Social relations as contexts for learning in school. *Harvard Educational Review, 47,* 198-213.

Moffett, J. (1983). *Teaching the universe of discourse.* Boston: Houghton Mifflin.

National Council of Teachers of English Task Force. (1979). Standards for basic skills writing programs. *College English, 41,* 220-222.

National Council of Teachers of English Task Force. (1982). *Essentials of English.* Urbana, IL: National Council of Teachers of English, 1-4.

Nystrand, M., & Himley, M. (1984). Written text as social interaction. *Theory into Practice, 23,* 198-207.

Perl, S. (1979). The composing process of unskilled college writers. *Research in the Teaching of English, 13,* 317-339.

Petrosky, A. R. (1982). From story to essay: Reading and writing. *College Composition and Communication, 33,* 19-36.

Petrosky, A., & Bartholomae, D. (Eds.). (1986). *The teaching of writing: 85th yearbook of the National Society for the Study of Education.* Chicago: The University of Chicago Press.

Piazza, C. L., & Tomlinson, C. M. (1985). A concert of writers. *Language Arts, 62*, 150–158.

Piazza, C. L., & Wallat, C. (1987). Performance-based teacher evaluation: Steps toward identifying excellence in the teaching of writing. *English Education, 19*, 44–50.

Read, C. (1975). *Children's categorization of speech sounds in English.* Urbana, IL: National Council of Teachers of English Research Report No. 7.

Smith, F. (1973). Twelve easy ways to make learning to read difficult. In F. Smith (Ed.), *Psycholinguistics and reading* (pp. 183–196). New York: Holt, Rinehart, & Winston.

Sommers, N. (1980). Revision strategies of student writers and experienced adult writers. *College Composition and Communication, 31*, 378–388.

Sowers, S. (1985). Learning to write in a workshop: A study in grades one through four. In M. Farr (Ed.), *Advances in writing research, Vol. 1: Children's early writing development* (pp. 297–342). Norwood, NJ: Ablex.

Stallard, C. K. (1974). An analysis of the behavior of good student writers. *Research in the Teaching of English, 8*, 378–388.

Taylor, D. (1983). *Family literacy: Young children learning to read and write.* Exeter, NH: Heinemann.

Vygotsky, L. S. (1978). *Mind in society.* Cambridge, MA: Harvard University Press.

About the Editors
and the Contributors

Ernest Balajthy is Assistant Professor in the Department of Elementary and Secondary Education and Reading at the State University of New York at Geneseo. He is President of the Microcomputers in Reading Special Interest Group of the International Reading Association, and author of *Microcomputers in Reading and Language Arts* and *Computers and Reading: Lessons from the Past and the Technologies of the Future.*

Marilyn Cochran-Smith is Associate Director of Programs in Teacher Education and the head of undergraduate and graduate programs in Elementary Education at the Graduate School of Education, University of Pennsylvania. She currently directs both the "Microcomputers and Writing Development" study and "Project START," a collaborative teacher-researcher program involving cooperating teachers, student teachers, and university supervisors. She is the author of *The Making of a Reader.*

Colette Daiute is an Associate Professor at the Harvard University Graduate School of Education. Previously, she was a member of the faculty of Teachers College, Columbia University where she earned her Ed.D. She is the author of *Writing and Computers*, an introduction to uses of computers for teaching writing. In addition to her ongoing research on uses of computers for writing, Ms. Daiute is currently doing research on the role of play in the development of writing abilities.

James L. Hoot (Editor) is Associate Professor of Early Childhood Education and Director of the Early Childhood Research Center at State University of New York at Buffalo. He holds a Ph.D. in Early Childhood Education from the University of Illinois. In addition to his interest in technology, his research has focused upon programs designed to develop improved intergenerational and international understandings. He is the editor of *Computers in Early Childhood Education.*

Mary A. Johnson is Assistant Professor of Education at the University of Texas at Tyler. She received her Ed.D. at Texas Woman's University and has done research on using the language experience approach to reading with young Hispanic and deaf children. Her research has also centered upon potential benefits of word processing with younger children.

Jessica Kahn is a doctoral candidate and an instructor/researcher at the Graduate School of Education of the University of Pennsylvania, where she teaches courses on the role of computer technology in education. A former elementary school teacher, she is interested in the potential for reconceptualization of teacher training, research, and classroom practice that computers offer.

Ruth J. Kurth is Professor of Education at the University of North Texas, Denton. She holds a Ph.D. from the University of Wisconsin, and has done research in the fields of reading comprehension and computer assisted reading and writing instruction.

Catherine Cobb Morocco is Director of School and College Programs at the Education Development Center in Newton, Massachusetts. She directs several classroom-based research projects related to integrating computers into instruction for special needs children. She has a doctorate from Harvard University and has taught writing, language development and the teaching of language arts.

Susan B. Neuman is an Associate Professor in instructional technology and literacy at the University of Lowell. Her major research interests include communication theory and the effects of technology on literacy development.

Cynthia L. Paris is a doctoral candidate at the University of Pennsylvania and an instructor of Elementary Teacher Education at the University of Pennsylvania and Rutgers University. She has served as a research associate in the "Microcomputers and Writing Development" project and is currently Associate Director for the "Teacher to Teacher" dissemination phase of the project.

Carolyn L. Piazza is Associate Professor of Education at Florida State University. She holds a Ph.D. in Language Communications from the University of Pittsburgh, and publishes in the areas of language and literacy development and computer applications for teaching writing.

Teresa J. Rosegrant is Associate Professor of Early Childhood Education at George Washington University. She received her Ph.D. in Education from the University of Illinois. She is the developer of several early language software programs including the Talking Text Writer.

Terry S. Salinger is Coordinator of Reading for the National Assessment of Educational Progress at Educational Testing Service. She has been a faculty member at the University of Cincinnati and the University of Texas at El Paso, where she also coordinated the early childhood program. She is author of *Language Arts and Literacy for Young Children*.

Steven B. Silvern (Editor) is Associate Professor of Early Childhood Education at Auburn University. He has conducted numerous studies on children's interaction with microcomputers, and has published articles and chapters on video games, Logo, and children's writing with computers. In addition, Professor Silvern is Associate Editor of the *Journal for Research in Childhood Education.*

Index

Abilities: theories about, 10-21
Access: to computers, 3, 44-45, 77, 79-80, 147; to printers, 82-83, 112
Addy, P., 193
Alphabet Authors [software], 190
Alpha Letter Drop [software], 190
Assignments, 5, 36-37, 44-45, 47, 48
Audience: and Quill, 200, 201, 202, 203, 204-5; and talking word processors, 149, 153-54; writing for an, 30-32, 100, 198

Backups, 27, 36, 88
Balajthy, E., 103, 193
Bank Street Writer [software], 44, 99, 119, 147, 148, 177
BASIC [software], 147
Bereiter, C., 128
Bork, A., 3
Bradley, V., 79
Burg, K., 164

Calkins, L. M., 160
Cameron, J., 188, 192
Campbell, D., 185
Casad, K. H., 188
Cheating, 37-38
Cinquain [software], 33
Cioffi, G., 57
Cognitive structures, 12-14
Cognitive theories. See also Piaget, Jean; Vygotsky, Lev
Cohen, M., 86
Coke, E. U., 169
Collaboration: and access to computers, 80; and cheating, 37-38; computers as a tool for, 19-20; and ESL students, 116-17; and illicit writing, 37; and LD

students, 123, 126-27, 130; and learning word processing, 37-38, 57-58; and placement of computers, 45, 77; and scheduling, 86; teachers' perceptions of, 45; and word banks, 115
Communication approach, 17, 28-29
Composing: and access to computers, 79; and editing, 86; as a focus of writing, 25-27, 34, 38; and the introduction of computers, 59, 60-61, 65, 80-81; and keyboarding, 60, 61, 151; and LD students, 137; and LEA, 92-96, 102-3; and learning word processing, 56; and Quill, 200, 201; research about, 197; and talking word processors, 149-56; and the writing process, 4-5, 59, 81
Computer experts, 33, 51, 53, 58-59, 71, 76
Computergarten [software], 190
Computers: role of, 3, 8, 19-20, 64-65, 75, 80, 107-8. See also Word processing
Computers, introduction of: and children's use of computers, 54-59, and computer experts, 58-59; and learning strategies, 49-50, 53-54; research about, 68-70; and school policy, 70-73; and teachers, 44-45, 48, 50-54, 75-76, 88; and timing, 44-49, 53-54; and the writing process, 59-63. See also Word processing
Conceptual "bugs", 55-56
Content. See Composing
Cooper, M., 190
Cooper, Russell, 144

Cosgrove, S., 111
Critical ear, 149
Curriculum: and computers, 88;
    keyboarding in the, 186-93

Daiute, C., 4, 17, 19
Decentering, 12, 14, 199
Decision making, 52-53, 53, 71, 138
Dialogues, 57-58, 91, 129-32, 150
Dictation, 61, 64, 91, 97-98
Diel, M., 171
Direct instruction, 128, 131-32,
    132-33, 134
Discovery, 15-16, 19, 203-4, 212
Diskettes: caring for, 83-84, 88. See
    also Public access to writing
Drafting, 77, 81, 93, 197, 200, 202,
    203-4. See also Composing

Edit files, 101-2
Editing: checklist, 163; features,
    124-28, 132, 137; groups, 28, 77,
    86, 87, 153. See also Revising
Eiser, L., 173
Electronic mail. See Networks
English as a second language [ESL]:
    and collaboration, 116-17; and the
    LEA, 109-19; and literacy needs of
    students, 108-9; and motivation,
    118-19; and self-esteem, 117-18;
    and teachers, 118-19
Environment: importance of, 18-19,
    196, 198, 200, 204, 205
Epistle [software], 162
Equalizers: computers as, 65
Equipment, 78-79. See also name of
    specific piece of equipment
ESL. See English as a second language
Evaluation, 13, 123, 127, 151, 155,
    172-73
Experienced/novice writers, 24-25, 93
Experimentation with language, 116,
    154-56, 202, 209. See also
    Discovery

Facilitators: computers as, 64-65;
    teachers as, 212
Feedback: from peers, 25, 64-65, 151,
    165, 205; from teachers, 14, 151,
    157, 166-67, 205, 212; and LD

students, 133; and the process
    approach, 17; and printing, 63;
    purpose of, 199; and Quill, 205;
    and revising, 62, 64; and social
    interaction, 14; and talking word
    processors, 146, 150, 151-52, 154,
    155; and text analysis, 164, 165,
    166-67, 171, 175; timing of, 155;
    and Writing to Read, 211. See also
    Spelling checker
Files, 27, 87-88, 98, 99, 101-2. See also
    Public access to writing
Format, 20, 32-34, 205
Form of writing, 4-5, 20, 198. See also
    Mechanics
Fraggle Rock [television program], 30
Frase, L. T., 171, 175
Freeman, R., 185

Games, 15, 99, 190, 206, 207
Ghost Writer [software], 162, 177
Go-Bots [television program], 30
Graphics, 23-24, 33, 83, 87, 119, 125,
    210
Graves, R. L., 4

Hall, M. A., 110
Handwriting, 23-26, 28-29, 65, 181-82,
    188-89
Hardware, 82-83. See also name of
    specific piece of hardware
Hines, S., 189-90
Humphrey, M., 116

Illicit writing, 36-37
Imitation. See Models
Incidental learning, 171
Inner voice/internal speech, 14, 19,
    149-51

Johnson, M. A., 6, 117-18
Jungck, S., 75

Keyboarding: and composing, 56, 60,
    61, 151; and conceptual "bugs",
    55; in the curriculum, 186-93; as a
    form of producing print, 181-83;
    and handwriting, 181-82, 188-89;
    instruction in, 183-84; and LD
    students, 136, 137; and learning

word processing, 35, 55-56, 82, 97, 112-13; and placement of computers, 78; research about, 185; speed, 183-84, 187-88; and teachers, 192; and typing, 35, 186-87, 190-91
Kids on Keys [software], 190
Kiefer, K. E., 171
Kisner, E., 188, 190, 192
Kleinman, G., 116
Knapp, L., 182, 188-89
Koala pad peripherals, 125
Krashen, S. D., 118
Kurth, L., 79
Kurth, R., 79, 128

Language: as an object, 17-18; awareness, 17-18; development, 199; experimentation with, 116, 154-56, 202, 209; oral, 198, 208-11; and play, 18; as a social phenomenon, 109, 198-99; and symbolism, 17-18; writing as a process of, 198-99
Language experience approach [LEA]: cautions of using word processing and the, 97; and composing, 92-96, 102-3; and ESL, 109-19; teachers' roles in, 102-3; uses of the, 90-92; and word processing, 96-103, 111-19
Layout, 32-33, 38
LD. See Learning-disabled
Learning: and collaboration, 37-38; computers as a means of, 34-36; incidental, 171; and the introduction of computers, 34-36, 49-50, 53-59, 75, 84-85, 97, 136-37; and programs, 36; and social interaction, 37-38, 57; strategies for, 49-50; teachers' views of, 49-50, 69-70, 71; transfer of, 170-71
Learning-disabled [LD]: and approaches to teaching writing, 128-32; and collaboration, 123, 126-27, 127, 130; and a model of writing instruction, 133-36; and motivation, 138-39; and teachers' approaches to writing, 132-39;

and the teacher's role, 136-39; and word processing features, 124-28; and writing instruction, 123-24
Leo the Lop: Tail Two [Cosgove], 111
Listen to Learn [software], 147-48
Logo [software], 33, 125, 147
Losing text, 35-36, 97, 100, 137

Martin, John Henry, 205-6
MasterType [software], 191
Mathinos, D., 75
Meaning, 196, 197, 198, 199, 209
MECC Speller [software], 177
Mechanics: and the communication approach, 28-29; and editing, 86; and evaluation of writing, 13; as a focus of writing, 25, 34, 38; and hand-written materials, 25, 28-29; and the introduction of computers, 63, 64, 65, 80-81; and LD students, 123-24, 127, 138; and the writing process, 16. See also Text analysis
Memory, 14
Models: and apprenticing, 16; skill, 83, 102, 103, 201; teachers as, 14, 47, 81-82, 93, 100, 119, 157, 213
Model of writing instruction, 133-36
Monitors, 78, 82, 97, 103, 126, 133
Monologues, 57-58
Moore, D., 168-69
Motivation: as a benefit of word processing, 29-34, 103, 108, 122, 138-39; and the communication approach, 17; and environment, 200; and ESL students, 109-10, 118-19; and LD students, 138-39; and LEA, 103; and the process approach, 160; and purposive writing, 29-34, 38; technology as, 103; and text analysis, 171; and typing, 185
Muskowitz, S., 109

Naymark, J., 75, 79, 88
Networks: electronic mail, 20, 201, 205
Newman, J. M., 118
Newspaper, class/school, 17, 19-20
Newsroom [software], 20

Oksendahl, W., 185
Oral language, 198, 208-11. *See also*
　　Talking word processors
Ownership of writing, 47-49, 123, 130,
　　133, 135, 138-39, 166, 167

Papert, S., 182
Peers: and conferencing/feedback, 25,
　　64-65, 151, 165, 168, 205; and
　　illicit writing, 37; and the role of
　　computers, 64; and social
　　interaction, 100; tutoring/help by,
　　33, 48, 165, 168, 171-72; and
　　writing as communication, 17. *See
　　also* Public access to writing
PFS Write [software], 148
Piaget, Jean, 11-14, 15-16, 17, 18-19,
　　21
Pictures, 16. *See also* Graphics
Placement of computers, 45, 76-78
Plaisant, C., 75, 79, 88
Planning, 19, 86, 123, 135, 200,
　　203-4
Planning programs, 23, 203-4
Playing, 18, 20, 55
Polin, L. G., 88
Pretend writing, 47
Prewriting, 4-5, 50, 59, 60, 77, 79, 81,
　　85, 93, 95, 200, 213
Printers: access to, 82-83, 112
Printing. *See* Publishing/printing
Print Master [software], 87
Print Shop [software], 87
Procedural instruction, 128, 130-31,
　　132-33, 134-35
Procedures: need for, 124
Process approach: and cognitive
　　development theories, 15-16;
　　definition of, 45-46, 197; and
　　feedback, 17; and the introduction
　　of computers, 59-63; and LD
　　students, 123; and motivation,
　　160; as a recursive/linear process,
　　46, 59-60, 67, 168, 197, 202, 203,
　　209-10; research about the, 4-5,
　　203-4; revising, 168; steps in the,
　　93, 197; teachers' views of the,
　　46-49. *See also* Computers,
　　introduction of; Quill; Writing to
　　Read

Programs/software: availability of, 5,
　　29-30, 83, 119; incompatibility of,
　　36; and LD students, 137; learning
　　to use, 36; and motivation, 29-30;
　　need for teachers to understand,
　　6; selection of, 83, 119, 170,
　　172-77, 196; and talking word
　　processors, 144-46; use of, 3. *See
　　also specific name or type of
　　program*
Prompting programs, 20
Proofreading, 163-64
Public access to writing, 27-28, 29, 30,
　　64, 100, 103, 128, 138-39, 201, 202
Publishing/printing: and LEA, 96; and
　　learning word processing, 59, 63,
　　64-65, 81, 86-87, 98, 99, 108, 113;
　　and Quill, 200, 202; and revising,
　　25, 28, 160; and sharing with
　　others, 25, 28, 63, 64-65, 86-87,
　　108; as a step in the writing
　　process, 93; and talking word
　　processors, 149, 156
Purposive writing, 29-30, 34, 36, 38,
　　86-87, 198, 200, 202, 204-5

Quill [software]: 196, 197, 199-205,
　　213-14

Rainbow Keyboarding [software], 190
Raskin, R., 173
Rauch, V., 184
Reading: computers as an impetus for,
　　21
Repetition, 152, 154-55, 156, 168
Research. *See name of specific
　　researcher or topic*
Revising: benefits of, 38, 160-61;
　　children's attitudes about, 63; and
　　cognitive structures, 13; and
　　content/composing, 86; ease of, 5,
　　6, 21, 26-27, 63, 96, 103, 108, 153;
　　and editing, 86, 125; and
　　experienced/novice writers, 24-25,
　　93; and hand-written text, 24-26,
　　28-29, 65; and internal dialogue,
　　19; and the introduction of
　　computers, 47, 49-50, 55, 59,
　　62-63, 64, 81; and LD students,
　　124-25, 132, 133, 137-38; and